I0866859

Illegal Immigrants/ Model Minorities

In the series *Asian American History and Culture*,
edited by Cathy Schlund-Vials, Shelley Sang-Hee Lee, and Rick Bonus.
Founding editor, Sucheng Chan; editors emeriti, David Palumbo-Liu,
Michael Omi, K. Scott Wong, and Linda Trinh Võ.

ALSO IN THIS SERIES:

Chia Youyee Vang with Pao Yang, Retired Captain, U.S. Secret War in Laos, *Prisoner of Wars: A Hmong Fighter Pilot's Story of Escaping Death and Confronting Life* (forthcoming)

Kavita Daiya, *Graphic Migrations: Precarity and Gender in India and the Diaspora* (forthcoming)

Timothy K. August, *The Refugee Aesthetic: Reimagining Southeast Asian America* (forthcoming)

L. Joyce Zapanta Mariano, *Giving Back: Filipino Diaspora and the Politics of Giving* (forthcoming)

Manan Desai, *The United States of India: Anticolonial Literature and Transnational Refraction*

Cathy J. Schlund-Vials, Guy Beauregard, and Hsiu-chuan Lee, eds., *The Subject(s) of Human Rights: Crises, Violations, and Asian/American Critique*

Malini Johar Schueller, *Campaigns of Knowledge: U.S. Pedagogies of Colonialism and Occupation in the Philippines and Japan*

Crystal Mun-hye Baik, *Reencounters: On the Korean War and Diasporic Memory Critique*

Michael Omi, Dana Y. Nakano, and Jeffrey T. Yamashita, eds., *Japanese American Millennials: Rethinking Generation, Community, and Diversity*

Masumi Izumi, *The Rise and Fall of America's Concentration Camp Law: Civil Liberties Debates from the Internment to McCarthyism and the Radical 1960s*

Shirley Jennifer Lim, *Anna May Wong: Performing the Modern*

Edward Tang, *From Confinement to Containment: Japanese/American Arts during the Early Cold War*

Patricia P. Chu, *Where I Have Never Been: Migration, Melancholia, and Memory in Asian American Narratives of Return*

Cynthia Wu, *Sticky Rice: A Politics of Intraracial Desire*

Marguerite Nguyen, *America's Vietnam: The* Longue Durée *of U.S. Literature and Empire*

Vanita Reddy, *Fashioning Diaspora: Beauty, Femininity, and South Asian American Culture*

Audrey Wu Clark, *The Asian American Avant-Garde: Universalist Aspirations in Modernist Literature and Art*

Eric Tang, *Unsettled: Cambodian Refugees in the New York City Hyperghetto*

Jeffrey Santa Ana, *Racial Feelings: Asian America in a Capitalist Culture of Emotion*

Jiemin Bao, *Creating a Buddhist Community: A Thai Temple in Silicon Valley*

Elda E. Tsou, *Unquiet Tropes: Form, Race, and Asian American Literature*

Tarry Hum, *Making a Global Immigrant Neighborhood: Brooklyn's Sunset Park*

Ruth Mayer, *Serial Fu Manchu: The Chinese Supervillain and the Spread of Yellow Peril Ideology*

Karen Kuo, *East Is West and West Is East: Gender, Culture, and Interwar Encounters between Asia and America*

A list of additional titles in this series appears at the back of this book

Heidi Kim

Illegal Immigrants/ Model Minorities

THE COLD WAR OF CHINESE AMERICAN NARRATIVE

TEMPLE UNIVERSITY PRESS
Philadelphia • Rome • Tokyo

TEMPLE UNIVERSITY PRESS
Philadelphia, Pennsylvania 19122
tupress.temple.edu

Published 2021

Library of Congress Cataloging-in-Publication Data

Names: Kim, Heidi, author.
Title: Illegal immigrants/model minorities : the Cold War of Chinese American narrative / Heidi Kim.
Other titles: Asian American history and culture.
Description: Philadelphia : Temple University Press, [2021] | Series: Asian American History and Culture | Includes bibliographical references and index. | Summary: "Illegal Immigrants/Model Minorities thinks through two figures-the Chinese illegal immigrant and the Chinese model minority-during the Cold War. Reading the two together sheds light on how the discussion of Chinese Americans in both literature and archival materials grapples with these constructs and creates competing usages of and perspectives on Chinese American history"—Provided by publisher.
Identifiers: LCCN 2020019246 (print) | LCCN 2020019247 (ebook) | ISBN 9781439919019 (cloth) | ISBN 9781439919026 (paperback) | ISBN 9781439919033 (pdf)
Subjects: LCSH: Chinese—United States—History—20th century. | Chinese—United States—Public opinion. | Chinese Americans in literature. | Model minority stereotype—United States. | Immigrants—Government policy—United States. | China—Emigration and immigration—History—20th century. | United States—Emigration and immigration—History—20th century.
Classification: LCC E184.C5 K48 2021 (print) | LCC E184.C5 (ebook) | DDC 973/.0495—dc23
LC record available at https://lccn.loc.gov/2020019246
LC ebook record available at https://lccn.loc.gov/2020019247

♾ The paper used in this publication meets the requirements of the American National Standard for Information Sciences—Permanence of Paper for Printed Library Materials, ANSI Z39.48-1992

Printed in the United States of America

9 8 7 6 5 4 3 2 1

Contents

Acknowledgments

This work was supported by my wonderful colleagues at the Department of English and Comparative Literature at the University of North Carolina, Chapel Hill (UNC), and a semester-long faculty fellowship at the UNC Institute for the Arts and Humanities (IAH), as well as a fellowship at the Columbia University Center for American Studies.

I am grateful for helpful and stimulating conversations with many people, including Leslie Bow, Tim Carter, Cindy Cheng, Sylvia Chong, Jennifer Ho, Madeline Hsu, Cathy Schlund-Vials, my fellow IAH Fellows and program director Michele Berger, and Ted Chapin of the Rodgers & Hammerstein Organization. For their support, I also thank Priscilla Wald and John McGowan. Special thanks go to Ji-Yeon Yuh, in whose graduate seminar I read several books of Asian American history and, although I didn't know it at the time, laid the foundations for this study. Jared Brown-Rabinowitz provided valuable assistance with legal research and interpretation, as well as Chinese translation. Bibliographic and data assistance was provided at different times by research assistants Kevin Pyon and Dylan Thompson. A portion of the discussion of *Flower Drum Song* in Chapter 2 was previously published as "'Flower Drum Song,' Whitewashing and Operation Wetback: A Message from 1961" in the *Los Angeles Review of Books* on September 22, 2016. Thanks to Sarah Munroe and Sara Jo Cohen for their support throughout the review process and to all the other Temple University Press staff members who worked so hard, even during the COVID-19 pandemic, to bring this book to print.

Research for this book was conducted at many institutes and archives across the United States. My research on the papers of Jade Snow Wong at the Library of Congress was funded by a Florence Tan Moeson Fellowship and facilitated by the staff of the Asian Reading Room, particularly the indefatigable Pang Xiong; on another trip, the staff of the Music Division assisted me in looking at the papers of Oscar Hammerstein. I thank Mark Ong for his permission to quote from the papers and works of his mother, Jade Snow Wong. I also thank the staff of the Princeton University Seeley Mudd Manuscript Library; the New York Public Library for the Performing Arts; Special Collections at the main branch of the New York Public Library; Columbia University Rare Books and Manuscripts; the Bancroft Library at the University of California, Berkeley; and the Hoover Institution at Stanford University. Last, the assistance of librarians and staff at my own institution has always been essential, particularly that of Tommy Nixon.

Finally, as ever, my thanks to my supportive family and friends, especially my newest and most cherished little family member.

Illegal Immigrants/ Model Minorities

Introduction

Illegal Immigration in the Cold War

Richard Rodgers and Oscar Hammerstein's musical *Flower Drum Song* (1958/1961), remembered as one of their lesser hits, concludes its light-hearted look at the lives of Chinese Americans in San Francisco with a scene in which girl gets boy—by informing on herself. "My back is wet," she quaintly announces, precipitating a romantic happy ending. Astonishingly, Rodgers and Hammerstein were able to appeal to a popular middlebrow audience by making light of illegal immigration, while Chinese American authors of the same period struggled to normalize and justify the Chinese presence, many of them quietly suppressing the stories of their family's own immigration strategies and deceptions.[1]

Illegal Immigrants/Model Minorities: The Cold War of Chinese American Narrative examines how Chinese Americans sought to address a Cold War–driven official narrative of the pervasiveness of illegal immigration, as the wave of "Chinatown novels" and memoirs coincided with immigration scrutiny and investigation on a massive scale. Whether hiding it, explaining it, countering its stigma through a proto-model minority embrace of assimilation and the nuclear family formation, or later, even boldly embracing it, Chinese American writers responded with remarkable strategy and specificity to the developments in immigration policy and surfacing of new public histories. Like the memoirs and novels it examines, this study tells a tale of two narrative authorities about Chinese America: the U.S. government, as told in laws, court opinions, and media appearances, and the voices of Chinese Americans in the same period. In particular, I focus on the public and private responses of authors in the 1950s and their retrospectives in later decades on the government investigations and attacks on Chinese American immigration. These narratives are inextricably intertwined with the history of immigration that authors seek to conceal and justify simultaneously, offering their own lives in the United States as proof and, later in the era, politicizing fraudulence as resistance.

Across these authors and this archive, two disciplining formations arise in this period: a racialized illegal immigrant and a differently but equally powerfully racialized model minority. Stemming from many of the same social formations and negative stereotypes, these two categories are defined against and in dialogue with each other, as Chinese Americans often wielded the second against the negative image of the first. Both, in the Cold War era, serve to contain the foreign presence within the United States. Indeed, the rise of both of these terms in the 1960s demonstrates how the need to narrativize the rapidly growing Chinese American population during China's communist upheavals led to the creation of new public identities and consciousness for Chinese Americans.

Although Chinese Americans were not estimated to constitute a large percentage of immigrants entering fraudulently or without documentation, the public identification of them as illegal immigrants rose in connection with fears of communist infiltration from China. Decades of restricted and gender-imbalanced migration paved the way for further restrictions and policing. After the "fall" of China in 1950, a cascade of government investigations, specialized programs, and deportations poured forth in concert with rising numbers of attempted family reunifications and refugee entrances. In particular, the high-profile attempted subpoenas of Chinatown family associations and the Chinese Confession Program, initiated by the U.S. Immigration and Naturalization Service (INS) in 1956, created an atmosphere of suspicion and fear over the course of the 1950s that perhaps has never died away.

However, long before the term "model minority" was invented, one side of Asian stereotyping in the United States focused on Asians' diligence, thrift, quiet behavior, and reliability. The narrative of progress and of good, fully legal and legitimate Chinese Americans was furthered by governmental, media, and community sources during World War II. Ellen Wu and K. Scott Wong have described how World War II military service in particular legitimated the Americanness of Chinese at the same time that the ally status of China placed them as the "good Asians," in contrast with Japanese and Japanese Americans. Madeline Hsu suggests that the students and elite refugees of the postwar era became the "good immigrants," worthy and valuable additions to a booming economy and society. As I chiefly argue, the coherence and stability of the Chinese American family also became a key point of definition for the model minority formation as it was defined in the 1960s as a means of further pathologizing African American socioeconomic problems. The nuclear family functioned to counter decades of the stereotype of pernicious clans, tongs, and bachelor Chinatowns, then, in the 1950s, to counter attacks on family reunification immigration and to tap into narratives of assimilation and social suitability. Thus, the need to publicly counter government narratives of fraudulent immigration directly fed into the establishment of the model minority. The nuclear and (paradoxically) even the extended family became the primary way for Chinese Americans to normalize their identity and exemplarity *because* the Chinese American family was constantly under attack by immigration investigation through interrogation, blood testing, and court proceedings. However, these narratives could not fully counteract the stigmatization of Chinese Americans as possible infiltrators and illegal immigrants. As Mae Ngai writes, "The community could not entirely redeem its virtue. Cold War politics and the sensationalized investigations against fraud reproduced racialized perceptions that all Chinese immigrants were illegal and dangerous."[2]

Chinese American writers in this period take on the mantle of speaking for an entire community, many of them explicitly, understanding that their stories represent the group to a mainstream public largely ignorant of this small but growing population. *Illegal Immigrants/Model Minorities* sets out a rubric by which to understand the literary landscape of illegal immigration in the 1950s, as Chinese American writers in this era reenvisioned national belonging, family, blood ties, and history. Within novels, memoirs, and literary archives, as well as government documents, court cases, and mass media, the battle for narrative authority and Chinese American identity evolves over the course of the Cold War. I create a new understanding of the stigma and anxiety of illegal immigration as it affected the image of the entire Chinese American community and was recontextualized by immigration reform and ethnic activism in the 1960s and 1970s, leading to a politicized revelation of family secrets. This book illuminates the rapidly shifting political and social pressures on Chinese American writers, as I examine not only published works but also revisions, adaptations, and private family narratives. I recognize that a peril of the binary framing of my title is that I may seem to reaffirm the separate categories of illegal immigrant and model minority. However, I believe that close attention to these writers' negotiations reveals how definitions were historically navigated and combated by many different individuals during this era, working against the narratives of the nation-state.

Blood tells. Interrogation searches. Confession reveals. Law defines. But Chinese American literature can perform all of these and more, selectively concealing, revealing, and reconstructing. As with the discussion of silence and speech, the lines between history and fiction have been blurred significantly by theorists of the past few decades, who work against the reification of "truth" and "fact" and instead have exposed the mediated and constructed nature of history and historical narrative. The concept of immigration itself, as Bonnie Honig, Mae Ngai, and others have theorized, is a narrative that promises citizenship, belonging, and inclusion. Thus, the racialized exclusion from the "normative teleology of immigration," as Chinese Americans were tainted with fraudulence in the Cold War era, depended on the construction of other narratives.[3] The hostile narrative of Chinese fraudulence and illegality is continually countered and undercut in this era by strategic Chinese American speakers who appeal to the broader public with narratives of Americanness and belonging, beginning with proto-model minority tales but eventually encompassing even the independence and rebellion of an illegal immigrant identity.

Before I continue, a note about terminology: I have chosen, despite some qualms, to employ the terms "illegal immigration" and occasionally, as in my title, "illegal immigrants," because historically we see them being increasingly used and solidified in this era around particular ethnicities to specific political ends. Other terms were also frequently used, and I employ them, as well: "passport fraud," "smuggling," and more. "Fraud" was the government's most frequently used word in the 1950s for Chinese immigration. But "illegal immigration," which has become so pejorative in our time, was a general, popular term that encompassed many different aspects of undocumented or fraudulently documented immigration, and it was employed by many in different fields of endeavor. We see Chinese American writers working deliberately with and against this term, starting when Lin Yutang is told by his editor that he must explain how his characters could enter "legally" in *Chinatown Family* (1948); Maxine Hong Kingston embraces it in her imagination of "illegal" and "legal" versions of her father in *China Men* (1980).[4] I felt that this term, especially in conversation with the other term, "model minority," that developed over the course of the Cold War to describe Asian Americans, most accurately conveys the warring narratives that Chinese Americans faced.

Creating the Confession Era

The framework of my study is highlighted not by the traditional global or Eurocentric events that initially dominated Cold War study, but by the U.S. immigration policies of this era, such as the special prosecutions of Chinese immigration cases and the revised acts of 1952 and 1965. However, these policies are parallel with and inextricable from the Cold War, particularly as affecting Chinese Americans, because of relations with Communist China and the consequent increase of surveillance on Chinese America; therefore, although I do not continue this study all the way through the popularly conceived end of the Cold War in 1991, I use the terms "Cold War era" and "the era of immigration scrutiny" or the "Confession era" (referring to an INS program for Chinese Americans) somewhat interchangeably in this study to indicate the political entanglements of the period from the end of World War II through the 1970s, examining the literary history and aftereffects of immigration reforms in the Cold War political context.

Writing about Chinese American identity takes place in the context of the United States' struggle during the Cold War to maintain and further its democratic ideals at home, particularly in the struggle for civil rights. Cindy Cheng, in *Citizens of Asian America*, importantly develops a historical framework in which immigration activism and reform during the Cold War, as well as stigmatization as political subversives, become part of the civil rights struggle for Asian Americans, continuing to enlarge civil rights studies beyond the sphere of the domestic body politic. As both Cheng and Wu discuss at length, the rising communist tide in Asia placed Chinese Americans and other East Asian Americans in public relations peril but also gave them new opportunities to redefine a community identity through what Wu describes as an anti-communist "nationwide crusade." The author Jade Snow Wong's overseas tour to Asia, as well as those of other artists and public figures, formed an important part of that reshaping; not only could Chinese Americans serve as a virtuous and integral piece of American society within, but they had a special efficacy in the fight for democracy outside. However, Charlotte Brooks and Peter Kwong have described the deep rifts that political and social differences caused within developing Chinatowns, showing how a small ethnic population was buffeted by Cold War shifts that differently affected individuals based on immigration and class status.[5]

Paradoxes and contradictory policies governed immigration during the buildup of a large bureaucratic apparatus that led to an impossible subject position for small immigrating communities. Hiroshi Motomura exposes the wide discretion that the government applies in regulating and enforcing immigration restrictions, "replac[ing] the predictability and uniformity that is usually associated with the rule of law." Such unpredictability cascades into the different roles and interests that govern the integration of migrants into U.S. society. Mae Ngai and Elliott Young have examined the contradictory laws, public agitation, and labor conditions that created the illegal immigrant as a figure that was an "impossible subject," in Ngai's titular term, excluded and policed, and yet an "alien nation," in Young's, moving transnationally and sometimes eluding the scrutiny of the state. Such a complex history and confusing policies surface in the split rhetoric that the INS and other government agencies often applied to Chinese (and other) immigrants, who were characterized by turn in sympathetic and condemnatory tones. I likewise link this split rhetoric to the establishment of what I call the proto-model minority, looking at the young Chinese Americans of the 1950s whose writing and work enters into this unpredictably policed society. It should not be surprising that some constructed public personae as close to unimpeachable as they could, navigating the uneasy terrain of coercion and complicity, as Ian Haney López calls it.[6]

The terrain of Cold War Chinese America was the culmination of a gradual process of comparative racialization as economic forces collided with protectionism and nativism. The economic "yellow peril" and associated xenophobic fears surfaced in gender- and class-inflected fears of Chinese immorality, heathenness, unassimilability, and pernicious influence that lasted for decades as the policing of immigration and citizenship was created at the federal and state level. Constantly shifting state or federal policy, corporate or business interests, and labor opposition clashed with more favorably disposed politicians, charitable and Christian groups, those concerned with foreign policy in Asia, and the growing political agency and activism of Chinese Americans themselves.

The constantly shifting restriction of Asian immigration and the attempted conflation of immigrant, resident, and citizen in government prosecutions did much to shape the perception and political position of Asian Americans in the second half of the twentieth century. The common pressures of defining the white, the foreign, and the citizen in legalized processes fell hard on the small but growing Asian presence. Over the decades, as immigration restrictions shaped the Chinese American community, Chinese immigration also shaped the means of modern immigration restriction to a degree out of proportion with mere numbers. Over time, Chinese Americans gradually gained (in greater numbers) the right to immigration, to family reunification, and, in the mid-twentieth century, to refugee status and naturalization. In 1965, with the lifting of national origins quotas, some of the stigma lifted, but legal peril did not. Also, Hsu has presciently noted that the history of *inclusion* must be added to the history of immigration exclusion and deportation. Indeed, as she argues, the active assistance of educated immigrants and political refugees can be read as an origin of the model minority stereotype.[7]

Starting in the mid-nineteenth century, the gradual but steady influx of Chinese laborers into the West led to concerted political opposition. The Chinese Exclusion Act of 1882, passed amid great political contention over its initial severity, strove to protect the U.S. population and the labor market by excluding all family members of Chinese in the United States except for those of a certain class status, chiefly merchants, students, and diplomats. This created, on the one hand, a group of separated transnational families, with women and children in China and men in the United States. In the United States, it created what were and are erroneously referred to as "bachelor" Chinatowns, mostly male social worlds that consequently were described as homosexual, pedophilic, diseased spaces; Nayan Shah has brilliantly described how San Francisco Chinatown suffered from characterization in the nineteenth century by white politicians as "an immoral bachelor society of dissolute men who frequented opium dens, gambling houses, and brothels . . . [a] transient working-class world." Even into the twentieth century, these spaces were so pathologized that Louis Chu's 1961 novel *Eat a Bowl of Tea* is generally hailed as the *only* depiction of a bachelor Chinatown. *Tea*, however, shows a bachelor society already in decline, superseded by young families, as I discuss further in Chapter 3. Nor were women exempt from these depictions. In 1875, the Page Act laid the foundation for wider exclusion by excluding Chinese forced laborers and prostitutes, chiefly enforced to keep out the immoral Chinese female influence, decades before prostitutes of all races were excluded. The perceived lack of morality and Christianity of Chinese raised fears not only that they were unsuitable for assimilation but that they were unsuitable simply to be present in the West amid white settlers.[8]

With the increasing migration arose the issue of citizenship. Asians were barred from naturalization in 1870 alongside Chinese exclusion. Perhaps the most famous early legal case, *Wong Kim Ark v. United States* (1898), established the principle of birthright citizenship—that is, by birth on U.S. soil (*jus soli*). Wong Kim Ark was born on U.S. soil and denied reentry after a trip to China; the judicial recognition of his citizenship represented an important step in law at the time. Furthermore, his citizenship trumped the Chinese Exclusion laws, so the permission to reenter also represented an important, albeit limited, recognition of citizenship rights over race-based immigration policy. Different cases regulated or increased the power of the state over noncitizens as the bureaucratic regulation of certificates of residency increased.[9]

At the height of the nativist era, the immigration acts of 1917 and 1924 sought to further cut off immigration from Asia, first by demarcating an "Asiatic Barred Zone" and later by creating a circular logic, excluding aliens not eligible for citizenship—a move highly damaging to relations with Japan and other Asian nations. Likewise, the racial barrier to naturalized citizenship for Asians was upheld by courts, cemented by the *Ozawa* (1922) and *Thind* (1923) Supreme Court cases, until World War II for Chinese. In 1952, all general racial prerequisites for immigration were finally ended. The alienness and precarity of Asians, even citizens, thus remained a matter of fact and law right up until the Cold War, reaching its height with the mass detention of Japanese Americans during World War II.[10]

Just as Chinese immigration shaped the laws of entry and citizenship, it shaped the apparatus of deportation and the federal power over immigration as a national security concern. The bureaucracy of immigration grew immensely over the exclusion period. The Geary Act of 1892 required certificates of residence to avoid deportation, something that Jade Snow Wong would openly reflect on late in her life (see Chapter 4). *Fong Yue Ting* (1893) cemented the federal government's immigration powers as separate from criminal punishment and relieved it of the evidentiary standards and burden of proof of the criminal justice system. Torrie Hester convincingly traces how the federal government then took steps to integrate the special clauses of the Exclusion Act into larger federal policy, removing many judiciary procedures and making it much easier to deport Chinese migrants. At the same time, the judicial system protected the rights of citizens, whose claims were in most cases granted a judicial trial, as well as the rights of Chinese who had entered as merchants under the Exclusion Act to change jobs so that the federal government could not readily deport those who fell from merchant status, an economic aspect revisited in later deportation laws and cases regarding other Asian ethnicities.[11]

In the late nineteenth and early twentieth centuries, industries and circuits of fraudulent immigration sprang up to achieve entry and family reunion. Men who returned to China periodically would report the birth of a child, thereby opening up a slot—real or fraudulent—for the immigration of this child in the future. Immigrants entering falsely through these slots were nicknamed "paper sons," although women also entered in this manner. Names and identities were bought and sold, invented and charted for memorization, and sometimes could hardly be distinguished from biological family members, who also struggled to remember exactly how many animals the family had owned or the year of their grandfather's birth. The "power of immigrant resistance and agency" is demonstrated, as Lee notes, by the fact that more than 300,000 Chinese managed to immigrate during the exclusion era (1882–1943), most of them laborers and farmers, despite the attempt by the Exclusion Act to admit only the merchant and elite classes. Women gradually entered in numbers closer to those of the men, coming not only as wives but also as widows assuming control of businesses and as miscellaneous workers of all kinds.[12]

A couple of officials and Angel Island detainees estimated that 90–95 percent of entrants were falsely documented in the 1920s–1930s; by the end of the Confession Program in 1965, 13,895 people had confessed, closing 11,294 potential slots. Exactly how many were deported was not heavily publicized. The sheer number is not surprising. Certainly, Wen-hsien Chen's sociological study showed no compunction on the part of immigrants about helping others, because they felt that exclusion was racist, unjust, and "inhuman in separating families." To elude exclusion, the birth certificates, coaching books, and other documents were insufficient; to back up these proofs, they had to maintain these identities and networks to avoid raids and deportation.[13]

In parallel with the development of Chinese immigration policies and the modern apparatus of immigration enforcement, the wrangling over citizens' or residents' *rights* racialized the Chinese (and other Asians) as a separate group, holding a tenuous position socially and legally. These cases and laws laid the groundwork for the illegal immigrant/model minority binary in the Cold War. In the first half of the twentieth century, activism by Asian Americans and their allies, including many religious and civic organizations, often urged assimilation via language, dress, religion, and other socially visible measures, and in their political advocacy they appealed pragmatically to the need for better relations with Asian nations, as well as to American and Christian ideals of civic virtue.[14] Thus, the seeds of the model minority were already contained in the efforts to combat exclusion or prejudice.

The slow shaping of Fourteenth Amendment protection at the national level seesawed with anti-Asian laws. *Yick Wo v. Hopkins* (1886) barred discriminatory laws that were written, on their face, as racially neutral but did not settle the question of classification. As Neil Gotanda points out, Justice John Marshall Harlan dissented in both *Plessy v. Ferguson* and *Wong Kim Ark* based on the race and foreignness of Chinese; Harlan noted that Jim Crow laws did not specify the status of Chinese, leaving it to be presumed that they might enjoy the higher social status of whites. Though only a footnote in *Plessy*, the economic and social rights of Asians would prove to be intimately tied to the racialized perceptions of them as everything from dirty and economically threatening to quiet and diligent, perceptions shaped by and shaping immigration policy. The early and deeply negative stereotypes of Chinese were cemented in the California state ruling of *People v. Hall* (1854), which enlarged a statute ensuring that no "Black, no Mulatto person, or Indian" could testify in the trial of a white man, citing the "mendacity" and "impassible difference" of the Chinese, "inferior" and "differing in language, opinions, color, and physical conformation." Such words echoed and justified the restrictions that went into place in 1863 in California and then in the Exclusion Act and its companion laws; indeed, the 1892 congressional dictum that one white witness could substantiate legal residency for a Chinese person was in many ways the twin of *People v. Hall.* Yet only a few short decades later, during Reconstruction, Chinese were imported to replace and subjugate black labor in the South because of their presumed docility and diligence, perhaps the earliest proto-model minority formation and one that would last to modern economic patterns of globalized industrial labor.[15]

Out west, where the black-white binary was less crushing, the civil rights of Asians were more directly attacked. The Alien Land Law (1913 and 1920) in California, the best known of the similar state laws, kept Japanese farmers at an economic disadvantage for a generation by forbidding sales or long-term leases of land to aliens ineligible for citizenship, which in turn empowered exclusive unions, professions, and other certifications. The culminating cases of Asian American civil rights in this era were the Japanese American incarceration cases, which failed to strike down racially based confinement, tacitly endorsing perceptions of foreignness and unassimilability, but also ruled that citizens could not be indefinitely held.[16]

After the war, the inclusion of Asian Americans, who had also pursued school desegregation cases, in the enforcement of desegregation after *Brown v. Board of Education* (1954) served as only a run-up to the social inequities of the 1950s on which the authors included in this book reflect. The practice of racially restrictive private covenants, which I revisit briefly in Chapter 2, rose in the 1920s in response to the Great Migration and immigration and lasted in private agreement until 1968, though unenforceable by courts after the 1948 case *Shelley v. Kraemer*, in which a black family in St. Louis ran afoul of a covenant excluding owners of the "Negro or Mongolian race." Such covenants were typical, aimed in different geographical locations at different races or ethnicities and serving to enforce segregation and further economically disadvantage the excluded group. During this era, individual cases of discrimination and segregation, as with contestations of antimiscegenation law (see Chapter 3), saw intermittent progress or rejection at the state level but ultimately were most often decided at the national level in the late 1960s, as with *Shelley* or *Loving v. Virginia* (1967), in cases that featured African American plaintiffs but included other races in decision or enforcement.[17]

The Chinese American community went through large changes and growing pains during the World War II and postwar period, as Xiaojian Zhao has discussed: geographical mobility, new waves of immigration (including more women), family reunification and formation, and political conflict in China, to name a few. The supposed reforms of the Immigration and Nationality Act of 1952, better known as the McCarran-Walter Act, did little to open the gates to entirely new Chinese immigration, but family reunification led to demographic shifts in the community. A paltry one hundred Chinese per year were allowed to immigrate freely, a number including mixed-race individuals and ethnic Chinese of every national origin; the bulk of the immigrating population in this era, unsurprisingly, entered through other means, whether as refugees or family members (who did not count toward the quota). Nor did the Refugee Relief Act of 1953 do much to relieve this pressure, though as a federal assessment of the act pointed out, the two thousand dedicated slots for Chinese were ridiculously in excess of those allowed under the 1952 Immigration Act, and three thousand more "Far East" slots were often used for Chinese. However, in comparison with the total of 214,000 aliens allowed by the Refugee Relief Act, and the million refugees in Hong Kong, it was but a small addition. The sympathetic attention paid to Chinese refugees was likewise proportional, as most of the dialogue focused on different situations in Eastern European countries and the growth of communism in Europe, also addressed by the Displaced Persons Act, which focused on Europe but allowed Chinese students stranded in the United States to officially claim asylum.[18]

My focus is not on the numbers, though those provide important context, but on the construction of narratives that could support either the government crackdown or the better assimilation and acceptance of Chinese Americans in U.S. society, particularly as a U.S.-born generation began to burst Chinatown's boundaries and demand housing, economic opportunity, social acceptance, and even interracial marriage. The struggle around immigration and this personal and community identity formation took place in part on the page, where writers struggled to reconcile the demands of family and community with those of self and state. Political discussion of the decade focused on "fraudulent" or "illegal" immigration of Chinese, particularly the reunion of families but also other filings for entry and citizenship immediately before and after immigration reform. What is more, the legal peril of Chinese Americans or any person found guilty of immigrating without proper documentation created lasting fears and silence because this status could never be trumped even by the most model of model minorities.

The Literary Cold War

As difficult as the Chinese American population found this era, the mainstream treatment of Chinese illegal immigration encompassed not only the serious, in news coverage of trials and investigations, but the silly, as in the light-hearted *Flower Drum Song*. Illegal immigration reached the awareness of a solidly middlebrow, well-to-do white U.S. audience in the 1950s through fairly frequent coverage in both media and the arts. Nationally known Chinese American writers, whether engaged in fictional or autobiographical accounts, were working within a quickly shifting but still white-dominated publishing landscape. Almost all of the narratives that made their way to publication adhered to middle-class mores; authors dealt individually with the hurdles of manuscript review and editorial intervention, not to mention critical reception. Archives reveal this editing process as a form of censorship (or self-censorship) and expose immigration secrets that authors sought to keep hidden for the sake of the community.

The Cold War U.S. literary landscape was characterized by tremendous overall production, as in other consumer industries, and wavering artistic trends, with the slow descent in reputation of recognized masters such as William Faulkner and Ernest Hemingway and the rise of younger, more radical, and increasingly diverse writers such as Ralph Ellison. Work by or about Asian Americans made up a relatively small portion of mass-market publications, though I have written elsewhere about the presence of the Asian in the Cold War imaginary. Only a few works in this era explicitly took on the project of depicting Asian American experience, including genre fiction such as mysteries and a few works of children's fiction. (Notably, a short-lived comic book series, *Yellow Claw*, posited a Chinese Communist supervillain against a Chinese American FBI agent, explicitly making the clash of this book's title manifest.) Chinese American literature was a relatively robust field within Asian American literature at this time, meeting a new interest from a U.S. audience. The first novel about Chinese in San Francisco Chinatown (as opposed to thrillers merely set there) was *When the Living Strive* (1940), by the sociologist Richard LaPiere and his collaborator, Pardee Lowe. (Though the novel appeared only under LaPiere's name, both referred to it in correspondence as "our" novel, and Lowe received 25 percent of the royalties.[19]) The novel, a rather clunky tale of a Chinese immigrant who is determined to return to China but accidentally passes his whole life in the United States, was chiefly notable—at least to the *New York Times*—for its novelty, but it paved the way within the publishing industry for more works.

The literature chiefly divides into two main categories, both at least superficially realist: memoirs or nonfiction by transnational elite refugees, such as Helena Kuo and Mai-mai Sze, and a slowly growing roster of memoir and fiction by American-born children of earlier working-class immigrants, such as Jade Snow Wong and Maxine Hong Kingston. Focusing as I do on the topic of illegal immigration, my interest is naturally chiefly in the second category, among which there is strong anxiety over illegality regardless of personal status, which serves to differentiate it all the more strongly from the tales of the Court of St. James from Sze or the Harvard- and Yale-set anecdotes of Buwei Yang Chao and her husband (more famous for the cookbook *How to Cook and Eat in Chinese*).[20] There are others who also complicate this neat division, such as the Chinese-born, San Francisco–dwelling C. Y. Lee, stranded by the Chinese Civil War on his U.S. student visa in the late 1940s, who wrote widely about the Chinese diaspora, including Chinese Americans, and Lin Yutang, the most famous of the transnational elite, who felt compelled to write a novel about the Chinese American working class surrounding him in New York, also drawing on the sociological work of U.S.-born Pardee Lowe. I therefore look at works by a diverse set of Chinese American authors that treat the important topic of illegal or falsely documented immigration, though this list skews toward the U.S.-born.[21]

The literary output of U.S.-born Chinese Americans in this era was mostly memoir or so-called sociological (which I do not use as a negative, though many critics have) fiction that bears a heavy burden of storytelling through the vehicle of the family. Asian American life writing has been well studied, as by Rocío Davis, who postulates family stories as a mode of conveying a psychological journey: "The history of Asian American life writing, because of the imperative to explain or understand immigrant cultures (for oneself and mainstream America), very often privileges the intersection of generational and cultural issues, focusing very specifically on family stories."[22] The telling of family stories turns into a political journey that informs the psychological. In what I refer to as the *reconciliation plot*—an Asian American play on the marriage plot—the protagonist's union with the body politic or the mainstream culture is typically effected through an eloquent pronouncement or some vivid bicultural tableau in order to create a sense of a happy ending. Because so many of these books for the most part aim at a mainstream middle-class audience, it is unsurprising that they adhere to a positive narrative of American belonging, but as we shall see, the reconciliation plot only thinly papers over the ruptures and difficulties of immigration that threaten to surface.

This trend aligns with a period in which best-selling white American literature followed a trend of exposing the drama behind happy family formations nationwide, in regionalist works (all made into films) such as the soap operatic *Peyton Place* (1956), set in a New England town seething with rape, murder, and class rifts; *Marjorie Morningstar* (1955) and its unhappily assimilating New York Jewish eponymous heroine; or *The View from Pompey's Head* (1954), by Jade Snow Wong's friend and champion Hamilton Basso, featuring a Southern returnee to a society rife with race and class prejudice. Such novels pointed fingers at the hypocrisy and familial breakdown in postwar American society but usually ended by confirming social formations, particularly white heterosexual procreative marriage. Stalwarts such as Faulkner, James Agee, and Conrad Richter likewise meditated on the breakdown of the family in this era of change, while the dawn of the Beats and the rise of a new generation of African American writers marked a willingness to challenge the social status quo. Chinese American literature understandably, as a new entry into the market, hews more closely in form and content to the mass-market mainstream, similar to the perfect happy families on the television shows that took off toward the end of the decade. However, this does not mean that the literature refrains from critique or transformation of the symbolic power of the family, especially as social mores shift over time. Instead, Chinese American literature betrays an increasingly critical attitude toward the literary construction and portrayal of these families.

This book's heterogeneous group of Chinese American writers—both sexes, both coasts, with different political and social views—obviously houses many political vantage points on the issue of illegal immigration, an anxiety that manifests differently. Yet, as Wu and Christina Klein have theorized about the Asian domestic and cultural presence, and Ali Behdad has theorized more generally about the American relationship with foreigners, while Asians benefited from racial-liberalist theories of assimilation and a narrative of progress, their work to earn citizenship and inclusion contrasts forcefully with those whose native Americanness was unquestioned. That work and the effort of depicting that work cuts across political differences, manifesting in all of the works that I examine. The dichotomy of foreigner and native or American and Asian is complicated by "good"/"bad" and legal/illegal immigrant, increasing the pressures of self-depiction for Chinese Americans, among others.[23]

Juxtaposed against the Chinese American literary archive, which in the 1950s reveals caution, erasure, concealment, and revision, I posit the political and legal framework of the 1950s, which demands exposure, confession, and revelation. Within a strikingly short period of time, the changes wrought by the 1965 immigration reforms and growing ethnic nationalist movements allowed younger authors and public historians to start to work within a narrative of memorialization and celebration instead, though one still fraught by the lingering trauma of decades of scrutiny and secrecy. The lack of a homogeneous politics among these writers may, at first, seem to undercut my attempt to understand the stigma of illegal immigration as a site of artistic production. However, that heterogeneity is, as Lisa Lowe set forth, a paradigmatic aspect of Asian American culture, particularly in the testimony of individuals who critique the lack of inclusion or the deception of inclusive ideologies.[24] The confusion of testimony, in the Cold War era, works against the liberal individualism and multiculturalism described by Klein; it is a particularly fraught concept for Chinese America, racked by decades of interrogation.

The Asian American Archive

In another sense, this project takes up the Asian American archive as its primary focus, from the voice of Benjamin Gim, the first Asian American lawyer to be lead counsel on a case in front of the U.S. Supreme Court, to the correspondence and drafts of Maxine Hong Kingston. The archival work that I perform is essential to understand the shaping of both official narratives and individuals' voices. The tragic story of Ly Shew, a cook in Chinatown, might have been lost to history if not for his entanglement in the immigration crackdown of the 1950s, and still can be found only at the nexus of lower court opinions, small newspaper mentions in local papers (both Chinese American and mainstream), and a few scattered legal documents. As I outline it in Chapter 1, Ly's story and that of his family illuminate the efficacy and persuasion of narrative, as his fate was left in the hands of judges adhering slavishly to a prevailing narrative of fraud, and his legal and public defenses proved to be too little, too late. These historical narratives are essential to understanding the definition of racial, ethnic, and legal categories in this era, just as the conversations between writers and editors or adapters demonstrate the pressures and limitations of artistic production.

In considering the Asian American archive, I am thinking not solely of a body of texts for study but also of the more institutional definitions of archive, a gathering of documents that establish legal and political authority or a place in which materials of historical and cultural value are gathered for future generations to study. Richard Harvey Brown and Beth Davis-Brown, librarians themselves, argue for the genealogy and importance of archives as bulwarks of modernity, tied intimately and institutionally to the rise of the nation-state. Their argument, based on Benedict Anderson's characterization of the nation as an imagined community centered on certain common cultural materials—a daily newspaper or, as in the Browns' focus, an archive—stakes out an explicitly conservative origin for archives as sources of "social stability and solidarity," deliberately excluding certain narratives from the nation, which now struggle to create new knowledge, as well. Jacques Derrida's theorization of the originary archive as a body of state papers that not only constitutes order but also hermeneutic power (to interpret and then to enforce) gives an even more abstract and absolute notion of the linkage between authority and the archive. The turn toward a more subjective view of history as a constructed narrative and the understanding of representation rather than truth as a prevailing mode of understanding the world have, in turn, the Browns argue, undercut the progressive narrative of the archive as a place that charts the large scope of human progress or offers the free access necessary to democratic government. Such an attitude toward the archive as a place of state power and contestation undergirds my study.[25]

Indeed, it could hardly not, as Asian American voices so often become difficult to retrieve from the writings of officialdom. Gayatri Spivak warns us of the impossibility of retrieving a lost subjectivity from the archive in her examination of one rani "caught in the cracks between the production of the [British Raj] archives and indigenous patriarchy, today distanced by the waves of hegemonic feminism." Nonetheless, "The account of her representation is enough for the book. To retrieve her as information will be no disciplinary triumph. . . . [T]here is no 'real Rani' to be found." Facing a similar lack in the official archive, I must focus this study on the writings of public figures instead, who have some few archives preserved, though I do also try to highlight other stories retrieved from legal cases and newspapers. In line with Spivak's warning, perhaps there is no real Ly Shew to be found, but the archive allows us to make our last, best attempt at resurrecting such stories in order to complicate our understanding.[26]

The well-theorized call to "queer" the archive, to put an evasive, lost, and missing archive in conversation with the preserved archive in order to recontest the definitions of gender, sexuality, and sex, as well as to find archives of queer experience, serves as a useful model to understand how the preservation and reclamation of an Asian American archive may operate twofold to recontextualize racialization, immigration, and the structures of surveillance and juridical power during the Cold War. Furthermore, the queering of an archive demands that we consider just how broad and yet how biased the archive is that controls the definition of such broad terms as "sex" and "gender."[27] In this book, I interrogate how the archive has constituted the categories of Chinese/Chinese American, immigrant, and illegality/fraudulence. We must look to as broad an archive as possible in order to fully understand the construction of these conceptions. Here, I look across media, the literary archive, and legal and other governmental documents and statements, seeking to contextualize the construction of Chinese Americans as inherently fraudulent and illegitimate and, in opposition, as exemplary and exceptional. At the same time, I attempt to reconstitute an Asian American archive of that process.

As important as legal and historical work is to this volume and to the Chinese American authors who signify on the historical record (in the spirit of Henry Louis Gates's signifyin[g]), I want to focus for a moment on the Asian American *literary* archival research that I perform extensively here, looking at authors' papers and their less-well-known or all-but-unknown works, from C. Y. Lee's other novels to Maxine Hong Kingston's essays. By including *Flower Drum Song* and white editors' and collaborators' voices, I am inherently adhering to those who eschew authorial ethnic/racial identity as part of the definition of Asian American literature, but that is not my primary goal. As part of my approach to recovering the author's relationship to history, *Illegal Immigrants/Model Minorities* delves deep into the available archive with a particular focus on authors' drafts and correspondence, as well as their short (usually periodical) writings, which are much less well known than their novels and memoirs. This gives further voice to these authors, many of whose publication in the mainstream was shaped by white editors and industry pressures; their private papers and drafts serve not as a corrective but as a supplement that allows us to understand how they negotiated and reimagined the categories of Chinese American and immigrant identity in this period.

This type of archival examination is not very common in Asian American studies; expansion of the archive has advanced more vigorously in the crucial directions of microhistory, oral history, digitization, and further ethnic and geographical diversity, often simultaneously. The complications of literary archival work for Asian Americanists are a combination of market forces, copyright issues, geography, and linguistic barriers, all related to a relatively short time frame in which Asian American literature has been recognized as work worthy of collection and preservation. Its relative lack of representation in author collections at major literary archives within the United States speaks to its precarious state; while a few major authors have deposited their papers at universities in California, Asian American literature as yet appears very little in mainstream archival powerhouses such as the Ransom Center and the Library of Congress—both of which I am personally indebted to for their sponsorship of my archival research. Indeed, the Library of Congress's relatively new and very small collection of Asian American individuals' papers, housed in the Asian Division and, at the time of this writing, being reviewed for new placement, raises questions as to the place, quite literally, of Asian America in a national archive.

From the outset of what we might call a field or discipline of Asian American literary study, the archive has always been conceived of as one full of loss and gaps—pyres, even, that reflect the political and physical violence of the racial formation of Asian America. These represent what Derrida might call the death drive of the archive, the "violence of forgetting," a willful forgetting by a racist and discriminatory society and publishing industry. The story of John Okada's lost second novel, burned by his widow, represents this loss at its most anguished and its most subjugated; Frank Chin and Jeffery Paul Chan used this symbol to substantiate their politicized call for an Asian American literature that reflected their own burning vision of Asian America. The apocryphal tale that they recounted, based on a conversation with Okada's widow, Dorothy, was one of exclusion from the official archive; when Dorothy offered the manuscript to the University of California, Los Angeles, for its collection of Japanese American incarceration papers, the politically opposed project curators supposedly refused and pointedly suggested to Dorothy that she destroy his papers, which she did. As Min Song writes, "Asian American literary studies was partially founded on the need to salvage what could be salvaged from this past" of manuscript loss and destruction. I mention this example not to set Asian American literature up as merely a reflection of political occlusions, omissions, and violence. Indeed, as Colleen Lye has noted, given the relative weakness and expansiveness of the Asian American racial formation, literature (and, increasingly, other cultural forms) may well be one of the strongest backbones of Asian America as a political and social entity. It is, however, one in which physical preservation has always been imperiled.[28]

Literary archival research for this monograph thus has been an almost forensic search online for small collections here and there; through periodicals of the era; publishers' papers (archived or not); or finding someone who knew and might help me speak to descendants or obtain privately held family papers, in which I was singularly unsuccessful, being perhaps too far personally and geographically removed to forge connections, a failure that speaks to the problems of a lack of preservation and access. What archival theorists have agreed in the past decades is that there is no perfect history to be reconstructed with the aid of archival research. And yet the importance of archival work remains, particularly in discovering the currents of power that have shaped cultural production. Edward Said exhorted us to read the entire "cultural archive . . . not univocally but *contrapuntally*, with a simultaneous awareness both of the metropolitan history that is narrated and of those other histories against which (and together with which) the dominating discourse acts." Following this behest, in cases where I was not able to find archival documents I nonetheless do my best to read the cultural archive, from the well-known to the all but forgotten, in order to better understand how these productions reflect immigration history.[29]

The literary archive provides a method for reexamining the narrative construction of Asian America by looking at specific works, as well. The examination of manuscripts and editions has traditionally tended to be a search for the ideal text, the ideal often being characterized by the author's original or unadulterated intentions. Asian America has been more often in the position of reissuing out-of-print texts than the more privileged one of desiring to reconstruct better versions of them—assuming that the available and preserved manuscripts would even permit such reconstruction. In any case, the pursuit of the ideal text is necessarily a fraught one, and here, as I argue for this group of literary texts, the desire to disentangle author from editor would erase some of the political pressures that irretrievably also made these artists and artistic productions who and what they are. As Richard Jean So writes in his call for more Asian American literary archival work, "Such a method provides some necessary relief to long-standing debates over defining an Asian American aesthetic, and locating authenticity within Asian American literature," though I would not use the word "relief" so much as "complexity."[30] Archival work, in addition to illuminating the material conditions in which a work of literature is produced, illuminates the particular concerns and choices of each author and the dialogue, whether resistant or accommodating, nationalist or assimilationist, that constitute the development of this literature.

In this variant of textual criticism that I employ in looking at drafts, editorial correspondence, and different versions, my goal is not to ascertain the authoritative status of any given version or to uphold authorial intentions as inherently superior, but to look at these writings as historical documentation of the lifelong struggle between secrecy and revelation as inflected by personal and political events—here, related to illegal immigration. (Indeed, because of the paucity of resources, in some cases this literary archive is also a source of biographical and historical information.) My chief concern is instead to ascertain how the Chinese American community in this era stakes its uncertain claim to its own archive—to the ability to narrate and preserve not only individual histories but also wider tales of the community and of Chinese American identity formation. How to do so, then, with few public forebears on whose narrative authority to build and in a political era in which Chinese Americans have such questioned narrative authority? In a time when the authority of family narrative itself is under siege by the government, so that everything from minute details of a house to blood relation itself is considered unreliable by the interlocutor and desperately rehearsed and memorized by the narrator, the archive shows us how Chinese American artists learned to assume their own authority, sometimes from tentative amateur beginnings such as that of Jade Snow Wong, or from a Yale-trained but racially disenfranchised ambition such as that of C. Y. Lee, rebuilt by writing in community newspapers. The anxieties, dissension, and assertions of the archive themselves construct the claiming and reclamation of Chinese American narrative authority.

The archive also allows us to consider an intertextual and dialogic approach to the construction of Asian American literature within a booming midcentury literary industry in which Asian Americans are only newly and fractionally empowered. Asian American literature, which from the anthologizing of the 1970s has reached back to reconstruct a history of the field and the people, signifies, in my thinking, most prominently on the politico-legal texts and mass-media stereotypes that wrote them into being in the first several decades of a substantive Asian American presence (the late nineteenth to mid-twentieth century). The narration of Chinese American experience emerges as a blend of literary and historical work for these authors, who in order to explicate ethnic experience for a mainstream audience, necessarily must create, as Davis states of life writing generally, "a significant degree of intersection between the personal and the public, generally enacted by the incorporation of substantial historical information—dates, places, names of politicians, descriptions of battles, discussion of ideological commitments, and so on—to supplement the relatives' stories."[31] The self-reflexive construction of family history, ethnic history, and personal narrative based on an uncertain archive constitutes the political and literary formation of Asian America in the 1970s and beyond.

Illegal Immigrants/Model Minorities puts published texts, already imbricated with official history, into dialogue with available literary archives and a broad array of historical documentation that are necessary to "queer" the archive that defines race and ethnicity through the immigration process: legal cases, immigration documents, immigration law, political debate, mass-media coverage, and more. By incorporating both but never privileging the official over the personal, this context allows us to see how writers construct stories of self and family or fictional families in relation to the political structures of the nation that are allowing or disallowing their presence, their citizenship, and their blended identity. Far from seeking to undo generations of academic work on the creation of history and narrative, I hope to show yet more of its entanglement on the highly fraught, over-narrated issue of illegal immigration and how Chinese American narrative moves toward an acceptance of the constructedness of history.

The Cold War of Chinese American Narrative

Each of my chapters offers a transhistorical look in miniature, focusing on a particular thematic aspect of the Chinese American negotiation of illegal immigration stigma during part of the Cold War and concluding with a section ("Post-") that reflects on the later literary transformation and remembrance of those experiences. Chapter 1 lays the foundation of this negotiation in my project as I narrate the intertwining of "Narrative Cold War: Public Faces of Chinese America": the insistence in government narratives on a community identity of illegal immigration and the constant protest, by the claiming of exemplarity and a solidly American identity, of Chinese American public figures throughout the Cold War. By the mid-1950s, the stigmatization of Chinese America was at its height, and government statements and actions from the famous Drumright Report to the multitude of immigration court cases painted Chinese Americans as inherently fraudulent and foreign, an image that community leaders contested publicly with portrayals of their law-abiding and Americanized lives. Jade Snow Wong's foundational 1950 memoir serves as one bookend, as her archive exposes her strategic private and public concealment of immigration secrets about her family over the next half-century as a political counterpoint. The battle over the construction of Chinese American identity in the 1950s also ranged from nineteenth-century to contemporary race-targeted policies, as government officials and Chinese American leaders and editors contested the history of Chinese America and the claims of Chinese Americans to constitutional rights and protections. I conclude the chapter with Kingston's 1970s meditation on her experiences of suppressed immigration stories, bred by the 1950s Confession era in which she grew up, and her desire to find a way to speak freely of immigration in her experimental memoir. The struggles of the 1950s thus become embedded in both form and content in Chinese American literature, necessitating the reconstruction of Chinese American identity.

Chapter 2, "Happy Families: Modeling the Minority in the Era of Immigration Reform," encompasses perhaps the most important social formation that Chinese American writers could invoke rhetorically in order to defend themselves from the stigma of immigration: the nuclear family. As attacks on family reunification immigration escalated, the nuclear family and the extended family were, at various points, the public face of Chinese America. Government and popular rhetoric in the early 1950s characterized the strength and the non-nuclear structure of the family formation in Chinese and Chinese American society as everything from old-fashioned to pathological, but later in the era, the sociological development of the model minority concept paradoxically espoused Chinatown's kinship and clan structures as its strength. Wong carefully concealed the rifts and "horror and pain" in her own family, all of which threatened her literary construction of a proto-model minority family—a family that must be not only nuclear but happy. Many Chinese American writers were already expressing a more ambivalent attitude toward the supposedly all-powerful nuclear family formation, instead turning to other grounds to stabilize their American identity and image and to redeem the virtue of extended families, clans, bachelor Chinatowns, and, by extension, illegal immigration. I compare the extraordinary cases of two works deliberately revised to include illegal immigration as a plot device by white Americans: first, by the editor Richard Walsh, and in the other, much more popular case, by the foremost musical playwriting duo of their day, Richard Rodgers and Oscar Hammerstein II. In the first case, Walsh pushed Lin Yutang to include an explanation of illegal immigration methods in the novel *Chinatown Family*, ultimately composing it himself. In *Flower Drum Song*, Hammerstein and his collaborator Joseph Fields introduced the plot thread of illegal immigration, making reference to its global nature and ultimately creating a cross-racial comparison to Mexican immigration; their unceasing revision reveals the sensitivity of the topic, which they nonetheless used as a key to the understanding of Chinese American culture. The resolutions of both suggest that love and family are, once again, the vehicles of American acceptance, but *Flower*

Drum Song's politics of confessing and informing leave us in grave doubt as to the price that the community must pay. I conclude by looking at Jade Snow Wong's late-in-life reflections on the hidden stories and subjectivity of her mother, a picture bride, and her mother-in-law, a concubine, written at a political and personal moment when she finally felt free to dwell on other family formations and their surprising happiness.

Turning from family structure to family ties, Chapter 3, "Blood Tells: The Attack on Chinese American Family Ties," discusses how Chinese Americans have uniquely labored under intersecting judicial and immigration attacks on marital and blood relationships. I commence by discussing *The Woman Warrior* and *Eat a Bowl of Tea*, with their concern about illegitimacy and bastardy, as responses to the policing of paternity of "paper sons." In the early 1950s, the INS went as far as to require blood tests to verify paternity of entering Chinese immigrants, though even then some officials saw matching tests as proof of collusion, thereby undermining any evidence of family connection. However, the rise of literary depictions of interracial sexual intimacy and even intermarriage in this era starkly contrast with stories of all-Chinese American families. I reread the historical case of *Naim v. Naim* (1955) to show how immigration difficulties were inextricable from the social pressures of interracial marriage, a problem that C. Y. Lee adapts in his dark early works set in a multiracial, multiethnic San Francisco. *Lover's Point* (1958), the little-known follow-up to *The Flower Drum Song*, argues for love and understanding between Chinese American and Japanese American protagonists caught in a common immigration tragedy of overseas marriage and unhappy war bride marriages. The figure of the mixed-race child, in Lee's and Kingston's works, haunts the protagonists as proof of their inability to fully enter U.S. society. These conflicting drives for racial purity and fears of illegitimate, mixed-race, or illegally married families show how the nuclear family ideal was held out of reach by immigration and discriminatory domestic policies and social pressures. However, I conclude by considering the lighter, more optimistic narratives that appear after *Loving v. Virginia* (1967) struck down anti-miscegenation laws nationwide. Lee's late work *The Land of the Golden Mountain* (1967) and Kingston's famous ending to *The Woman Warrior* use the reconciliation plot to suggest that Chinese Americans may find a way to reconcile or translate themselves to the nation.

Finally, Chapter 4, "History, through Literature: Rewriting the Past after the Confession Era," delves into the reclamation of authority over documentary and legal history in Chinese American writing, particularly examining Wong's and Kingston's works in the context of the later Cold War. The legacy of debate over the uses of history can best be seen in the public controversy evoked by Kingston's claim of ignorance of her parents' immigration history in *The Woman Warrior*, which impels her literary journey to find stories that tell her origin. I contrast the orientalist delight taken in this secrecy by high-profile mainstream reviews with the anger from other Chinese American writers who found Kingston's ignorance implausible, at best, arguing for an unbroken line of historical transmission. While Kingston's assertions about silence and the need to reestablish family histories seemed to prevail within the Chinese American community, over time she herself both developed and embraced a more creative attitude toward history. By the mid-1970s, amid the rise of ethnic activism and nationalism, Wong and Kingston had both returned to questioning and probing documentary history, using the newly memorialized history of Angel Island and Chinese American immigration flexibly to inspire and politicize family stories, radicalizing what had previously been narratives of exemplarity. Kingston's manuscripts reveal how she split a more celebratory historical narrative off to become the short historical section in *China Men* while reserving a withering critique for Arnold Genthe's supposedly neutral documentation of turn-of-the-century Chinatown. Looking at Kingston's and Wong's last (to date, for Kingston) works, written after the Cold War, I conclude that they fully demonstrate to the reader that the archive inspires but no longer holds authority as a repository of "pure" or truthful history.

In the Epilogue, "The Failure of the Model Minority Narrative?" I end and enlarge this study—admittedly, somewhat bleakly—by looking at the ways that these narratives, particularly the pressures for undocumented immigrants to become exemplary, resurface in our contemporary political discourse. However, the unceasing attacks on even the most exemplary political figures suggest that our era of divisive debate about undocumented migration and refugeeism has undercut even the dubious power of the model minority to protect. Looking at contemporary literature, Ha Jin offers us an equally profound critique of the model minority image to protect from the greatest enemy of all: one's own emotional insecurities as an immigrant. The literature may, I suggest, at least serve as a road to better understanding the narratives and strategies of communities afflicted by the racialized stigma of "illegal" immigration, even as the model minority defense plainly fails in political efficacy in our own time.

The shift that Chinese America made over the course of the Cold War was nothing short of extraordinary; the postwar transition as China's "fall" to communism turned it from World War ally into new Cold War enemy was itself a huge shift in identity formation, as was the liberalization of Asian immigration that slowly occurred throughout the 1950s, culminating in the 1965 Immigration and Nationality Act permitting Asian migrants, including my parents, to enter the country in numbers never before seen. Chinese America literally wrote itself into being in this era, authors grasping the authority to create their narratives in the literary sphere to speak of and for the growing and diversifying population in the nation. The stakes of recovering this literature of illegal immigration is in the uncovering of our own critical and narrative biases, which post-1965 continue to be shaped by political pressures of normalization and Americanization. But importantly, we must also resituate the construction of ethnic literary narrative within the tangle of judicial, legislative, and popular narration about immigration that continues to shape the fates of many communities today.

1

Narrative Cold War

Public Faces of Chinese America

In *The Woman Warrior*, Maxine Hong Kingston recounts the fears and multiplicitous stories of a community fraught with fear of deportation. In a long exchange devoted to the Chinese Confession Program, which was designed to bring fraudulent documentation to light, she voices the debates and conflicts of a tight-knit community:

> "We might as well," somebody would say. "Then we'd have our citizenship for real."
>
> "Don't be a fool," somebody else would say. "It's a trap."
>
> "You go in there saying you want to straighten out your papers, they'll deport you."
>
> "No, they won't. They're promising nobody's going to jail or getting deported. They'll give you citizenship as a reward for turning yourself in, for your honesty."
>
> "Don't you believe it. So-and-so trusted them, and he was deported. They deported his children too."
>
> "Where can they send us now? . . . We don't belong anywhere since the revolution." . . .
>
> "Don't tell," advised my parents. "Don't go to San Francisco until they leave."
>
> Lie to Americans.[1]

This mistrust and fracturing of narrative runs throughout the book, shown in the rifts within the community and even within families. A long legacy of distrust of Chinese Americans' immigration stories has boomeranged back to create an intense distrust here of the government's claims. Relying on rumor, anecdote, and friendship, the community works to maintain the fraudulent identities that gave its members legal purchase.

An era of strategic Chinese American public writing was provoked by massive investigations and prosecutions, which commenced with the "fall" of China to communism in 1950. The decade cemented an oppositional relationship in which the government sought evidence of fraudulence that investigators were sure was hidden in community sources. Government narratives largely cast Chinese immigration as fraught with fraud to a degree that was inseparable from culture and history. The preponderance of documents and public discussion implicitly framed Chinese and Chinese Americans, alike in their probable fraudulence, in opposition to a U.S. immigration service seeking to find the truth and root out the fraudulent means by which communists might enter. The government's authority to narrate and characterize a community thus intertwines with the community members' supposed lack of Americanness and legitimacy.

Chinese Americans living through investigations and media reports in the 1950s found themselves stigmatized at a time when U.S. culture was tending toward containment and cohesion. These political and social pressures led to a culture of strategic silence and the evolution of a proto-model minority narrative, founded upon mainstream ideals and narratives, as the public face of an active segment of Chinese America. Finding themselves so often on the defensive, Chinese American public figures in this period sought instead to brandish their American credentials by seizing the narrative. Some chose the language of exemplarity, but others turned to a kind of civil rights language, appealing to their valuable contributions to America as well as their rights and protections as citizens and legal residents. In so doing, they attempted to redefine Americanness to include themselves and begin to construct a blended public Chinese American identity.

In this decade, a growing Chinese America faced new challenges and discrimination, partly as a backlash to increased wartime visibility and partly as a response to the fears of communism and illegal immigration. The Chinese population numbered 117,629 in the 1950 census (probably undercounting undocumented migrants), less than 0.1 percent of the U.S. population, and contained nearly twice as many men as women, reflecting past immigration restrictions and labor flows. Chinese America was coming out of a wartime boom that had greatly improved its mainstream economic opportunities, although different Chinatowns had different trajectories during this period, some faltering economically and some just commencing. Thirty percent of young Chinese American men had worked in defense industries, particularly after the fight for equity by the National Association for the Advancement of Colored People (NAACP) led to President Franklin D. Roosevelt's executive order against discrimination in the defense industry. More Chinese Americans were buying property, as well, due to increased eligibility from newly permitted naturalization and a wave of U.S.-born citizens coming of age. Nearly another third of Chinese American men aged fifteen to sixty had served in the armed forces, opening up new connections and opportunities to some extent; many veterans moved out of Chinatowns after the war and established families in other friendly enclaves, some in new suburban Chinatowns. However, as mentioned in the Introduction, such individuals also faced the reconfiguration of prejudice in restrictive housing covenants and community resistance, as well as foreclosed postwar work opportunities.[2]

As this growth and change was underway, Chinese Americans suffered through an era of high-profile, sweeping investigations of the community during which the U.S. Immigration and Naturalization Service (INS) allied itself with the Federal Bureau of Investigation and U.S. State Department, shoring up its own power within the federal government. In 1956, grand juries were impaneled in San Francisco and New York to investigate Chinese illegal entry, resulting in thirty-eight indictments. That same year, the San Francisco office of the INS announced the beginning of the Confession Program as a means of choking off possible communist infiltration by closing paper slots, suggesting but not promising that law-abiding residents who confessed would gain citizenship "if at all possible." Embracing the stigma might, then, lead to a life of new security and status. However, the description of the program itself was elliptical in the extreme, holding out the hope but not the promise of naturalization even through such methods as military service: "Chinese persons illegally in the United States who have long feared deportation or prosecution now make full disclosures knowing the Service will assist them to adjust their status *if at all possible* under the law." Ngai's tabulation of the INS reports shows that although many confessors were granted an adjusted status, not all were. Thus, the transformation out of fraudulence was not guaranteed, and there would have been grave doubt before the fact.[3]

Behind the unhappiness and confusion of depiction of the Confession era is the long history of stigmatization and confession that lasted for decades. As late as 2005, in an interview, Kingston expressed her enduring conviction of the fear in which the community labored, which in her childhood was specifically a fear of confession and informing, followed by deportation. Fae-Myenne Ng, born in the 1950s, wrote similarly in a 2009 essay focused on the Confession Program, in which she pointedly recounts the agonies of the Confession era. Ng characterizes herself as out-narrated by her father's confession in 1965 and his continuing feelings of rage and betrayal, expressed in outsize public cursing and shouting. Both Ng and Kingston portray a generation nearly stupefied out of their voices by fear. Trained to a protective silence and baffled by their parents' stories or scolding, they elaborate on the difficulties of revelation.[4] Such difficulties stem from the great weight of government narratives with which writers contend in the 1950s and even as late as the 1970s, when the stigma lingers.

Pitched by the government as a program of compassion (by relieving anxiety) but also as a way to weed out communists, the widespread campaign to obtain confessions and the possibility of deportation only further publicized the fraudulence that the government used to describe the Chinese American community for a decade. This led to a narrative crisis that the writers discussed in this chapter had to learn to navigate by piecing together favorable narratives about Chinese America. The Chinese American community had existed in a limbo in which personal narrative (the family histories given under interrogation at Angel Island) or even written, quasi-official versions of a personal narrative (in the form of affidavits and family papers) could always be trumped by the government's declaration. Consider, then, the extraordinary state not only of political but also of narrative confusion caused by the federal government's declaration that personal narrative was suddenly sacred if delivered in the form of a revelation of illegality. After decades in which stories of family relations were deemed fraudulent and questionable, the idea that confession would not only be acceptable but would magically deliver immunity from fraudulence was simply incredible.

Furthermore, these writers had to constitute a Chinese American identity without a clear consensus from their own communities about public speech, as Kingston's half-imagined, half-recollected debate shows. The small, tight-knit communities of different Chinatowns, linked by internal structures ranging from family associations to tongs and informal business networks, inevitably made it difficult for an individual to speak publicly without turning informant. Estelle Lau's study of "paper sons" suggests that in some ways, Chinese diasporic society became more strongly united by the structures and trust required, but that also means that the thought of betrayal was even more painful. Speaking outside the community, regardless of immigration status, required one to elude the interrogations, invitations to confess, and other nets that lay in wait for Chinese America during the Cold War.

The public writing and speaking of Confession-era writers must be interpreted in the context of the caution in which they lived for most of their adult lives and was not fully over even in the 1970s, so that even young authors—most prominently, Kingston—struggled to find narratives that could adequately combat the stigma of illegal immigration and fraudulence. Prosecutions of illegal immigrant-smuggling rings frequently made it into mainstream newspaper coverage from the 1950s through the 1970s. Many of these cases featured exemplary leaders of Chinatown, making them all the more dangerous for the image of Chinese Americans as a whole; if even these upstanding community leaders were conducting illicit immigration operations, the whole community was implicated. Public figures could only with difficulty avoid the topic, so prevalent was the coverage and consequent stigma. Likewise, Kwong and Brooks have discussed how political turmoil within different Chinatowns differently affected the communities, with a diverse, tolerant atmosphere in San Francisco and a conservative one in New York.

Though many of the most famous works of Asian American literature avoid addressing immigration explicitly, focusing instead on a protagonist-centered contrast of the United States with the Asian country of origin and a cultural clash set in the United States, careful reading shows the enduring anxiety of the movement between the two as framed by the public discussion of immigration and fraudulent documentation. Chinese Americans sought to contest the government's implications of fraudulence in both personal and group/community histories, creating different versions of exemplarity and Americanness while hiding or minimizing illegal immigration. I begin by examining the formation of the public identity of Jade Snow Wong, whose carefully crafted image elides the history of fraudulent immigration within. Starting from her earliest media appearances, Wong learned to craft an image of exemplarity as a cultural bridge, both in her own person and among her family members. I then turn to the clashes of the 1950s, after the publication of Wong's first memoir, when government officials and Chinese American public figures struggled to control the image of Chinese America, and examine the competing narratives about Chinese America as written by the INS, Chinese American newspaper editors and community leaders, and the mass media. Their battles over American fairness and equality, as well as the roots of Chinese American history, sought to create an image and genealogy of Chinese America based on freedom and patriotism rather than fraud. Finally, Kingston's reflections on the traumatic and lasting impact of this era, as remembered from childhood, give us a clearer understanding of how the inability to speak publicly about illegal immigration inspires not only her childhood attempts at model behavior but also her narrative form.

The Making of Jade Snow Wong

Chinese American literature in the 1950s was kicked off by the bestselling coming-of-age memoir *Fifth Chinese Daughter* (1950), by Jade Snow Wong. "Many feel it is a book of permanent importance in interracial understanding," wrote one gushing columnist, calling Wong "a beautiful girl with a beautiful name."[5] The delight with which her most famous piece of writing was generally received in 1950 shows that, at the very least, it struck a sympathetic chord with its mainstream readers. Wong, whose fame had already been on the rise as a ceramic artist, was thus launched on a long career, the epicenter of which would be her Bay Area home but that would take her around Asia on behalf of the U.S. State Department and see her pottery reach the collection of the Metropolitan Museum of Art. Wu and Cheng have argued that Wong's State Department tours served to construct an interstitial Asian identity as an ambassador of both Asian American achievement and American racial tolerance.

Wong's memoir appeared years before the most fear-inducing investigations of the mid-1950s, but it coincided with the "fall" of China and waves of postwar immigrants and refugees that would soon lead to the immigration act of 1952. In 1950, the INS detailed false documentation (theft or forgery) "schools" coaching applicants for false slots and the lack of records, stressing the extreme difficulty of and necessity for investigation. It promised an era of intense scrutiny, noting, "It will be apparent that these cases are such as to require very exhaustive examination and thorough investigation because of the possibility that the claim of relationship may be fraudulent."[6] *Fifth Chinese Daughter* thus entered a landscape of increasing doubt about the legitimacy and legality of Chinese Americans, offering a sentimental and domestic tale that papered over any doubts or skepticism of this particular Chinese American with its appealing descriptive writing, cultural conflict between parent and child, and solidly Californian yet exotically Chinatown setting. Avoiding mention of fraudulent immigration, not to mention communism or any other politics, Wong implicitly proffers a tale of praise for American society in much the same manner that Chinese American public officials would later in the decade, though their statements would be made with an explicit political goal.

Fifth Chinese Daughter, famously narrated in what was received as a charmingly modest (and typically Chinese) third person, opens in Wong's early childhood and narrates the love, labor, economic makeshifts, and celebrations of her large and tightly bonded family, supported by her father's garment-manufacturing business in San Francisco Chinatown. The strength of the family and their work ethic are highlighted by traditional Chinese values, as well as strong Christian beliefs. As Jade Snow grows up, she increasingly embraces what she characterizes as American independence, as well, venturing out to earn her own money, go to dances, and attend college. The memoir ends with the launch of Jade Snow's pottery business and a reconciliation in which her independence is met with her parents' love and acceptance. The memoir normalizes cultural and racial differences through her femininity and domestic accomplishments, as well as her many positive experiences outside Chinatown. *Fifth Chinese Daughter* received glowing reviews for its timely portrayal of a young woman who combines the discipline of her strict Chinese father and the liberation of American society to become, first, a worthy contributor to the war industries, and then an independent craftswoman and entrepreneur during the postwar economic boom.[7]

The dualities and difficulties of Wong's offering have created a mixed reception and legacy. Because Kingston dubbed Wong the "Mother of Chinese American literature," Wong has maintained an unquestioned historical status even as her mainstream remembrance or instructional use has dwindled in the past couple of decades. Critics have explored or deplored the politics of Wong's memoir: its politics of personal responsibility and denial of institutional racism; its food pornography; its wielding of a prefeminist guise for its narrator in order to bolster the relationship between American individualism and Chinese discipline. Leslie Bow has neatly described the ambivalences and complexities of Wong's politics, which conceal the creation of an economically driven common cause between two disparate cultures.[8] More recent critique has focused on the establishment and subtleties of her double voice or narration and a corresponding divided subjectivity; this, however, runs the risk of reifying a binary American and Chinese identity. However, all of the techniques that Wong employs to create a public self for the reader work to screen her family's true history at a fraught moment.

My investigation into Wong's papers, now held by the Library of Congress, exposes the highly self-censored construction of her family's immigration history in *Fifth Chinese Daughter*, comparing it with her private accounts, as well as new information given in her last, unpublished book manuscript, *Chinese American: Burden and Prize*, a blend of history, Asian travelogue, and memoir written in the 1990s and 2000s. This information allows us to view her proffered exemplarity anew as a deliberate attempt to screen the topic of illegal immigration, casting new light on the careful politics of *Fifth Chinese Daughter* as it grows out of Wong's publicity materials and interviews.

Let me state clearly that the point of this investigation is not to chide Wong for her concealments or constructions, or to correct the historical record, though it may incidentally do that for those interested in the biographical details of this important cultural figure. Rather, I probe the excision of immigration as a topic in order to create the family image that she early learned brought acceptance and fame.

The greatest silence in Wong's public writing and speaking surrounds the fact that her mother was her father's second wife, a fact that had dropped out of public knowledge but that her papers allow me to elucidate. The discord in Wong's presentation of this information clouds a remarriage after her father's first wife's death, which seems in no way unethical or, by her family's Presbyterian beliefs, irreligious. Only after her mother's death at the age of 102 did Wong, in the very last drafts of *Chinese American*, finally reveal the reason for her silence and tell her mother's story at length in a separate and evidently newly composed chapter. I give the opening of this story in her own words:

> My mother was my biological mother, but she was my father's second wife. My father's first wife died after giving birth to four children, of whom three survived. My maternal grandmother emigrated here as wife of my maternal grandfather, who was a merchant in a fish and poultry store in Chinatown. Grandmother was a seamstress in my father's factory. When Daddy's first wife passed away, leaving four children with two under ten years of age, she introduced my mother as a picture bride. My mother was twenty-two, and my father was forty-three.
>
> To comply with immigration laws, Mother sailed with my Fifth Uncle, also a merchant in the shirt business, and entered the United States as his wife. I do not know if my mother knew that she would be a second wife to a much older man, nor if she knew that she would care for stepchildren.[9]

Wong finally reveals the reason for her many elisions and silences: her mother, Jang Shee, had entered the United States fraudulently, in a fairly common manner, accompanying Jade Snow's Fifth Uncle as his legal wife but then "marrying" Wong Hong once she arrived and assuming his first wife's legal identity. She was determined to be an "exemplary, virtuous stepmother," and Wong seems to have learned from her example. The awkward rifts in the family and Wong's strange narrative contrivances result from her desire to avoid this topic entirely. Her careful concealment of the exact family configuration most centrally buries her mother's immigration story in a way that she could not have done if she had mentioned a second marriage, while also protecting her mother's legal status. Only her mother's death frees her to speak. Wong's suppression of this history even in the initial drafts of a late work that is focused on exposing the unsavory details of Chinese exclusion and anti-Chinese racism is particularly noteworthy. She answered questions very similarly in an interview in 1995: when asked how her parents got married, she deceptively replied that her father, as a merchant, was able to send for his wife.[10]

Bow, in her discussion of Wong's memoir in terms of its historical repression and its inability to resolve the contradictions of a plot that attempts to contain its feminist conflict and social critique in a classic tale of immigrant self-reliance and rise, presciently pointed out a discrepancy in dates in Wong's two published books that led Bow to speculate that Wong's father had two wives and perhaps had committed bigamy overseas. Perhaps the most telling discrepancy that Bow points out is the mention of "Daddy's wife" having two-and-a-half-inch bound feet, yet "Mama" loves to walk all over San Francisco. The sudden shift in terminology to "Daddy's wife," since she is usually referred to as "Mama," also seems very telling. (In a hilarious personal anecdote, Bow recounts how Wong eluded her questions during a brief encounter in 1987.) While, with the exception of Bow's deductions, little is usually mentioned about Wong's biography outside her memoirs, her blended family was evidently known in some circles, perhaps primarily local ones. The San Francisco ethnographer and historian Judy Yung wrote to Wong inquiring specifically for information about her half-sister in 1997; Wong wrote back calling her a stepsister instead, perhaps to preserve her emotional distance. It was quite easy for Wong to continue this conflation, repeating as late as 1994, early in a draft manuscript of *Chinese America*, that her father "sent for his wife and two little daughters, one of whom had been born just before he left China. More children were born here; neither he nor my mother ever returned to China."[11] As in her previous writing, the syntax plainly pushes the reader to assume that the "wife" and "mother" are the same.

The explosive secret was not a shameful bigamy that would explode conceptions of the 1950s nuclear family but more dangerous immigration secrets that would have an even worse effect. Mention of her father's first marriage surfaces only fleetingly once, early in Wong's public life, in a *Saturday Evening Post* feature. Thereafter she conceals it carefully, a combination of the desire to present a united family front and, as I discovered in Wong's public and private papers, to conceal the cascade of immigration secrets and illegalities that accompanied her mother. The classic tale of immigrant self-reliance or American pioneer families that was popular in the 1950s demands, first and foremost, an unsullied family.

Wong does not excise immigration because of a lack of interest. It is clear from one early piece of writing that Wong did care deeply about the racial and ethnic inequities of immigration—enough to speak out publicly. In a heretofore unnoted letter to the editor of the *San Francisco Chronicle* in 1943, she protests the views of H. J. McClatchy, executive secretary of the California Joint Immigration Committee, which notoriously opposed Asian immigration and advocated heavily for Japanese American incarceration during World War II. McClatchy had evidently been quoted in the *Chronicle* opposing the repeal of Chinese exclusion, in which he said that "60 years' work has kept the Pacific Coast white." In response, Wong offers her most strongly worded critique, calling his views "obviously ridiculous" and calling the exclusion laws "laws originally passed in hysteria." However, the grounds on which she argues this are standard model minority arguments about the "law-abiding, hard-working and loyal people, who have a much lower crime rate and have caused less civic trouble than an average group of white people." She avoids all mention of her family and their immigration methods. What is more, Wong falls into the pit of gaining acceptance by employing antiblackness, repurposing McClatchy's language: "[Why would] allowing Chinese citizenship and to enter on quota add half a dozen Oriental problems to the present Negro one?" Acknowledging racial strife but distancing herself and her race from it, Wong lands far from an ideology of racial equality, relying instead on assimilation and exemplarity already at this young age to make her political points about immigration, which, in any case, she distanced herself from as she grew older.[12]

The very first public profile of the Wongs as a family—a splashy, celebratory *Saturday Evening Post* feature by George Sessions Perry in 1948 titled "The Wongs"—shows how the public pattern of Wong's exemplary family and immigration concealments commenced at her still young age. By this time, Wong had published very short profiles of her father and her youngest brother that easily skirted the topic of immigration by their brevity and comic nature. "The Wongs" appeared in a series about diverse white and nonwhite families in the United States: Chinese, Mexican, Norwegian, Italian, German, African American (then termed "Negro"), Jewish, Acadian, and "the pure blood of those salty old dogs who settled this nation in the first place"—that is to say, English.[13] In the feature, the emphasis on the Americanized family subsumes the only published acknowledgment of Wong Hong's second marriage, establishing the Wong nuclear family image.

"The Wongs" is written as a chatty profile, as Perry employs a first-person tone of discovery at times and then takes on a tone of authority in offering background information. Some information about the family clearly draws on the minutiae of two short essays by Wong about her family in *Common Ground*, which have been more studied than the *Post* feature because of her authorship (a third about Chinatown also made it into *Fifth Chinese Daughter*).[14] "The Wongs" recasts these details, as Perry alternates between exoticizing and Americanizing the Wongs, all while extolling their virtues to impossible heights. After he first introduces the "Wong family, in the Chinese sense of family . . . , a river 3000 years long," he then focuses himself on "Wong Hong's immediate family, which includes children ranging in age from the forties down to a five-year-old lollapaloosa named Prosperity from Heaven" (24). This contrast between all-Americanness and gentle exoticism, and even Perry's alternating register of discovery and authority, can also be seen in much of Wong's later writing. Since Wong continued to consult with Perry on the composition of his piece long beyond his interview of the family members and was herself in the process of writing *Fifth Chinese Daughter*, it may have been either inspiration or a sort of co-authorship, but either way, the narrative of "The Wongs" was the model to which she largely adhered for the rest of her life.

Perry narrates the family as a happy, inseparable unit culturally spread across a spectrum from Chinese to American, but with a solidly acceptable American exterior. He takes a strong tone in establishing the children's Chinese American identities, referring to them by both translated Chinese and Western names and describing their careers and activities rather than fully orientalizing them, as well. Americanizing the children for the middle-class white reader, he notes, "And, as may be true of your own family, any of these children can usually be found, three minutes after getting home, protruding stern-to, from the refrigerator." The color photos of all the Wongs in Western dress and mostly plastered with smiles finalize their image (105, 109–110). Notably, the older siblings are not pictured; their estrangement from the family, which is only delicately alluded to in *Fifth Chinese Daughter*, was documented in an unpublished interview with Esther Wong, the oldest child (in her forties), discovered by Judy Yung among the responses to the Survey of Race Relations conducted in 1924 while Esther was at college.[15] Perry's article omits any mention of strife, with these siblings' omission from the photos our only clue.

As for the Chinese interior, he describes the virtual cloistering of Jang Shee in orientalist tones. Perry says that Jang Shee "speaks no English and almost never goes out" (109), thereby connecting the two, and further notes that Chinese ladies are often so cloistered as to allow a doctor to see only their wrist and hand, though this is clearly not the case with Jang Shee, as she sees Perry. Thus, when Perry notes that Jang Shee "sits at the [sewing] machine where, except when sleeping, cooking, or dressing babies, she's sat for twenty-seven years" (110), the reader is primed to accept this as "dells of Oriental family privacy" (105) rather than evidence of a rather crushing working-class poverty.

Though the profile presents the Wongs in only the most positive and charming (if also quaint and orientalist) light, Wong struggled mightily with the revelation of too much information about the family for reasons that she publicly obscures. She wrote at length but vaguely about this in her first drafts of *No Chinese Stranger* (1975): "When her parents had learned that Jade Snow was working on an autobiography, they had expressed disapproval, for publicity was loathsome. [Perry] had spent three weeks trying to find a family who would consent to be featured. He complained, 'The Chinese seemed to disappear into holes in the wall.'" Wong glosses over any reason for or analysis of this fear of publicity, continuing, "Eventually, he was introduced to Jade Snow and she had talked her family into being interviewed and allowing pictures to be taken." That was putting it mildly, as she wrote to the Perrys in a self-parodically orientalist fashion, "I practically had a tong war with Daddy." This hatred of publicity was drastically compressed in the final publication of *No Chinese Stranger*, which attributes the family's dislike of Perry's article to the drawings by Miné Okubo, which showed the Wongs "in peasant clothes, with unkempt hair, without shoes or stockings. It mattered little about the words Jade Snow had written; the illustrations antagonized her family members."[16] Thus, their disapprobation reads as a desire to adhere to a proper middle-class, assimilated appearance, a laudable mainstream goal, not a hatred of publicity due to fears of immigration investigation. Even in the draft, no explanation at all is given for a desire for privacy, and the invocation of Perry's complaints about *all* Chinese makes this yet another piece of quaintness—or inscrutability. The historical record, of course, tells us with great clarity why so many Chinese American families shrank from publicity. Even before the investigations of the mid-1950s, the questionable entry methods of many wives and paper sons were not something their families would submit to mass media scrutiny.

What is evident from her personal papers is that Wong did not conceal this information privately and that Perry became her coconspirator in its public concealment. Wong became very close to the Perrys, up to and including Perry's tragic disappearance and death in 1956. A chatty, personal letter from Claire Perry to Wong in 1948 breaks off her discussion of clothes and household china and Wong's book project to note that the *Post* had moved up the schedule of publication of the family profiles and that "we had no time to send the galleys on to you as we had planned. However we corrected yours with extreme care. I believe we added all the things your father wanted, and were very careful in the re-defining of your mother's new status. That is, we just spoke of her as your father's second wife, with no details that could conceivably cause any repercussions."[17] What details Wong had confided to the Perrys, and what they had unwisely put into their first draft, are not clear from their exchange, but it seems clear that she had told them enough that the information could have revealed a questionable immigration status, the only thing that could cause "repercussions." Given the generally flippant tone of the piece and the year of its publication, before the full-blown publicity about Chinese illegal immigration, it is entirely possible that Perry would have framed it with the best of intentions as quaintly Chinese, not thinking of its possible effects on the family. Wong's first major public appearance thus deliberately sets out to conceal issues of immigration and familial blending, trying instead to offer an unimpeachable exterior. The positioning of Jang Shee as the cloistered interior of the family thus turns into a doubled metaphor.

The article deliberately sweeps aside consideration of the two marriages through its bright insistence on a single, large family and the skillful deployment of Perry's orientalist phrases. Looking merely at the staggering range of ages, from forty-something down to five, of the carefully cataloged Wong children, one might already wonder about this large family, especially as the elder children are not pictured. It is possible for a *Post* reader to do some speculative mathematics and further reading between the lines here to unravel the family history: Jang Shee is in her forties, close in age to the eldest daughter (107). But in Perry's colorful article, the images and writing tend to gather the Wong children into a happy tangle. Specific mention of the first wife is all done with orientalist imagery, relegating her to an old-fashioned Chinese past. Halfway through the article, the existence of a prior marriage is subtly buried in a list of items that Wong Hong keeps in his safe, including "a tooth that belonged to his first wife" (106). Perry eventually explains briefly, "Mr. Wong's first wife, who had bound feet, has returned to her ancestors. His second wife, still in her forties, is named Jang Shee" (109). The gratuitous note about bound feet, a familiar feature of Chinese culture to the general public, is of more note than anything else about the previous marriage. He does not belabor the point, referring to Jang Shee's influence on "the children" as if she had borne and raised all of them. Indeed, as this explanation only appears quite late in the article, he has already presented the Wongs as a unit, not specifying which are Jang Shee's biological children.

As the adorable little jitterbugger, the youngest child, Little Jon/Prosperity from Heaven, serves as an all-American capstone by supplying comic relief and, more importantly, a domesticating presence, as his loving sister Jade Snow serves as his "outside mamma," a detail mentioned in every single piece of writing about him by Wong and Perry. The use of Jon for Americanization is ironic and may well be symptomatic of an unease that is particular to his birth and his name, pushing Wong and Perry to Americanize him as thoroughly as possible. Jon's last name created a considerable legal problem for years because of his parents' questionable marriage status. Wong cautiously referred to the reasons behind this in a letter in 1948 to Esther Dayman Strong, the beloved dean for whom she keeps house in *Fifth Chinese Daughter*, and her husband, Stuart Strong, pertaining to an insurance application with which Stuart was helping her. Wong wrote, "The reason Jon and Mother's names and relationships are so given have to do with legal and passport difficulties. Esther knows all about the difficulties and can explain them to you." Later that year, perhaps driven by continued confusion, Wong threw caution to the wind and set some of the story down in writing for Stuart: "Jon Wong Ng should be Jon's full name. He is supposed to be Cousin Ng's son. His mother is Jang Shee because Chinese women keep their maiden name when they marry (Jang). The 'Shee' is added upon marriage as the equivalent of 'Mrs.' O.K.? However, Jon's last name is Ng."[18]

The reasons for Wong's great care are evident, since Jon's name certainly could have raised all kinds of questions that ultimately would reveal her mother's deceptive immigration paperwork. I speculate that Wong and her younger sister were able to take the name Wong because of less regimented paperwork in the earlier decades or because they may have been born at home instead of in a hospital, with their births registered later by their father, as was common practice. In addition to the later public writings, the federal censuses of 1930 and 1940 show the Wongs living together as a family and all of the members listed as Wongs, including Jang Shee (spelled with several variants).[19] The care over Jon's last name may also reflect the political situation in 1943, the year in which he was born, and some uncertainty over whether revocation of exclusion might have had some meaning for improperly documented immigrants or their children. No echo of Jon's different last name ever surfaces in any of Wong's own public writings or, for that matter, in "The Wongs," but it does provide yet one more reason the Wongs might initially have flinched from national publicity and explains Wong's caution in *Fifth Chinese Daughter.* Without this information, Jon completes the happy family picture, entertaining the reader, and leads them away from the contemplation of immigration details, a role he would continue to play from birth in *Fifth Chinese Daughter* (see Chapter 2).

Wong's development in her public life of an exemplary and blended Chinese and American (rather than Jon's all-American) image continued to snowball as she gained in confidence and savoir-faire. Some of this care safeguarded not only her family's continued residence but Wong's increasing fame on a local and national scale. Perry's profile singled out Jade Snow among her siblings for special praise as "shining with a bright-blue flame" (107), detailing some of her achievements, but still positioned her as a bridging figure with two names. Over time she adopted Perry's method of selective orientalism, choosing to use the transliterated moniker "Jade Snow" for business rather her given name, Constance; friends addressed her as Connie, never by her Chinese name or Jade Snow, her papers show. Indeed, when launching her early pottery business, she wrote quite coolly to a friend of her intention to "play up the Chinese angle" in order to distinguish herself from the competition. Her famous use of the third person in *Fifth Chinese Daughter* likewise distinguishes her from non-Chinese memoirists from the outset.[20]

Wong likely had learned a great deal about how her Chineseness could be favorably depicted from the way she was being portrayed elsewhere in mainstream media; this became a reciprocal relationship as she gained more control of her public image. For Wong, the expectation of exemplarity and cultural bridging was everywhere manifest as her profile rose even before the publication of *Fifth Chinese Daughter.* Early praise of Wong set up the image that she perpetuates in her memoir. *Mademoiselle* magazine, awarding her one of ten Merit Awards, mentions her achievements in ceramics but heavily emphasizes her cultural "struggles and adjustment" as she "weighs the values in the formal patterns of her Chinese heritage with the enterprise of her American homeland." Notably, none of the other winners' achievements are framed in racial or any other terms of affinity, except one who concisely exemplifies "Quaker humanity." The African American winner Hortense Williams's race is not even mentioned; it is simply left to be assumed from the photograph. A *House and Garden* feature on California craftsmen more subtly alluded to the popular Chinese-versus-American dichotomy, contrasting Wong's "war work in a shipyard" with her "potter's wheel in the China Bazaar."[21]

In addition to the influence of Wong's already public persona as a Chinese woman who could move freely in the mainstream, editorial advice to a young, uncertain author produced a slightly redacted memoir and shaped its cultural politics. The greatest influence Wong's editor Elizabeth Lawrence had on the politics of the memoir was in shaping a properly reconciliatory ending. She clearly states her view in a particularly important directive to her inexperienced writer in February 1947: "Even though you cannot say everything in this one book, it should come to an end at the right point artistically. This point should lie near the conscious moment of your acceptance of both the Chinese and American cultures. It might be when you chose a career. It might be Jon's birth. Only you can decide certainly."[22] Framing the cultural bridge as an "artistic" necessity, Lawrence dictates that Wong must describe a moment of conscious acceptance, thereby imposing both a binary and a reconciling framework on the narrative. Unsurprisingly, Wong chose a quiet domestic moment with her parents to reinforce her family narrative rather than a scene of worldly success.

Such an attitude was entirely typical of editors at the time in approaching Asian American work. Lawrence was a highly influential editor at Harper and Brothers and was particularly active in the midcentury with women and ethnic writers; the most famous work she edited was Betty Smith's *A Tree Grows in Brooklyn.* Richard J. Walsh, Lin Yutang's editor, suggested similarly that *Chinatown Family* (1948) end with an overt comparison between life in the United States and life in China, resolving cultural duality through a tableau such as a Chinese wedding or through the aged mother's thoughts rather than merely ending with a love match, which would normally be a classic ending to a novel. Wong's memoir was thus unexceptional in being shaped into the required sentimental reconciliation plot early in her process, a plot that fostered the hope of an individualized East-West bridge typical of Cold War orientalism.[23]

Wong's papers reveal much about the shaping of her memoir, which critics have wondered at over the years since her casual mention in an interview that Lawrence cut "two-thirds" of her memoir. Lawrence's influence, as well as that of one of Wong's English teachers, was strong because of Wong's uncertainty about professional writing. Correspondence shows that Lawrence first contacted Wong in 1946 to see whether she was in the midst of writing a book; her attention had probably been drawn by Wong's comic articles about her family, which overlap in subject matter (though not in writing style) with *Fifth Chinese Daughter.* Lawrence's heavy persuasion got Wong started on a book, which she had not thought to try for many years. However, while Lawrence did urge many cuts over the next three years, they were not always in contradiction with Wong's own impulses. For example, Lawrence suggested that Wong cut lengthy description about the various families she worked for as a domestic; much of this description of the families' social pretensions was quite sarcastic and biting compared with the published version. Wong herself worried constantly about being too critical, asking Lawrence to help her edit the tone, and had already made many cuts to this section herself. Likewise, she softened criticisms of her family.[24] Lawrence's edits gently guided Wong to a more positive, triumphant memoir of cultural harmony, with humorously softened lows that might have criticized either white mainstream or Chinese culture too much—the two poles that stabilized her public identity as the exceptional success from a worthy American family.

Wong's exemplarity during post-publication publicity only grew with her economic success, increased Americanness, and marriage. Interviews dwelled not only on her new married life and her exotic but feminine beauty but also the continued presence of her father, who attended awards banquets with her. Eager questions about what had happened since her memoir revealed that since retirement, "Daddy's learning to be a citizen; spends all day at it," properly taking advantage of his newly available naturalization rights. Wong's tale of economic rise also continued, as a radio profile only a year after the memoir's publication reflected on how far she had come at the opening party for her new studio, "so far removed from the little shop window Jade Snow Wong first startled Chinatown with, as her workshop."[25] Wong's success in creating this public persona and later taking it abroad firmly covered over her family's secret, one that she would keep for five more decades.

An American War of Words

During the 1950s, government reports and crackdowns on Chinese illegal immigration created a nearly constant furor in the media. Countering a stigmatized identity of a fraudulent and illegitimate community, Chinese American leaders turned to several different narratives that appealed to American ideals, emphasizing their service, their citizenship, and their uprightness. The narratives started to create a new proto-model minority identity for Chinese America, one of exemplarity not only in their own behavior and achievements but as exemplars of America's goodness. Like Wong's memoir, which quietly demonstrated not only her family's virtue but also the possibilities and inclusiveness of life in America through anecdote, Chinese American community leaders' narratives offered powerful counters, substituting a larger group for positive scrutiny in place of the fraudulently immigrating individual. But these leaders spoke of not only a family or individual, but an entire community's legal rights and privileges, as well as their virtues. Amid the haze of immigration cases and investigations, the alternative narratives that these speakers sought to create were narratives of American identity and constitutional protections, offering protest on these grounds such as would not be seen openly in the literature for many years. The vehement public stand that Dai-Ming Lee of the San Francisco newspaper *Chinese World*, in particular, takes in his editorials demonstrates a historical understanding of these issues that presages the ethnic nationalism of the 1970s by several years. In a way, part of this discourse actually overleaped the proto-model minority discourse, claiming legal rights and Americanness as a matter of justice and equality, though many still pled the community's deserving status. They steadfastly maintained a relative silence on the issue of individual fraud, referring to it only in passing, substituting a history of their patriotic and civic-minded actions.

The McCarran-Walter Act, by putting an age limit on applications for derivative citizenship (citizenship via a parent's U.S. citizenship), engendered a flood of applications in 1952; a *New York Times* article in 1956 cited 750 cases still in process. Everett F. Drumright, then the consul at Hong Kong, sent the long "Report on the Problem of Fraud at Hong Kong" to the U.S. State Department in December 1955, describing a crisis in the consulate's ability to check identity and therefore to "exclude Chinese Communist agents or criminal elements." He thus indelibly cast the problem of illegal immigration and that of communist infiltration into a single mold, characterizing the need to root out fraudulence as a strong Cold War imperative. The report would give force to a series of investigations and subpoenas that would occupy the Chinese American community for the greater part of an entire year and continue to plague them over the next decade. It is important, however, to note that the Drumright Report was not the start of such policies or theories in the government. Rather, it was a powerful statement of them at a key moment: the ideas themselves were circulating years before, as other documents show.[26]

While Drumright's political goals were complex and not aimed at the complete ending of Chinese immigration, an examination of his report reveals the strong, even extreme narratives that he employed to persuade. The report employs such statistics as are presumably available, but its body consists largely of proof by storytelling, piling example on example to impress the reader. Naturally, all of these anecdotes are stacked on the side of fraud; Drumright does not dwell on legal or truthful immigration or citizenship; nor does he linger on the danger of excluding citizens. While he details some of the cultural practices that create difficulties, such as adoption, polygamous marriage/concubinage, and a different naming system, he does so to further narrate the difficulty of determining fraudulence, not to exonerate. Cultural difference is thus framed as grounds for suspicion rather than leniency, explaining why so many Chinese American public figures worked to establish a firm American cultural identity. The stringent warnings of the Drumright Report would quickly influence the policies of the INS and the State Department as a whole. The report was confidentially submitted to the State Department in December 1955, but a summary of it was made available to the Appropriations Committees of Congress at the end of February or beginning of March 1956, and the entire report was later declassified.[27]

While the Drumright Report did not itself make the mainstream national news—immigration investigations and cases tended to instead—it provoked a barrage of responses from Dai-Ming Lee that countered the report's narrative with equally strong narratives of its own. *Chinese World* was a newspaper with an English-language front and a Chinese-language section; while it circulated primarily within Chinatown, it was at least possible for Lee's protests to reach much further. Lee, a U.S. citizen born in Hawai'i, was a leader in the community and a staunch anticommunist who was not intimidated by controversy or even possible physical danger. "Even those who didn't agree with him wanted to read him. . . . 'Take a look at what Dai-ming Lee is saying about things,'" said his friend Gilbert Woo. Lee's death in 1961 would end a highly active journalistic career after a particularly fraught decade in which he ceaselessly advocated for Chinese American equality and a third-party solution to government in China both in print and at political meetings.[28]

In the spring of 1956, *Chinese World* ran nearly daily coverage and editorials attacking the Drumright Report and the investigations of Chinese immigration. In his extensive editorial responses, Lee did not respond to the details of Drumright's accusations of fraud or his detailing of Chinese culture, focusing instead on the ethics and legality of this immigration scrutiny, which he generalized as an attack on all Chinese Americans. Lee focused heavily on the unethical and harsh interrogation and other investigative measures of the consulate, performing some impressive close readings. He used his months of daily editorials to create alternative narratives around the principles that he saw Drumright's report violating: racial equality; Sino-American friendship and cooperation in the fight against communism; and the lack of constitutional protections, since Drumright's actions were legally shielded from judicial review. He heaped repeated scorn on the report on all these fronts, suggesting that "it should provide Hollywood with scores of melodramatic plots." These editorials were eventually issued in a pamphlet or short book form by *Chinese World*, sold in both Chinese and English.[29] Addressing a Chinese American audience and acting as his own publisher, Lee was able to stake out clear political positions beyond those of the memoirists and novelists of this era, who were addressing a mostly white publishing industry and audience.

In offering a community defense, Lee made strategic pleas for leniency, only touching lightly on undocumented or falsely documented immigration by pleading that the "sins of fathers and grandfathers should not be visited on innocent children." He reframed Chinese emigration in sympathetic terms, calling the migrants "refugees" in order to appeal to the contemporaneous laws permitting political refugees (including Chinese, but chiefly from Eastern Europe). Describing the earlier migrants as both economically and politically subject to "Manchu oppression," Lee very simply called them refugees in search of "an honest living" but who were subject by the exclusion laws to separation from their families on the basis of their race. This set out a different paradigm for current immigration, emphasizing a communist refugee situation that was omitted from the prevailing narrative of fraudulence and infiltration.[30]

Lee chiefly offered political critiques of the government and its failure to live up to its own constitutional obligations. On one occasion, he unusually used a small individual tragedy to turn his rhetoric to Chinese American service and patriotism. In early 1957, he wrote about the tragic immigration case of a man named Ly Shew, who had been convicted of immigration fraud and committed suicide in his jail cell while awaiting sentencing. Lee had to discuss fraudulence here, but he acknowledged only the finding of Ly Shew's fraud by noting that he "pleaded guilty" and that "government investigations discovered his claims to be false." While these might seem to be unequivocal statements, in the context of Lee's skepticism of government investigations and prosecutions, it represents a possible sideswipe at the reliability of these findings in order to stress Ly's worthiness as an American.

Ly Shew was an undisputed U.S. citizen by derivation (via his father) and had arrived in the United States in 1912. He later visited China multiple times, marrying a woman in his home village and fathering multiple children. He brought three children, two boys and a girl, to the United States in 1947. In the early 1950s, Ly Shew, living in San Francisco Chinatown and working as a cook, attempted to bring two younger children to the United States. However, their immigration cases went through prolonged and unusual legal reversals and wrangles, which ended in their deportation. (Although none of the court cases specify, it is historically likely that the children had to remain in INS custody in northern California throughout their three-year judicial process.[31]) The aftermath of this case can be traced only in local newspaper stories published before Lee's editorial, including *Chinese World* coverage that suggests the case was well known in the community. Perhaps in consequence of the failure of these immigration cases, Ly Shew was caught up in the ongoing grand jury investigations and charged with fraud. He fled to Mexico but was either persuaded to return to California and then arrested or was illegally "arrested" by two State Department security officials without proper extradition. He and his wife then pleaded guilty in federal court; she had in fact been brought to the United States in 1947 as his paper daughter.[32] This common dodge came to what the judge called, with considerable understatement, "a rather tragic ending": on or before January 28, 1957, Ly Shew hanged himself in the San Francisco County Jail at San Bruno, where he was being held awaiting sentencing after pleading guilty to perjury and conspiracy. He was survived by his wife, who was spared deportation by the judge, and four young children of that marriage in addition to his elder children.[33]

Mainstream newspaper coverage referred to Ly Shew only as a Chinatown or Chinese cook. This simple phrase cloaks him in a firmly ethnic identity, associating him with then exotic Chinese restaurants in an ethnic ghetto and ignoring his U.S. citizenship. Ly Shew's supposed children's Americanness and their intent to assume their Americanness had also been deeply questioned during their trials by skeptical judges. Lee turned this rhetoric around to argue Ly Shew's Americanness as a last eulogistic proof of his worth. Supposedly, Ly Shew had feared being deported to "Red China," and Lee used the suicide to plead against deportation to a communist country as a general policy, as well as implicitly noting Ly's anticommunist politics. He prominently noted that Ly Shew had seen service in World War I—certainly possible, though I was unable to verify it—thereby instead asserting his contributions to his country of citizenship as part of his life story. Lee cast this fatal tragedy, the suicide of a veteran and family man, as the symbolic culmination of a terrible year of attacks for the Chinese American community.[34]

Lee's discussion of Ly Shew, although minor amid his much more voluminous arguments about constitutional rights, partakes of a larger discourse of American belonging employed by other Chinese Americans during the year. Following close on the heels of the Drumright Report, the grand jury investigation of Chinese immigration sent out a mass subpoena of the family associations of San Francisco Chinatown, when many Chinese American individuals were also being investigated and indicted. The Chinese Consolidated Benevolent Association (better known as the Six Companies), the Chinese American Citizens Alliance, and twenty-two other benevolent and family associations were subpoenaed for, in the case of the Six Companies, all books and records showing their officers, and for the other twenty-three associations, "All lists, rolls, or other records of membership of the Association during the entire period of the Association's existence; all records of dues, assessments, contributions and other income of the Association; and all photographs of the membership or any portion thereof." The hope was to find family records that would disprove assertions made during immigration proceedings.[35]

As soon as the subpoena was issued on February 29, 1956, the community leapt into political action, backed by several supportive California and Chinese Nationalist politicians. The legal course was ultimately the one that garnered relief, but Chinese American community leaders began a public relations battle that was the forerunner of the large public history projects and debates in the 1970s (see Chapter 4). The Six Companies took the lead on all public statements, beginning with a back-to-back press release and statement on their history and mission in mid-March. They articulated clearly that this was a racially based attack on the entire community, stating, "Whether intentional or otherwise, [government officials] are having the effect of stigmatizing the social and family status of a respected community with criminal coloration." The community, not defined in this particular line, was elsewhere defined very clearly as "an entire community and a whole people of a specific racial ancestry." Their statements relied on the racially defined identity of the group as a way of invoking the protection of civil rights, an idea that, as we must recall, was being newly wielded in the 1950s.[36]

In this discourse, community spokespeople's public statements generally skirted the question of immigration fraud or guilt, relying instead on the language of equal rights and government overreach. In 1957, 124 delegates from Chinese American organizations across the country gathered in Washington, DC, to discuss matters related specifically to U.S. domestic issues, oddly avoiding the recent furor over immigration. In a statement and series of resolutions issued publicly, the conference delegates focused heavily on the tiny immigration quota and limited slots in the Refugee Relief program rather than on the equally obvious immigration investigations. However, they did, in resolutions related to hardship cases, ask for judicial and administrative review of "unreasonable, capricious, and arbitrary [consular] power" in a probable reference to Drumright. As had Lee, the conference critiqued government overreach in investigation while quietly putting the issue of illegal immigration to one side.[37]

Notably, although these public statements heavily emphasized the racial inequities of Chinese immigration scrutiny and noted that a blanket wrongdoing was being laid on an entire U.S. racial group, the legal case did not, as a matter of fact, invoke equal protection of the laws, which had proved its efficacy when used only two years previously in *Brown v. Board of Education* (1954). It relied instead on the patent overreach of the government, invoking the better-established case law on Fourth Amendment protection against unreasonable search and seizure. (Invoking equal protection of the laws would not only have trod on relatively new legal ground, but it also might have raised the question of whether it applied to noncitizens.) The public defense was thus ahead of the legal realm in this regard. The verdict was hailed both by those who saw it as a repeat of the outrages of King George III and those who saw it as racial profiling, such as the San Francisco African American newspaper the *Sun-Reporter*.[38] Nonetheless, Chinese American spokespeople may have understood that there were limits to the power of racial equality as a narrative to defend themselves.

As a replacement, they relied on asserting their status as law-abiding citizens cooperating with investigation and resisting unjust investigation, relegating any fraud to a minor and hypothetical percentage:

> If any citizens or aliens of Chinese ancestry in the United States are legitimate objects of inquiry with respect to violation of immigration or other laws, we would be the last to deny the government's right to take every appropriate action against them and to receive every pertinent record required in the prosecution of its case. But where, in an effort to adduce evidence in support of intangible suspicion of wrong-doing, an entire community is subject to calumny and the inference of wholesale wrongdoing, we believe that it is our right and our duty to protest, as Americans, against such injustice. This we do.

From beginning to end, the press release reaffirms their identity as "patriotic loyal and (law) abiding American citizens [*sic*]" and, consequently, devotion to and deserving of civil rights. This would remain the line of Chinese spokespeople throughout, creating an alternative narrative to the presumption of guilt.[39]

Meanwhile, the New York Six Companies showed support with symbolic telegrams to President Dwight Eisenhower, Vice President Richard Nixon, and a number of other prominent U.S. government officials. This patriotic solidarity, clearly invoking American identity by appealing to the highest U.S. officials rather than to Chinese Nationalist figures, would continue amid the investigation and stigma that continued even after the subpoena was quashed. Jade Snow Wong, aware of the same need for authentication although remaining apart from the public discussion of these investigations, made some of the same moves in her article "How to Get the Best Chinese Food" (1955). While describing the specialties of various Chinatown restaurants, Wong recounts the story of a private luncheon that she had organized in 1951 for the wives of important delegates to the Japanese Peace Treaty Conference in San Francisco. "Mrs. Dean Rusk, wife of the then Assistant Secretary of State," asked Wong to arrange the outing for "Mrs. John Foster Dulles, Mrs. John D. Rockefeller, III, . . . and Lady Carl Berendsen," among others.[40] She lists the menu for the luncheon, which includes some of the dishes and recipes that appear later in the article. Thus, at the same time that she invites white middle-class readers into San Francisco Chinatown, she assures them of its safety and suitability by invoking the wives of white U.S. dignitaries. Far from simple, vain name-dropping, Wong's invocation of these names and the Six Companies' telegrams place them as Americans in close communication with powerful mainstream political figures. Such ploys for connections to the body politic could serve to establish Chinese Americans' citizenship rhetorically, if not legally.

Ultimately, these self-representations were not enough to win the day; the associations applied for relief to the courts. Judge Oliver Carter noted in his ruling that the subpoena was indeed unduly onerous, though the volume of the papers was not at issue so much as the sheer extensiveness of the subpoena, which covered all time periods and all of these associations without showing their precise relevance. His ruling quashed it in decided terms, stating that the grand jury's investigation "must necessarily be related to individuals, or groups of individuals," but that the subpoena's "broad demand smacks more of the fishing expedition which was condemned" previously, targeting and smearing the entire community in the hope of finding proof of fraud rather than fraudulent individuals. The effects of this subpoena went much further than the months of legal wrangling, as the community was galvanized into public speech asserting that a patriotic national identity could override the presumption of fraud.[41]

The Stakes of History

The American lives and rights of the contemporary community did not exist as the only divergent narrative of government officials and Chinese American public figures. The second, interestingly, focused on the creation of Chinese American history as a path to understanding the present-day situation. At a time when one side questioned the truthfulness of personal history and the other largely subsumed the personal in its defense of the community, a history of the community instead became a place to argue for or against a presumption of fraud for the individual; the stakes of history and who gets to write history, particularly a U.S. ethnic history, have rarely been so clear. In retelling the story of coolie labor, racist violence and laws, and exclusion, writers on opposing sides of the immigration debate cast it as a history of racial prejudice and oppression leading to present persecution or a history of false identities and, however sympathetic, present resentment and illegal behavior. These laid out wildly different precedent and identity to argue logically that the community was either rife with fraud or patriotic and put-upon. The repeated usage and apparent efficacy of the government's history of Chinese America made this narrative equally essential for Chinese Americans to combat.

Drumright, in his report, recast the history of Chinese Americans in terms of immigration fraud, from the days of coolies imported to build the railroad through the claims of citizenship after the great San Francisco earthquake of 1904 and the repeal of exclusion during World War II. Although the report sympathetically recognizes the "horrors" of the origins of Chinese in the United States, it assigns next to no responsibility to the U.S. government or American actors. Notably, he condemns certain injustices of the past in the strongest possible terms, particularly the coolie trade and the racist basis of the exclusion laws. Early in the report, Drumright describes the coolie trade in extremely strong and specific language, comparing "the overcrowding, filth, and horrors of these trans-Pacific passages" to the transatlantic Middle Passage of the slave trade. The conditions of the coolies' labor, working off the debt of their passage, are mentioned, and he critiques the idea of "voluntary status" and the ships' captains who would rob coolies of their fares as they tried to sail home. He thus frames the report in terms of what we might now dub social justice; at the very least, it may read as a sympathetic framing of Chinese American history, though he then undercuts some of his own critiques. He displaces blame for the trade onto the "feeble" Chinese Imperial Government and notes that coolies often "returned home within a few years after making more money than they could have saved in a lifetime in China." In addition, he cites the historian Foster Rhea Dulles in saying that, later in the nineteenth century, "The people of California . . . saw in the activities of the Six Companies an attempt to maintain a system of forced labor," thereby displacing the coolie trade onto the Chinese themselves (ironically, though he does not note it, this is an argument frequently used about African chattel slavery, as well).[42]

As a closing for a frame of just evaluation, the report returns to the anti-Chinese sentiment of the late nineteenth century that led to exclusion but with an astonishing rhetorical reversal. Drumright touches on violent hatred briefly in the course of his initial history, citing "labor agitators and political demagogues [who] preached a doctrine of riot and lynch law." However, he then cites the lasting American shame over the "approach of [Dennis] Kearney [of the Workingmen's Party] and other Western rabble rousers" as the reason that so many illegal loopholes have been left alone. He goes further in saying that "anyone attempting to call attention to the problem had to run the risk of being considered anti-Chinese or prejudiced."[43] Evidently, Drumright was aware of the charge of prejudice, and his citing of past injustices and consequent guilt-induced lack of enforcement read as self-defense for the measures that he wants to implement.

Responding to Drumright, Dai-Ming Lee and the Six Companies also undertook to renarrate Chinese American history in light of the current political situation, delving into the nineteenth century to explain the present, but casting history as a continuum of racist persecution. Like Drumright, Lee organizes his comparisons by drawing the reader in with a tale of the past, only later establishing the contemporary parallel. In April 1956 in particular, he focused on rebutting the report's account of history, scathingly calling the report "truly a 'white paper'" and noting that it "goes back more than a century and attempts to trace the roots and causes of events that occurred beyond the memory of living man." Of Drumright's review of nineteenth-century immigration, Lee complains that "implicit in his report is the theme that all Chinese who entered the United States a century ago did so illegally." Drumright "ignores the fact that Chinese labor contributed to the development of America's Far West," Lee instead notes, a now familiar argument about Chinese American contributions to American infrastructural greatness. Instead, the report focuses on the long and ineradicable roots of false identities, presenting for the reader the "eighty-three years [that] have elapsed since Exclusion and twelve since the repeal of Exclusion." The Six Companies issued their own statement about the association's history on the occasion of the mass subpoena in March 1956. The Six Companies describe themselves, "beginning with the historic Gold Rush of 1849," a well-known moment of Americanness, as systems of organization of "mutual help and protection," though they do not go so far as to say why the Chinese population needed protection. The negative and criminal connotations of "tongs" are written off as part of the "turbulent growing stage—as in the American wild west frontier days."[44] Like Lee, the Six Companies appeal to familiar aspects of western Americana, attempting to incorporate Chinese American history into familiar U.S. narratives rather than allowing it to be constructed by Drumright as indelibly separate and foreign.

Like Drumright, Lee draws close parallels between past and present contemporary immigration and invokes the short passage of time since the repeal of exclusion. But to connect Drumright himself to those prejudiced officials of the past, he reminds his readers that "it is only a little more than a dozen years since exclusion laws were repealed. . . . [I]t is therefore not surprising that remnants of out-moded thinking still exist." Lee also depends on the converse of Drumright's claims of current leniency as compensation for a racist past, instead establishing historical connections between the exclusion era and the new wave of deportations. The longest and most extensive rhetorical comparison he makes is between the modern interrogation of Chinese applying for citizenship and the interrogations of the past on Angel Island. Decades before its "rediscovery" in the 1970s, Lee invokes the memory of Angel Island very clearly for his readers, recalling the years that people spent there, in some cases, while submitting to INS examination. He asks why fraud was not discovered during these extensive interrogations, "if any existed." Once again highlighting the problem that Drumright is free from judicial review, Lee suggests that Drumright is trying to support his claims of wholesale fraud by rewriting history to suggest that "all immigration decisions affecting the parents and grandparents of Chinese in America were wrong." Ultimately dubbing the new policing "Drumright's Exclusion Laws," Lee insisted on the continuity of discrimination and interrogation over the previous several decades as a counter—or, at least, an accompaniment—to the history of immigration fraud.[45]

Elaborating his historical trajectory in one column, Lee describes the domestic forms that discrimination took in addition to restrictive immigration law, discussing social and legalized discrimination against Chinese in the United States, from discriminatory housing laws and economic or occupational restriction to the verbal and physical abuse of Chinese who ventured out of Chinatown or associated with white Americans. However, Lee catalogs these injustices not merely to build up his reader's sentiments but also to draw a precise historical parallel: "Mr. Drumright's [report] is obviously an attempt to revive anti-Chinese sentiment." This was one of his few ventures beyond immigration law, but it painted the bleakest picture of what Lee believed could come of Drumright's unchecked power and the ensuing investigations.[46]

How one framed the history of Chinese America was far more important than a working knowledge of it; as far as basic events and laws go, Lee and Drumright rely on more or less the same major historical anchors, particularly the coolie trade and the Exclusion Act, and both clearly see the power of the historical narrative in persuading the reader of the justice of their stances. Such historical framing would often prove to swamp the facts of individual cases, as the judiciary also often depended on a historical justification for their presumptions of immigration fraud but adhered to a chronology of fraudulence. In one of the Chinese immigration cases that made it to the U.S. Supreme Court, *Lee Kum Hoy*, the government would revisit the debate as its counsel parroted the historical trajectory laid out in the Drumright Report to little reaction from the court (see Chapter 3). The *Ly Shew* cases and other, similar immigration trials for individuals likewise featured dueling versions of history that the government lawyers subjected to withering commentary. In Ly Shew's early case, Judge Goodman specifically declined to find anything about the Lys, saying, "The court does not find that the plaintiffs and their witnesses are not telling the truth. But rather I cannot tell whether they are or not." Instead, he focused on the larger context of immigration fraud, going back to its origins and describing the exclusion laws as a result of "a huge number of Chinese immigrants" during the Gold Rush, using this history to lay out a discussion of the legal basis of derivative citizenship.[47] The efficacy of Drumright's report in changing INS policy and the reach of this narrative into the judiciary would seem to indicate that his version of history won the debate. However, it was far from final, as Chinese Americans would renew combatting this identity of fraud with a much broader and wider-reaching public history in the 1970s, a topic to which I return in Chapter 4.

Post-Confession: Kingston's Model Minoritization and Rebellion

The memoirs and novels of the Confession era offer us an imaginative response to the political climate of their time in their self-reflexive meditation on the ownership of storytelling and narrative. It is the writer's ability to reconstruct and reshape narrative that ultimately allows each to create a sense of triumph (or rectitude, at least) regarding stigma, prejudice, or a sentimentally softened cultural difference. But this record would be incomplete without the inclusion of perhaps the most widely taught of all Chinese American literary works, which looks back to use the battles of the Confession era as the foundation of an ethnic identity. As her parents complain (and her mother and other relatives continue to complain in her later works), Maxine Hong Kingston's writerly investigations of immigration history are interpreted by family members as attacks similar to the INS investigations that she fears even in the late 1970s, long after the program was terminated. However, to Kingston, storytelling about the history of immigration is essential to her understanding of her narratorial self, which she constructs as a divided, conflicted speaker (though, for the sake of ease, I refer to the narrator often as Kingston, as most critics do).

The paradigm of *The Woman Warrior* is one of immigration secrets and fragile outside appearances, but the two have an uneasy relation to each other as the artist attempts to speak. Like Wong, Kingston is negotiating the need to conceal and the need for exemplary appearances, but rather than embracing this, she is rebelling against and reflecting on both. Her mother's paranoia when her sister, Moon Orchid, arrives in the United States circles around thoughts of immigration and rejection: "Ellis Island had been made out of wood and iron. Here everything was new plastic, a ghost trick to lure immigrants into feeling safe and spilling their secrets. Then the Alien Office could send them right back."[48] That fear impelled a pattern of model minority behavior that Kingston describes in *The Woman Warrior*, a desire to earn straight As and please authority figures. Writing after the explicit formulation of the model minority, Kingston reminisces about her blundering attempt at exemplarity and safety from a child's point of view.

The Woman Warrior portrays a girl narratively adrift during the Confession era, its formal structure mirroring her mental confusion as she composes composite narratives of autobiography and Chinese mythology to substitute for the stories that her family dares not speak because of their fraudulent immigration identities. After listening to the chatter of similarly handicapped children at school, the narrator asks, "Are there really flags in Chinatown signaling what stowaways have arrived in San Francisco Bay, their names, and which ships they came on?" Her parents dismiss the issue of stowaways altogether: "No. No, there aren't any flags like that. They're just talking-story. You're always believing talk-story" (183). Their heavy disdain forecloses the story at hand, illegal immigration, and its mechanisms. The implication is that they may be concealing the truth from their overly inquisitive child, just as they conceal it from government officials. The book is equally grounded in Kingston's desire to escape from this silence and to find a political and personal foundation for speaking out. She obsesses over the lack of safe history on which to draw, instead substituting the Hawaiian oral narrative form "talk-story," which she uses to designate the combination of stories, myths, and moral lessons through which she and her mother communicate. Their pastiche replaces stories silenced by the fear of betrayal and the exigencies of immigration law. Kingston's complicated narrative reflects in both content and form on the historical inability of Chinese Americans to exist and speak freely, a constraint that she still expresses at the time of writing.

The constraints that drive the young Kingston's attempt at perfect behavior come from the complicated web of immigration fears around her. The tenuous position of Kingston's family is exposed in one of the rare encounters with an unrelated Chinese American in the book, when the most powerful villager's wife comes around to critique her as a marriage prospect: "This woman was the giver of American names, a powerful namer, though it was American names; my parents gave the Chinese names. . . . She was a woman of such power that all we immigrants and descendants of immigrants were obliged to her family forever for bringing us here and for finding us jobs, and she had named my voice." When Kingston snaps at the critical woman, her mother hushes her quickly: "Maybe this lady was powerful enough to send us back" (192), Kingston reflects, and goes to the front of the laundry to work quietly. Her anger at the prospect of an arranged marriage later erupts solely at her parents, restricted by fear from attacking the powerful outsider who can betray them. Such a potentially abusive power dynamic was actually cited by the INS as a driver for the Confession Program. While these were often excuses for the severe and racially directed crackdown on immigration, they nonetheless reflected a very real result of fraudulent documentation, as Kingston's obedience and good behavior in front of this powerful woman demonstrates.

Silence, a necessity, becomes a stand-in for all of these fears. Unable to rebel against these larger political forces or even powerful individuals threatening everyone's safety, Kingston's fear and anger aims at silence itself. "Sometimes I hated the ghosts for not letting us talk; sometimes I hated the secrecy of the Chinese. 'Don't tell' said my parents, though we couldn't tell if we wanted to because we didn't know" (180). Kingston and her siblings know nothing of their parents' history because of their parents' alienation from their own children, who, they fear, might betray the illegalities of their immigration. "They would not tell us children because we had been born among ghosts, were taught by ghosts, and were ourselves ghost-like. They called us a kind of ghost. Ghosts are noisy and full of air; they talk during meals. They talk about anything" (183–184). Talking, which might lead to confession, is dangerous; hence, their desire for silence and the child torn between obedient silence and shouting.

Unlike Lee's contemporaneous editorial responses, confession itself is rarely mentioned in *The Woman Warrior*, aside from the passage with which I opened this chapter, but it is not even named there. But in one key mention, Kingston repudiates the idea of confession even between family members. An older Kingston—with white hair that her mother comments on—receives a visit from her elderly mother, who moans about her impending death. "I'm almost eighty," says her mother, triggering a debate. "But I thought your papers are wrong, and you're seventy-two, seventy-three in Chinese years," argues Kingston (100). Her mother dismisses Kingston's knowledge, as ever, maintaining both that her papers are wrong and that she is eighty. She commences to complain about her current labor in tomato fields and her life of hard labor in America, a torrent of words that Kingston calls "confessing, me maddened at confessions" (101). Despite Kingston's continual curiosity about her parents' immigration and earlier lives, when push comes to shove, she cannot bear her mother's confession. Her narrative suggests that this confession is simply too much, spilling out far beyond immigration, a confined and confining way to define Chinese America. Instead, her mother demands that the seeker for "truth" should hear the entire truth of her life.

The ability to speak out becomes a contested value in Kingston's narration, itself continually struggling to communicate clearly. As the Confession Program begins, Kingston mentions it as a key moment when Chinese Americans must make a decision about whether or not to tell speak out: "Occasionally the rumor went about that the United States immigration authorities had set up headquarters in the San Francisco or Sacramento Chinatown to urge wetbacks and stowaways, anybody here on fake papers, to come to the city and get their files straightened out" (182). This prompts the debate that opens this chapter. The Hong family may have escaped the most heated debate about the program by virtue of geography. Living in Stockton, in a tiny enclave that Kingston claims spoke a dialect of Chinese that she later found was so unintelligible to others that she stopped checking off "bilingual" on job applications, her family was less directly targeted, though no doubt peripherally affected by the possibility of family association records being checked. Her account of the program underscores a cultural secrecy but gets elided into secrecy about traditions, as Kingston drifts into an account of the constant scolding of the children for not knowing detailed taboos or observances that they have never been told. The obvious parallel between the children, reprimanded at every turn, and the Chinese American population, always in trouble with an authoritative government, goes unremarked by the narrator.

Kingston offers one anecdote about a classmate at school that illuminates the larger culture of immigration fears and the inability to speak:

> Last year the whole class had laughed at a boy who couldn't fill out a form because he didn't know his father's name. The teacher sighed, exasperated, and was very sarcastic, "Don't you notice things? What does your mother call him?" she said. The class laughed at how dumb he was not to notice things. "She calls him father of me," he said. Even we laughed, although we knew that his mother did not call his father by name, and a son does not know his father's name. We laughed and were relieved that our parents had had the foresight to tell us some names we could give the teachers. (177)

Though this anecdote is partially pitched as an embarrassing cultural confrontation, mentioning Chinese habits of address, it is a silence that is also strategic, related to Kingston's ignorance of her parents' real names. Tellingly, the rest of the Chinese American students are not giving real names; they are provided "some names" that they "could give" to escape this type of embarrassment, as well as the scrutiny of someone in power. This classmate's "dumb"-ness may well be a willful silence. But in explaining this, and ruefully looking back at her own childish cruelty toward this boy, Kingston reminds us how the community had to continually manage its secrets and its speaking.

However, Kingston's discussion of exemplarity, as befits a memoir of "girlhood," most often focuses on the everyday strivings of a child at school, attempts that nonetheless are urgently framed in contrast to illegal or illegitimate immigrants. She embraces a model minority identity in order to differentiate herself from a tainted community member, a mentally handicapped boy who, she begins to fear, is her parents' chosen husband for her: "I studied hard, got straight A's, but nobody seemed to see that I was smart and had nothing in common with this monster, this birth defect" (195). Sitting on the steps in front of the laundry, as she used to as a child, moaning and groaning in an unintelligible gibberish instead of English, the boy represents all of Kingston's fears about Chinese culture. As Michael Bérubé has noted, like Kingston herself, this boy is a figure of silence; both he and Kingston are disabled, in a sense, because they lack the ability to comprehend or tell a full narrative. Declaring her refusal to marry this boy to her mother, she shouts, "They tell me I'm smart, and I can win scholarships. I can get into colleges. . . . I can do all kinds of things" (200). Kingston sees her own anxiety about immigration reflected in this most forbidden of immigrants; number one in the list of aliens ineligible to be admitted to the United States were the "feeble-minded."[49] Regardless of the boy's citizenship, he, like Kingston, looks dangerously close to being illegal or, at best, unwanted, not only because of his disability, but also because he is presented in the context of fresh-off-the-boat hypothetical suitors, another set of possibly illegal immigrants, undesirable and dangerous to Kingston. All of these men are ineligible for narrative or naming: "I told nobody about the monster. And nobody else was talking either; no mention about the laundry workers who appeared and disappeared; no mention about the sitter." Silence is, for the moment, the only protection from the presence of these illegal entries, who might betray the entire community.

A misdirected attempt at speech takes the form of a much-discussed encounter with a soft, pampered Chinese classmate, whose persistent silence only enrages Kingston into embarrassing bullying. Kingston positions herself as an angry, loud American, which many readings have noted, but, in addition, she becomes a dangerous American interrogator and informant, while the girl is figured as a perfect, pink-and-white-skinned, feminine student. Kingston entraps the unnamed girl in a bathroom, shouting at her, "I am going to make you talk," saying that she has heard her yelling in at her own home (173). "If you're not stupid, what's your name?" Kingston demands of the perfect Chinese girl, who, like Kingston's parents, remains like the community at large: resolutely silent on the subject of names (175). Though, as many critics have noted, Kingston is enacting her anxieties of Chinese and feminine identity on this girl, the incident specifically mimics the interrogations of Chinese Americans that Kingston, even as a child, has to withstand, pretending not to know people's real names or occupations. Even the alien setting of the school bathroom becomes a hostile institutional space, reminiscent of the way Kingston describes Ellis Island or the airport offices, which might intimidate an unnamed Chinese American to confess. Only the exemplary girl can survive it.

Public speech is the path to resolution for Kingston, even in the present time of her writing; "A dumbness—a shame—still cracks my voice in two, even when I want to say 'hello' casually" (165). This twoness cripples her, ruining her ability to counter her stigmatized identity with overachievement. She fails her IQ test in kindergarten because she does not speak English and gets set back in school. She was—it seems—beaten up as a consequence. She becomes voiceless during her childhood at "American school," never speaking at school because she does not know what to say and getting sent to a speech therapist by her teacher. "We have so many secrets to hold in" (180), Kingston muses, implying that they cause her illness and her classmates' silence. Eventually, forced to find some kind of voice, she invents an "American-feminine" (169) voice for her American school and keeps yelling during her Chinese hours, splitting the body in two. The written record is her attempt at reconciliation, constructing a new self that can resolve the perfect student in American school with the daughter of a secretive Chinese household.

At the end of the memoir, the narrator speaks out, angrily asserting her own worth as a person (calling her work her self, her identity, and perhaps her land) and trying to retranslate her family's shouted words. Kingston confronts this dilemma as a Chinese American who has felt imprisoned in her model behavior, which she finally exchanges for action and activism. The myths of *The Woman Warrior* stand in for the narrator as a dream of action and activism, individual heroic action that could change leadership and political direction, but grounded in this early desire to confront immigration injustices. As a mythical warrior, she crosses many boundaries, leaving her family and sending away her husband and baby. As a narrator, she transforms from a child angry at her parents to one angry at their common enemy. In one battle, she briefly recounts her confrontations with bosses who are racist against African Americans, seemingly unrelated to immigration. She whispers her anger and defiance, linking it back to her own experience: "If I took the sword, which my hate must surely have forged out of the air, and gutted him, I would put color and wrinkles into his shirt. It's not just the stupid racists that I have to do something about, *but the tyrants who for whatever reason can deny my family food and work*" (49, emphasis added). The driving need to fight the "tyrants" of the immigration system that overshadowed her childhood has turned the would-be model child into the woman warrior at last. Like Lee, Wong, and other Chinese American public figures of the 1950s, who all combat the tyrants in their own way, Kingston embraces a need to speak out and to construct her own identity and beliefs around race and ethnicity. It remained for Kingston and other artists like her, after 1965, to negotiate with the images of the past as they imagined and wrote new identities into being.

2

Happy Families

Modeling the Minority in the Era of Immigration Reform

"The Chinese family is said, redundantly and monotonously, to be the basic unalterable unit of Chinese society, possessing superhuman ability to withstand social change, westernization, wars and other crises, with a tenacity that symbolizes indestructible China," wrote Rose Hum Lee in 1960.[1] Though in a work of nonfiction—a pioneering book-length sociological study of Chinese America—Lee's weariness echoes that of her contemporary novelists and memoirists who were centrally concerned with the presentation of the Chinese American family, also caught amid images of the Chinese family as inherently illegal and grotesquely extended, in contrast with mainstream images of the white nuclear family that pervaded screens and books in the 1950s.

This chapter examines literature about the Chinese American family—seemingly happy, strong families that prove their social worth, from the exemplary nuclear family to the extended or alternative family formations created by the exigencies of immigration. In literature, we see the brittleness and artificiality of the nuclear family as a counter to generations of immigration scrutiny and stigma as it transformed among several authors (and adapters) of the postwar era. The family doubles in all of these narratives as a vehicle to elude racism first in restrictive U.S. immigration policies, then in U.S. society after entry has been gained. The fame of Jade Snow Wong's first memoir, both at the time of its release and in early Asian American literary history, has cemented an idea that this era was one of assimilation, keeping up appearances about the family. Wong's drive to depict her family as a perfect nuclear family is explicitly embedded in the need to protect her mother's immigration secrets, as detailed in Chapter 1, but its deceptive surface reaches far beyond that, concealing internal rifts in structure and affection that she does not freely describe until the 2000s. Lin Yutang's *Chinatown Family* (1948), conversely, shows a family so loving that their virtue can even normalize their extended structure and their illegal means of immigration, which Lin's editor insisted on adding. Oscar Hammerstein and Joseph Fields likewise added illegal immigration as a plot thread to *Flower Drum Song* (1958/1961), their adaptation of C. Y. Lee's novel, attempting to contain it and give it a sympathetic glow with heterosexual romance and marriage. The literature, paired with the legal obstacles to family reunion and the attack on paper sons, shows not that Chinese Americans were blindly conforming to mainstream standards, but that they were highly aware of the problems that Chinese America faced and the power of the family as a part of their public image.

The 1950s saw a boom in marriage rates and earlier marriage, and correspondingly in birthrates, leading to an emphasis on the young family that Elaine Tyler May famously characterized as the "nuclear family in the nuclear age." Prosperous, growing, and yet full of anxiety about postwar readjustments and the growing anticommunist hysteria, postwar U.S. society contained the dangers of consumerism, technology, and shifting demographics and gender roles within the all-important home. The rooting of self-worth and identity in "familial and parental roles" and the new rush to establish single-family homes, often in the suburbs, shifted U.S. social formations, with lasting cultural but only temporary social effects. By the 1960s and 1970s, containment had failed—though May and Stephanie Coontz persuasively argue that in many ways, society merely returned to the model of earlier decades of the twentieth century: higher divorce rates, flouting of societal mores through untraditional or unmarried family units, and lower birthrates.[2]

Non-nuclear minority family structures troubled authorities, with the most famous exposition of the fear of social dissolution coming in the 1965 report *The Negro Family: The Case for National Action*, better known as the Moynihan Report after its author, Assistant Secretary of Labor Daniel P. Moynihan (later a U.S. senator). His assessment of the "pathology" of African American families suggested that absentee fathers and rising out-of-wedlock birthrates exhibited the familial "deterioration" of the lower-class black community and had led to welfare dependency. The extensive critique of Moynihan's white-centric and patriarchal political stance is well known, including Hortense Spillers's retort "Mama's Baby, Papa's Maybe," which roots the supposed "pathology" in the institution of slavery. Moynihan's analysis divided the country into three chief categories: white, a black middle class, and a black lower class. However, hidden was a reference to other minority groups that Moynihan implicitly held up as better: "A number of immigrant groups were characterized by unusually strong family bonds; these groups have characteristically progressed more rapidly than others." This positive characterization of immigrant groups included the Chinese, whom Moynihan favorably singled out in a footnote as having very low divorce rates; however, he then contributed to the problem of model minoritization as a racist weapon against African Americans by suggesting that immigrants' positive numbers prove that "statistics on nonwhites generally *understate* the degree of disorganization of the Negro family." Moynihan's discussion of the Chinese and other new immigrant groups as stronger in family bonds and socially superior precedes the invention of the term "model minority" by only a year.[3]

When "model minority" entered the language in 1966, its backbone was liberally construed to be the strength of the Asian family—in any form. A *U.S. News and World Report* article, "Success Story of One Minority Group in U.S.," famously instantiated Chinese Americans as a comparatively model minority, describing them as overcoming "even more prejudice than faces the Negro today" by invoking a past of anti-Asian discrimination while somehow failing to mention slavery or Jim Crow. It presents Chinese Americans as exemplary by the same terms with which Moynihan had adjudged African American lower-class deterioration: strong and stable families, *refusal* to go on welfare, thrift, and academic success. The theme of family cohesion and supervision runs throughout the entire piece in hyperbolic terms, even managing to make the formerly illegitimate and dangerous clan system into a cultural virtue. Starting from the "tight network of family and clan loyalties" that keep them off welfare, the article describes the "hundred cousins" who keep an eye on would-be delinquents, fear of Westernization leading to "increase in crime and divorce," and a "family group" in which the "parents always watch out for the children." Indeed, the article emphasizes the family a degree beyond even the more famous article earlier in the year in which William Petersen explicitly coined the term "model minority" in reference to the Japanese American population. From suspiciously large kinship networks that could hide illegitimacy, Chinese family structures had become methods of self-policing and assimilation—or, at least, "acculturation." Myron Cohen notes that the "large-family ideal" had appeared early in Chinese sociology and thenceforth dominated discussion to an almost unreasonable degree, citing studies in this era; though he does not explicitly mention it, it seems likely that the public discussion of large families during immigration may have kept this concern prominent.[4]

In what I call the proto-model minority formulation, the time in which the public imagery of Asians started to build this conception, there was a decided trend as Asian Americans reached media attention as exemplary nuclear family figures. As mentioned in the previous chapter, Jade Snow Wong's young wifehood and motherhood, as well as her filiality, served as a cultural bridge between the Wongs' Chinese and American notions of family, both portrayed as strongly nuclear. In 1952, Mrs. Toy Len Goon of Maine was named "Mother of the Year," receiving much media attention and meeting First Lady Bess Truman on a visit to Washington, DC. The historian Chiou-ling Yeh describes how Goon's publicity burnished the image of the United States as a land of equal opportunity, positioning Goon as an Americanized and assimilated immigrant, a perfect wife and mother; wrongly describing her as a citizen; and fictionalizing her takeover of the family business during her husband's World War I military service. However, as with Wong, the media used Confucianism and Chinese tradition selectively to exoticize Goon and even to chide undomestic modern white women. Further study of Goon, however, has suggested her agency in the construction of this image. The discovery among her possessions of four silk suits that she brought from China and put away, never worn in her entire Westernized life, evinces her conscious decisions about racial and ethnic performance.[5]

However, other images were circulating of Chinese American family life in this era, often contradictory and altered to suit the audience and political aims. Wu notes the frequent community newspaper discussions of Chinese American juvenile delinquency in the 1950s that were then followed with mainstream-facing claims of nondelinquency in order to "advance their social-political ambitions." Kwong blames delinquency at least in part on the triumph of the conservative Chinatown wing in New York, which then eliminated some of the community organizations that had been occupying and influencing youth. Contemporaneous observers sometimes admitted delinquency and sometimes denied or contained it within the community. S. W. Kung's description of the Chinese community relies on traditional virtues and a tight-knit system but ruefully admits that things have changed, though he still claims an extremely low rate of delinquency. He is also clearer than many about the diversity within the community based on generation and the parents' birthplace, education, and marital arrangements, including war brides and picture brides, noting that "it would be next to impossible to give any clear-cut definition of the typical Chinese family in this country." Only a few years later, in 1967, Betty Lee Sung's portrayal of the Chinese family turns the self-policing narrative on its head. While much of her information about Chinatown families is similar to that in the *U.S. News* article, she emphasizes the increases in crime and divorce rather than the kinship networks that police them. "What makes you think that Chinese youth, exposed to the process of Americanization and the conflicting values of East and West can escape what the Irish children went through, what the Italian children went through, and what the Puerto Rican and Negro children are going through?" asked the New York City Chinatown anthropologist Stuart Cattrell of Sung. However, his was a minority voice, drowned out by the outward-facing model minority discourse that relied on the supposedly almighty Chinese family to discipline the younger generation. Jade Snow Wong seems to have deliberately concealed any delinquency in her memoir, as she wrote only a few years prior in an essay, "My Chinatown," published in a San Francisco Junior College magazine, that she saw "children roaming in gangs on the street at . . . one o'clock in the morning, reluctant to return to noisy, crowded homes. . . . It is a wonder that the juvenile delinquency rate is as low as it is."[6]

Amid anxiety about attacks on the family, Chinese American writers, examining different family structures exacerbated by decades of exclusion-mandated separation and the ever-present fear of paper families, argued differently for their acceptance into American society based on different but equally strong structures. The Asian American family narrative has been a dominant literary model, partly because of the generational conflicts so commonly depicted but also because, as I address in the next section, the historical gender imbalances and prejudices against Asian America made the nuclear family a perfect vehicle of normalization and assimilation, not to mention of economic production. Many critics have described how the family narrative, particularly one of generational strife, has been a popular vehicle for model minority politics. This has made it, as erin Khuê Ninh calls it, a "politically discredited model," though one that more recent critics have regarded with a more tolerant eye.[7] Here, I delve into the political motivations for these family narratives, as well as the specific fractures of immigration that they often seek to conceal or protest.

The Chinese American Family at Midcentury

From the origins of their mass migration to the United States, the Chinese presented problems not only through the omnipresent threat that minorities posed through interracial marriage, but also through the differing social formations of the community—not purely imported cultural differences, as they were commonly designated, but also the formations that evolved through U.S. immigration policy. The gender imbalance of early Chinese America, caused by the importation of male coolie labor, threatened not only the small ethnic community but American society as a whole. Colleen Lye has demonstrated the economic threat of the Asian body, and the stereotyped erotic threat of Chinese villains and whores has been revealed by David Eng and many other scholars. These must be connected to their threat to the institution of family as a microcosm of the economy and society. As

May has discussed, the confused attitudes toward women's wage labor and gender roles in marriage followed a contradictory pattern from the late nineteenth century to the early twentieth century. Even as more women were working outside the home and enjoyed working independently, both men and women perceived husbands as the rightful breadwinners. Unease about traditional gender roles extended to those who visibly destabilized them, as in Robert Lee's "third sex" characterization of Chinese household workers and prostitutes. May writes, "Workers as workers were not held in disdain if they upheld proper sex roles and domestic duties. Rather, the Victorians were most alarmed by evidence of group power, such as labor unions, or public disorder, such as vice districts. These types of organizations and institutions posed a direct threat to the familial values and voluntaristic ethos that guided the Protestant middle classes—and kept them in positions of power." While May's study focuses on white Americans, her note of the threat to society is nonetheless highly appropriate in speaking about minority groups. As politically powerless as the Chinese were in the early days of immigration, their very presence in disorderly labor groups or Chinatowns posed a threat to the more ineffable "values."[8]

The emphasis on family structure in turn placed unrealistic pressure on an imbalanced, relatively new immigrant community. In the origin of Asians in the Americas as migrant workers, almost always male and already stereotyped, begins the skewing of the sexes that exacerbates the abnormality of Chinese American families by mainstream standards. While Asians have been present in the United States from its founding, chiefly as sailors or laborers, Asian American histories generally begin with the mass importation of workers from China in the mid-1800s. Moon-Ho Jung's study explains how this importation depended on the comparative racialization of African Americans as ignorant, rebellious, threatening bodies and the invention of the "coolie" as a dream of diligent, undemanding, Confucian-educated laborers to replace or bring the former slave into submission.[9] These coolies, with no family to support, soon became the subject of attack for their deviant lifestyle, which supposedly gave them an economic advantage. Hostile competitors complained that the Chinese were willing to live on little food in squalid conditions, while white laborers had to support a higher standard of living, as well as wives and children. The amorphous grouping of coolies and bachelor Chinatowns particularly posed a threat in their social arrangements and flickers of group power. Such homosocial worlds of the coolies existed in many places across the modern United States—in Hawai'i, the South, and the west—though we unfortunately have little documentation. We are left with the voices passed down through family oral histories of young men drinking and gambling in their spare time with their little spare money, then returning to the plantation, railroad, mine, or laundry. Indeed, in *China Men* (1980), when Kingston's mother finally arrives from China to join her husband, she breaks up a happy fraternal quartet.

More important, these labor flows placed new stresses on the family structure of Asian Americans. On the one hand, these stresses did perhaps result in some parallel structures to those of the dominant society. Erika Lee, in her study of immigration during the exclusion era, writes, "Most Chinese immigrant women, then, were dependent on men and their continuing relationships with them to gain entry and to remain in the country. This dependent status both mirrored and strengthened American gender roles and ideology in U.S. immigration law."[10] But it equally affected the family structure in China and perceptions of the Asian family in the United States. The model nuclear family, such as Jade Snow Wong's, acts as a normalizing technique to combat popular views of Asians as faceless hordes with vaguely threatening or mysterious kinship networks, legal and otherwise. Proving that conformity does not erase racism, as Chinese and Japanese Americans did gain more conventional family structures in the United States, opponents then complained that Asian wives and children labored long hours on the farm or in the laundry. This family labor supposedly gave Asians an unfair advantage, as if such collaboration was without its white pioneer equivalents or came without sacrifice.[11]

The other family formation strongly identified with Chinese America—the separated transnational family that resulted from the exclusion policies—was characterized as equally unnatural and pernicious, if later somewhat pathetic. Frank Chin and his colleagues' outrage at the popular family depictions of best-selling Chinese American literature particularly notes that "the frustrated bachelors of Chinatown, making up the majority of the Chinatown population, are symbolically rejected or totally ignored," an outgrowth of their social stigma. As awareness of the phenomenon of the separated Chinese family grew in the postwar era, Charles Frederick Marden coined the term "mutilated family" in 1952 to describe the structure in which the Chinese man lived and worked in America, rarely seeing his wife or children who lived in China. Sung had no hesitation in adopting this term, writing, "Family stability has been shaken up by the peculiar situations created by the reunion of mutilated families and the mass importation of brides." Citing Wong's and Lowe's memoirs as exemplars of earlier traditionalism and teenage rebellion, Sung's qualified conclusion, far from refiguring the Chinese family as a virtuous, cohesive whole, notes the rifts in the community and the terrible difficulties Chinese men face, though she softened it by sentimentally describing these men as deprived of the "benefits, joys, and warmth of family life." The term did not pass into common parlance, but the concept of "mutilation" marks the complete normalization of family life featuring the nuclear family under one roof. In addition, the U.S. government became more aware of the phenomenon, recording for the first time in 1960 the number of people married but who had, in the more reticent terminology of the census, "spouse present" or, significantly, "spouse absent," which was about a fifth of the married male Chinese population but scarcely any married women. (This record keeping may well have been part of the immigration crackdown; how accurately these numbers were reported is another question.[12])

Chinese family formations of all kinds thus became double-edged rhetorical swords over many decades, though as the postwar rush to conformity shows, the nuclear family became the favored vehicle of acceptance. In particular, the extended family formation with which Chinese were most commonly associated was disfavored due to the social movement toward nuclear families, as well as the official government attitude toward suspiciously extended families. In his 1955 report, Drumright had specifically related the Chinese kinship system to illegal immigration, claiming that the confusing Chinese systems of naming, multiple marriages, adoption, and other cultural differences formed "alibis" for illegal activity.[13] Their extended family system was thus characterized in government understanding as inherently unintelligible and foreign, too difficult for the consulate workers or other Americans to understand.

The census (though unreliable, particularly in counting undocumented migrants) shows how Chinese American demographics drastically shifted during the postwar era, first of all in the community's increase in numbers, but also in its shift toward families. The imbalance between men and women evened out greatly over the decade, thanks to family reunification, from a ratio of nearly two to one in 1950 to a much closer four to three in 1960. In 1950, the married male Chinese population older than fourteen outnumbered the single and widowed/divorced population, constituting 58 percent of the total. In 1960, this percentage was nearly the same, but a look at the marital data by sex reveals the huge shift from spouse absent to spouse present. The 1950 census recorded only marital status, and 36,484 men were recorded as married, while 18,341 women were recorded as married. Thus, about half of the married male population likely had a wife outside of the United States. In 1960, 80 percent of men had a spouse present, and the number of men and women with a spouse present was nearly equal. The conventional wisdom of the U.S. Chinese population balancing the sexes and becoming more family-centered is borne out by the available data, which amply illustrates the drastic changes in the community.[14]

The united marital or nuclear family unit thus became the demographically majority formation, encompassing not only reunited families and

TABLE 2.1. CHINESE AMERICAN POPULATION REPORTED IN THE U.S. CENSUS.				
	Male Total	Female Total	Male Married	Female Married
1950	76,725	40,415	38,484	18,341
1960	135,430	100,654	55,517 Spouse present: 44,352 Spouse absent: 11,165	44,526 Spouse present: 42,675 Spouse absent: 1,851

Note: Official census counts for 1950 and 1960. Information was not collected for spouses present or absent in 1950.
Source: 1950 Census of the Population, vol. 4: Special Reports, sec. 6: "Nonwhite Population by Race" tables 5, 12; 1960 Census of the Population, vol. 2: Subject Reports, pt. 1C: "Nonwhite Population by Race," table 12.

newly formed marriages among the younger generation of Chinese America, but also war brides and newly immigrating families, both those of refugee status and others. The nuclear family, rather than the extended family, largely triumphed in the 1950s as the public face of Chinese America, as well, sanitizing the image of Chinatown and Chinese Americans at a time when the construction of new housing was specifically tied to the postwar marriage and baby boom. Nayan Shah has shown how public relations campaigns about the modernization of living conditions helped to convert Chinatown from diseased ghetto to tourist destination and ultimately to an ark of happy families. As with literary representation, much of this was carried out by Chinese Americans themselves. "Chinatown public housing advocates denigrated the circumstances and indifference of Chinese bachelors while upholding the needs of 'deserving' nuclear families" in San Francisco, and, as Cindy I-fen Cheng discusses, in New York and Los Angeles, as well. Throughout the 1950s, San Francisco Chinatown activists successfully lobbied for new housing projects with all the latest "mod cons" to enable "family living." Only in the 1970s would this publicly extend to the non-nuclear elderly, once the remembrance of bachelor squalor had dimmed.[15]

The story of one Chinese American family's attempt to use their properly heterosexual nuclear structure to gain acceptance in the growing suburbs is a sobering reminder of the limitations of this rhetoric. Cheng examines the trajectory of Sing and Grace Sheng, who tried to buy a house in a southern suburb of San Francisco and, when the white neighbors protested, put it to a vote and lost by a landslide, sparking yet another national debate over the failure of democracy to uphold racial equality. In addition to citing Sing's veteran status and Grace's U.S. citizenship by birth, Cheng notes that the Shengs were able to play up their gendered and marital credentials in remarks such as, "You know how women are. She had it all worked out in her mind how she was going to decorate the house." The heretofore unpublished (as far as I know) end to the Shengs' story comes from the papers of Jade Snow Wong, herself a very similar figure, who wrote about encountering Sing in her travels in Asia. According to her, the negative vote disillusioned him so completely that he moved with his family to Hong Kong, where she met him as he was managing a large hotel (Wong was a travel agent and tour guide for many years, relinquishing her pottery business to take over the business after her husband's death).[16] Though one hopes that the Shengs prospered in Hong Kong, from a U.S. civil rights perspective this is an ignominious end to a high-profile story of restrictive covenants, betraying how the nuclear family formation failed to trump racial difference and segregation.

Standing in this contradictory period of model minority status and legalized discrimination, Chinese and other Asian Americans' family structures are a necessary but insufficient proof of all-American values and the right to societal inclusion, often argued on the battleground of housing and living arrangements. At this very moment, the federal government was also enacting and allowing restrictions against minorities, as famously dramatized in Lorraine Hansberry's *A Raisin in the Sun* (1959), which tells the story of an urban black family in Chicago and their internal struggle whether to insist on their rights in moving into a house in a suburban white neighborhood or to accept a payoff. It is no coincidence that *A Raisin in the Sun* is contemporaneous on Broadway with *Flower Drum Song* and other Asian-focused works that focus on the family and heterosexual marriage as a vehicle for sympathy and assimilation for minorities. When Wong dramatizes her family's move to a new building and her desire for a quiet room of her own in *Fifth Chinese Daughter*, she appeals to the dream of a single-family dwelling even in the midst of crowded Chinatown.

Legally, the favoritism shown toward the nuclear family continued well into the 1970s (and even beyond). *Moore v. East Cleveland* (1977), in the year of *The Woman Warrior*'s publication, struck down as unconstitutional a housing ordinance limiting single-family units to nuclear families. Justice Lewis Powell, in an opinion for the majority, wrote, "Ours is by no means a tradition limited to respect for the bonds uniting the members of the nuclear family. The tradition of uncles, aunts, cousins, and especially grandparents sharing a household along with parents and children has roots equally venerable and equally deserving of constitutional recognition. Over the years millions of our citizens have grown up in just such an environment, and most, surely, have profited from it." Justice William Brennan, a noted liberal voice, added more clearly in his concurrence with Justice Thurgood Marshall that race played a strong role in the conception of the family as nuclear:

> In today's America, the "nuclear family" is the pattern so often found in much of white suburbia. The Constitution cannot be interpreted, however, to tolerate the imposition by government upon the rest of us of white suburbia's preference in patterns of family living. The "extended family" that provided generations of early Americans with social services and economic and emotional support in times of hardship, and was the beachhead for successive waves of immigrants who populated our cities, remains not merely still a pervasive living pattern, but under the goad of brutal economic necessity, a prominent pattern—virtually a means of survival—for large numbers of the poor and deprived minorities of our society.[17]

While Brennan did not delve into the institutionalized racist reasons that the nuclear family and the white suburb had become almost synonymous, he astutely identified the incompatibility between the nuclear family mass image and the realities of extended family networks that existed and exist for Americans, particularly minorities (his opinion focuses on black families). The court was quite divided in this case, however, with multiple opinions and a split decision showing that extended or nonnuclear families of *any* ethnicity were by no means sure of protection or acceptance.

"Horror and Pain"

Jade Snow Wong explained her artistic decision to adopt the family narrative as her model as a reaction to the prevailing Chinese American depictions that she faced in the late 1940s: "At the time, movies were portraying Fu Manchu . . . , Anna May Wong was the toy of white men, and Charlie Chan was the pidgin-English Chinese, and I felt there was so much more to the Chinese culture than these Hollywood types. That's why I made my family training a very important part of this book."[18] By this standard, Wong presents a powerful argument in favor of the revolutionary nature of a family story, however conservative it may look today. As she no doubt remembered, the late 1930s and the 1940s were the comic detective Charlie Chan's heyday in theaters, with multiple films coming out every year, and could well be said to be the prevailing image of Chinese in America. Wong countered these negative stereotypes by fully embracing the prevailing social favorability of the nuclear family and, in particular, women's domesticity. In so doing, she made several important edits of her own family. The estrangements and unhappiness of the family, beyond a few moments of adolescent rebellion, are omitted or carefully transformed to an extent that her archive reveals.

One of the most important literary figures for the happy family image is her younger sibling Jon/Prosperity from Heaven, the "surprise child" whose birth halfway through *Fifth Chinese Daughter* allows Wong to uphold domesticity and the family's Americanness, as mentioned in Chapter 1. He functions to cement their parents' marriage and position Wong as a feminine, maternal figure. The archive reveals that Wong bowdlerized and Americanized the story of Jon's birth, omitting a highly emotionally fraught situation and her father's contemplation of illegal activities, particularly those stereotypically associated with Chinese, in order to deal with this unexpected late pregnancy. Furthermore, the self-censorship conceals not only her family's actions at the time of Jon's birth, but also continuing deceptions necessary because of her mother's immigration status. From an experience that at least in part was a source of family rupture and danger, Wong's memoir creates a depiction that frames the birth of the last child only as another source of unity for the family.

The discovery of the surprise pregnancy forms a brief but noteworthy part of *Fifth Chinese Daughter*, in which the college-age Jade Snow sees her mother as a woman—frightened underneath her dignity—for the first time and aids her as a companion, not as a respectful daughter, by gently insisting on taking her to the doctor for prenatal care. "She had by a cautious question confirmed" that her mother was pregnant (184). This adult relationship temporarily replaces the requisite filiality or presumptive parent-child bond with one based on an equality of adults and shared gender. However, the memoir then returns to Wong's usual filial duties: helping Mama, setting up the new home, and returning from college at a moment's notice as needed.

The original, unfiltered account of Mama's surprise pregnancy could hardly be more different. It appears in a letter from a hysterical twenty-year-old Wong to a close college friend, typed and hand-dated at 1:30 A.M. on February 4, 1942. "I am so full of horror [and] pain," she says. After being scolded and harangued for her unfilial neglect (hardly just considering she had not known about the pregnancy), she had taken her mother, who had been diagnosed first as pregnant and then with an ovarian cyst, to a doctor, who confirmed that she was pregnant. This news was far from welcome or greeted with the quiet resignation described in *Fifth Chinese Daughter*.

> Mother went haywire when we got home. She said she'd rather die than have the child. She was serious too. I think she'd just as soon kill herself. And my estimation of Daddy never fell so low as when I asked him what he thought. He said an abortion and a possible operation . . . were both UNnatural. But giving birth to a baby is very *natural*. It was God's will, said he, that she should have conceived. (I

> nearly shook him in outrageousness [*sic*]. Was it not HIS own doing as much, if not MORE than God's will?) [H]ereupon he made the classic remark to crown the day—that he advised giving birth *naturally* to the child, but *that does not mean the child has to live.* I was horrified when I finally grasped the meaning of those words. I personally think, in these calmer moments, that he is holding out for a *son*, that if it is a daughter, it would not sadden him greatly to do *murder.* But as my name is Constance Wong, If it is a son, he'd no sooner kill it than kill himself. But of course he didn't say so.
>
> He is supposedly a Christian, but he seems not to regard choking a baby as murder! I was sick. Mother said "Why go through the process of having one, to do that to it?"[19]

It is not only the shock of her mother's pregnancy and of her father's intentions that are expressed here; it is also the shock of a deep moral and cultural rift between parent and child. We are here reliant on Wong's interpretation of her father's insinuation of infanticide, though her mother's ending plaint seems to confirm it. The tone remains highly emotional and aggrieved throughout the rest of the letter. Her father's plans for infanticide highlight the contradiction of his character (or his characterization) as the modern man who refused to bind his daughters' feet and the traditionalist who would not pay for their college tuition, framed in *Fifth Chinese Daughter* as an American-Chinese conflict. In this less guarded personal moment, however, Wong attacks the contradiction directly, refusing to excuse it and making her own fierce assumption of her father's gender preferences. She herself casts the entire episode in the light of patriarchal family structures. "That Daddy had neglected me is *nothing* compared to what he intends to do now," she wrote bitterly. This continued dwelling on her father's neglect of her hews decidedly to one side of the family dynamic presented in *Fifth Chinese Daughter,* without the softening produced by writing for a mass audience or, perhaps, the mellowing of time and success. Regardless of the reason, Wong herself sees a continuum from his favoritism of her brothers to his disregard for her mother's emotions and wishes and his attitude toward an unwanted pregnancy. The family strife, the dismaying suggestion of alien customs and attitudes, and perhaps also, simply, the unwelcome news of a late-life child in a large and not wealthy family have ruptured Wong's sense of self, which she reclaims overtly—and American-style—by writing, "as my name is Constance Wong."

The letter goes on to discuss the family's continued but secretive discussion of what to do about the pregnancy, turning to yet another Chinese-identified practice. Wong, as usual the interface with the outside world, discussed the possibility of a legal abortion (which she also refers to as "doing away with it") with the doctor due to her mother's mental state. By the time Wong called her parents with the information that it would be possible, her father replied that they had come up with a compromise that satisfied everyone, which was to have the baby and then sell it. "Lots of women sold theirs regularly," he reportedly said in justification. Wong asked to speak to her mother, but her father said that she wanted him to do the speaking. A dubious Wong noted to Harriet that she would go to Chinatown to try to see her mother and make sure she had agreed to this scheme. None of Wong's siblings knew, so it could all be kept secret, her father had said.

Regardless of when or how her parents changed their minds about this surprise child, even assuming it was the very next week, Wong's account in *Fifth Chinese Daughter* not only deletes her own emotional register, as well as a factual account of contemplated abortion, suicide, and child selling, but overtly deceives, substituting the exact opposite for what happened in a few important instances. In her letter, Wong childishly seems to be most aggrieved about the way her father scolded her for unfiliality in neglecting to magically know to take her mother to the doctor. The memoir seems to deliberately substitute the perfect, filial daughter of her father's unreasonable desires, who perceives the pregnancy and volunteers to take her mother to the doctor, for the true story.

Switching emotions as well as actions to suit 1950s expectations of Chinese Americans, as well as mainstream American delicacy, she writes in her memoir, "Mama expressed *no emotion* and made no special preparations for the expected event. . . . Whatever was in her mind, whatever the feelings that Mama and Daddy shared about another child expected now fourteen years after the last one had been born, Jade Snow was *not told*, and she felt *no right to pry*" (184, emphasis added). This is false, as her letter reveals, and instead of her initial horror, which is too rupturing to be expressed, she wields an orientalized depiction of secrecy, stoic wifehood, and filial duty. The only facet of the experience that she retains in the memoir is an acceptable, suitably dutiful aspect of her own singular burden: "She was also carrying a family secret of stupendous implications—Mama was going to have another child!" (179). Phrased in delicate language suited to middlebrow memoir, Wong celebrates the import of childbirth to confirm her narratorial role as the chronicler and mainstay of this nuclear family.

In the letter, Wong reminisced about a seemingly equally shocking exchange with her mother:

> She started to talk with me, how happy Ruth and Lincoln [Wong's half-brother] were and that was the way for a bride to be. (They really are quite sweet). Then she was led to compare them with her own marriage, how she has worked all these years, and many of the

> things Daddy had done to her, and how he has never shown any concern for her future or given her any affection. Well, she started to cry, and I shall never to my dying day, forget how I clutched my dress and scissors in one had [*sic*] and with the other hand patted her in vain, trying to comfort her.[20]

This affecting moment in which Mama can only negatively compare herself to a stepdaughter-in-law does not make it explicitly into *Fifth Chinese Daughter*, which depicts her as a tower of strength. But for just a moment, Wong expresses how she views her mother with "pity" and empathy, seeing her emotional isolation even from her children "because affection had not been part of her training, and she did not give it in training her own" (185). Though an unusual moment in the memoir, it is far from the anguish of the letter, and it also positions Wong as able to act on and resolve the observation by reaching out to her mother, rather than the helplessness she felt in the moment.

How the family rift was healed is not contained in any correspondence that I reviewed (it was probably resolved in person or via telephone), though as readers of Wong's writings know, Jon/Prosperity from Heaven was born, not sold, and became the entire family's pet, as well as the all-American child of Perry's description. He was Wong's particular charge both in his childhood and later in life; correspondence years later revealed that she played a primary advisory role in his education and career decisions. Once again creating a united front for the Wongs, Wong uses an East-meets-West structure in *Fifth Chinese Daughter* to describe her mother's delivery of the new baby, displacing her own anger and concern onto a doctor, whose identity is not specified but who seems to be a white American. When Jade Snow explains that her mother does not want her father to see her "shameful" crying and suffering during labor, the doctor says, "Of course, he should see. I think a man little realizes what pain a woman endures" (186). It is her agency, rather than that of the silent and almost helpless Jade Snow, racked with nerves, that brings the two parents together and forces Daddy to recognize his wife's feelings. Wong's own anger at sexism and desire for her father to face his wife's suffering cannot be expressed, but an outsider can easily and almost casually force the confrontation.

Wong manages to end this episode happily in *Fifth Chinese Daughter*, relaying her father's happy and prayerful celebration with not even a tinge of irony, though perhaps the emphasis on the new "male heir" reveals a bit of protest of patriarchy. Certainly, no reader can help but rejoice at the successful conclusion of her mother's painful labor and the entertaining younger brother who enters the narrative. Wong offers these elements of her family's experience as the most exemplary and suited to the construction of a happy nuclear family, while repressing her most vehement anger against her father's traditionalism. Furthermore, in excising all mention of infanticide or child selling, Wong retains the ability to present Chinese tradition as ideally suited to the maintenance of a strong family.

Perhaps most bizarre and difficult to elucidate in this letter (though it is surely with difficulty that any reader can repress a fairly straightforward Freudian interpretation) is a handwritten postscript scribbled at the bottom: "I suddenly remember a horrible nightmare I had years ago when a little girl—that I saw a baby in a garbage can—my little brother, and Daddy was pouring boiling water on it from a steaming kettle, and gloating all the time."[21] Such gothic nightmares, as well as Wong's feelings of horror and pain, have no place in the happy family world of *Fifth Chinese Daughter.*

The dramatic tale of Mama's pregnancy may seem to have little to do with immigration aside from the need to preserve the image of a nuclear family, instead highlighting a rather boringly familiar contrast between the old world and the new. Yet in her letter, which in itself is enough to explode the Wongs' tight-knit family image, Wong obliquely refers to the immigration secrets about her family as the originary source of pain while musing on the hypothetical tragedy of a sister sold to another family. "There is enough mystery in my past ancestry as it is, without more mystery now," she writes in protest. Her mother's immigration status again complicates the open discussion of Wong's emotions and reactions. Wong's own association here of culture clash and extreme pain with her immigration secrets and relationships demonstrates the long shadow that these secrets seemed to cast over her family life, which was published in such censored form.

Family without Borders

At different political moments, other Chinese American narratives used a broader, shifting definition of family, very far from Wong's fictionalized front. Wildly different from the cracks and revelations that appear in Wong's public memoir and narrative when one looks at her private archive, Lin's *Chinatown Family* overtly stakes a public claim for the unfitness of the American nuclear family as an ideal for Chinese Americans, a much less popular model than Wong's would prove to be. Though the family is indeed the vehicle of sympathy and affection in the novel, a more flexible structure is not only admitted but, for the most part, celebrated as a source of stability and morality. This alternative narrative appeals to the strength of the community structure, leading up to its use in model minority discourse. As it does so, the characters do not forgo claims to Americanness. Rather, they create a different family foundation for their claims and a hybrid Chinese American identity that also critiques immigration restrictions as racist and unnecessary.

Appearing shortly before the "fall" of China to communism—and again, perhaps enabled by Lin's privileged transnational status—*Chinatown Family* uses a focalized narration through a growing and Americanizing child to justify and explain the closeness of the extended family that nurtures him. Tom Fong grows up into a Walt Whitman–reciting young American who serves as a proto-model minority, thus defending the normalcy of an extended family; if anything, Lin repudiates the idea of nuclear family structure, instead making a plea for the acceptability of this illegally immigrating extended family through their values and value to society. Published in 1948, early in the postwar period and a time when the United States was less concerned with individualism as a counter to communism, the novel stands as a rare defense of the Chinese extended family system and, by extension, a plea for family reunification. Lin slowly tempers the ideology of individualism and nuclear family with pleas for larger kinship structures, diaspora, and free movement across borders. Only at his editor's behest did he explicitly address issues of illegal immigration, against which the lovable but extended family's suitability for life in America makes an atypical appeal.

The Fong family is a constantly expanding and shrinking unit, with immigration and marriage as the chief method of subtraction and addition. Katherine Karle notes that several Fongs do not aspire to the American dream of the nuclear family. Loy, the oldest son, says to his wife, who asks when they will have a place of their own, "While the parents are living we are one family." This initially seems a risible statement to make, seeing that the family existed half in America and half in China for a dozen or so years.[22] But Loy and the rest of the Fongs seem comfortable with this divided family structure, a calm acceptance of a political and economic reality.

The extended family network is held as an ideal, while the nuclear family, to the Fongs, is dangerous to the family and to the marriage, a bold position to take in the postwar era. Freddie takes an apartment with his glamorous Chinese American wife, who rarely sees her in-laws even before she runs away with another man, taking her daughter with her. Tom, the youngest brother, stops by her apartment one night while Freddie is out of town on a business trip and sees her leaving with Freddie's white boss; the implication is that if Sing Toy lived with the family, she would have no opportunity, and perhaps no desire, to cheat on her husband. Living as a struggling nuclear family breeds discontent and immorality, but the extended family network, which Lin presents to the reader as a distinctly Chinese arrangement, fosters economic advancement and stable marriage. Lin thus normalizes the previously demonized Chinese extended kinship networks by describing them as inherently linked to American ideals of nuclear family stability.

The virtue of family, approvingly remarked on by contemporaneous reviewers, does not exist in a vacuum. Lin's novel, for all its light comedy, is no less complex or political, especially when the stress on illegal immigration and family formation is properly contextualized. In seeking to redeem Chinese immigrants from certain stereotypes, he unusually chooses the extended form of the family as a vehicle of anti-stereotype. The easily extended family network implies gender equality in certain spheres, blunting any stereotypes or assumptions of patriarchalism. However, Tom does hope to live alone with his wife, Elsie, a teacher; his mother, who apparently has not heard of the mainstream dangers of Momism, browbeats him into getting married while he is still a student, scolding him for his foolish dreams of being able to "support" his wife by himself. Both of his older brothers are able to do so, but to Mother Fong, more newly arrived from China, it remains a strange idea. Admittedly, the role of the husband as breadwinner was a subject of considerable economic and emotional stress after the war, and not just for Chinese Americans. May cites one survey in which two-thirds of middle- and upper-class women "considered their husband's most important role that of 'breadwinner.'" Both men and women felt that men should be the head of the family; intellectual and career compatibility was also seen as highly important from the point of view of fostering the husband's career.[23] Tom and Elsie's dueling philosophies of Walt Whitman versus Sun Tzu, assimilation refracted through intellectual debate, can be read in this light as a possible source of strife after marriage, perhaps a reason why Elsie is reluctant to marry Tom at first.

Tom's capitulation to marrying early—something he actually does want to do, after all—does not mean that the tension of competing visions of family are completely resolved. Elsie, who had been practically adopted by an older woman in Chinatown, also wants to return to China to live with *her* parents someday; Freddie, single again at the end of the novel, may or may not return; and what about the sister, little Eva? The last line of the novel comes from Mama, who says, "And now I have to think of Eva" (248). How Eva's future will play out we have no idea (since none of the sons married Chinese American women with families), but it is hard to imagine the Fongs letting Eva go too far physically or emotionally. Very little talked about in the novel, she is the Jade Snow or Kingston of the Fong family, growing up in a male-centered world and usually silent or silenced. Like Wong, Eva wants to go to college, but her family does not want to support her aspirations. Such issues are left open by the novel's ending. Eva's trajectory may indeed be a Jade Snow–like journey, adding to the family's complex Americanization.

However, it was this same spectacle of a large, loving, and only slightly feuding family that struck Lin's editor with its novelty and implausibility, leading to the interlarding of this depiction with explicit discussion of fraudulent immigration. Lin's early drafts of *Chinatown Family* had apparently skipped over the family's immigration methods altogether, mentioning only that the Fong wife and children had come to join the head of the family. Richard Walsh, Pearl Buck's editor and second husband, wrote to Lin in early May 1948, "You have to get round that immigration question somehow. I believe I am correct in saying that no Chinese entered this country legally between 1925 and 1944 except in the status of student, business man or diplomat—that is, an ordinary wife and children could not be brought over."[24] Walsh's sentence here is a little unclear (he later wrote to Lin that he was wrong about this), but his mention of an "ordinary" wife and children demonstrates his knowledge of the restrictions. When Lin failed to address the issue in his replies or subsequent drafts, Walsh wrote again:

> But I am very worried, indeed, about the immigration point, so much so that I have been consulting a good many types of persons about it. . . . They all agreed that you would be criticized severely by anyone who knows the facts about Chinese immigration, if you didn't give a plausible explanation of how the mother and two children came into this country. Burton [probably Rascoe, a literary critic] went furthere [*sic*] and said that he thought you would be missing a grand opportunity if you didn't dramatize the way in which they got into the country, which must have been illegal.[25]

It was thus not only Walsh's own interest in Asia and his advocacy for Chinese and Chinese Americans that led him to this concern, but the agreement of all of his friends among the literati. Buck was in frequent consultation about the project and presumably agreed on this point, as well. Their stress on clarifying immigration speaks to the identification of this issue with Chinese Americans at this time and the constraints on Chinese authors, even one as prestigious as Lin Yutang.

Oddly, although Walsh had been active in lobbying for the repeal of the exclusion laws, even testifying before Congress, he does not suggest to Lin that he is politically obligated to portray this aspect in order to render illegal immigration more sympathetic, though in my reading, this does ultimately become the thrust of the novel. Walsh instead expresses his concern in terms of adherence to literary realism, a selective demand that invoked the popular coverage of illegal immigration (his own selected primary news sources) and yet conveniently lapsed into ethnic stereotypes. Walsh continued to suggest that Lin "protect [himself] by letting the reader know that [he is] aware of the fact that the arrival of the family in this country in 1932 could not be legal and is, in fact, implausible." Protecting himself (Lin) from criticism is an oddly conservative way to render this concern. Further, Walsh suggested that Lin, far from making illegal entrance a dramatic feature, as Rascoe had suggested, invoke orientalism as a plot device! "Americans are always easily persuaded that the Chinese are very mysterious and ingenious and have all sorts of ways of accomplishing what they want," Walsh wrote—certainly an expeditious route to take, though entirely opposed to Lin's intellectual project up to that time, and, one would think, to the intentions of a publishing house and longtime editor devoted to the serious consideration of Asian issues.[26]

Perhaps out of a kind of passive-aggressive opposition or genuinely stressed by his upcoming appointment to the United Nations Educational, Scientific, and Cultural Organization (UNESCO) in France, Lin took the even more expeditious route of asking Walsh to "fix up a few lines" to "save [him] time."[27] Walsh did so, and the paragraph that he mailed to Lin, expanding on some specific thoughts in the letter, appears nearly verbatim in the final version, which is reproduced here:

> No, it was not easy. There were those immigration officials, and there were immigration laws, laws made, it seemed, especially to keep Chinese out of America, or to let in as few as possible. But Chinese are used to officials and know of old that there are ways to get around laws. Yiko's way had been to jump ship. But a mother and her children could not do that. Neither could they be floated ashore in barrels on the California coast or smuggled across the Mexican border. A laundry man certainly could not bring his family into the country legally. But a merchant could if the children were not yet twenty-one years old. And Uncle Chan was a merchant, with a fine busy grocery store in Chinatown. Uncle Chan was glad to help to bring his sister and her children over.
>
> So the legal procedures were taken to make Tom Fong joint owner of the grocery store with Uncle Chan. Thus in the somewhat blinking eyes of the law, Tom Fong became a merchant. Both he and Uncle Chan knew that this was a temporary expedient, to satisfy the law. It was irregular. But the thing was done.[28]

Walsh's original version of the passage added even more ambiguity and irregularity, probably to cover any other holes his account had left: "It was irregular, and perhaps there were some other irregularities too, for which Yiko or Old Tuck or someone else may have been responsible." In substituting the word "irregular" for "illegal," Walsh protects the Fongs themselves (other than Yiko) from the reader's ire by noting that they adhere to the letter of the law. However, he continues to explore the ways that others got around the law when they "could not" enter "legally." By opening with this discussion, the Fongs become exemplars of a community marked by fraudulent entrance. Likewise, Walsh resorts to the kind of orientalism that he had previously suggested to Lin, appealing to images of imperial officialdom and Chinese wiliness: "Chinese are used to officials and know of old" how to deal with them. On every level, then, Walsh seeks to mark the illegality, from one family's sole fraud to a cultural shadiness, while Lin's narrative seeks to explain their virtuous Americanness.

It seems that the oddity of an entire Chinese family immigrating loomed large in Walsh's mind, so that for all of his concern about the other aspects of Lin's admittedly hasty and flawed novel (lambasted by internal press reviewers), this one hole in the narrative overwhelmed him. He claimed that he did more editing on *Chinatown Family* than almost any other novel he had worked on, but the illegal entry was the only episode that provoked this much specific discussion in the correspondence. Walsh's concern is ostensibly all for realism and plausibility, but Lin, as careless as he was about doing the actual writing, exhibited some concern about the effects of his novel on the Chinese American community rather than his own intellectual reputation or the strictures of realism. In his few edits of Walsh's paragraph, Lin wrote, "I have cut out a few lines, not wishing to emphasize the irregularity. I see quite a few laundrymen's wives in this neighborhood [of New York City], and don't want to create any difficulties for them."[29] Lin's other mentions of the immigration obstacles position the Chinese as triumphant and, more sympathetically, desperate: "The immigration difficulties were nothing to laugh at, but you laugh at them when you have nothing to lose" (6). The driving emotion of this passage certainly hints more at Lin's concern for the community than Walsh's concern with accuracy.

Both Walsh's and Lin's characterizations of Chinese immigration implicitly assume the prevalence of fraudulence in the community and ignore details of law or regulation. Walsh in particular is ready to use this for literary convenience. The postscript to his second letter reads, "There is a big scandal in Philadelphia right now where the Commissioner of Immigration is on trial for getting Chinese into this country illegally, and two important men in Philadelphia's Chinatown are implicated. I'll get clippings on this and send them to you." The scandal to which Walsh refers was a sizable passport forgery ring involving "two former United States commissioners," "two former Federal District Court clerks and three Chinese" (presumably listed in order of importance) who sold hundreds or perhaps even thousands of documents "relating to American citizenship of Chinese." Lin failed to comment on the clippings; for that matter, Walsh's interpolated paragraph focused on the mysterious actions of the Chinese rather than the corruption of white American officials.[30]

"This might be elaborated, the idea being that Tom Fong pulled wires and did tricks and resorted to means too secret to tell about, because if told, it might do harm to many other people in Chinatown who got here in the same illegal ways," Walsh wrote. Implicitly, he relies on the idea of a community-wide prevalence and secrecy about these issues.[31] Even Lin's fears are not necessarily accurate. There was, for example, no reason that laundrymen's wives should not have entered the country, assuming that their husbands were partners in owning a laundry. Certainly, despite Walsh's concern with realism and even his interest in ongoing legal proceedings, he was uninterested in specifying details of laws and exclusions, preferring instead to summarize them all in quaint language as the "somewhat blinking eyes of the law." Indeed, considering the novel's generally focalized narration, Walsh's language positions the Chinese as ignorant of such things themselves, naively eluding an annoying mass of laws rather than exhibiting political consciousness and strategy. Likewise, perhaps it was easier for Lin, a transnational upper-class quasi-diplomat who never experienced the trauma of exclusion and interrogation, to skate over it swiftly and then to depict the entrants in a positive light, facing their adjustment to the New York Chinatown life without any fear of complications.

The intermittent and frankly flawed structure regarding this topic may not lend the novel the realistic heft that Walsh had hoped for, but it does (perhaps accidentally) add a different political critique. Illegal immigration is a singular event, not a lasting stigma, because the family's story overcomes it. Once "the thing was done" in the novel, it is done. Never will the Fong family members face any fears, betrayals, interrogations, or confessions in the course of their colorful American life as an exemplary—and extended—family. Hoping to prove that government protection is unnecessary (and in the case of a chaotic Chinese government, absent), Lin emphasizes that the family's existence is prosperous and peaceful in America, and that they are welcome after overcoming the Exclusion Act that bars their way. Indeed, he voids the novel of legal and governmental restrictions to a degree that may be interpreted as political commentary rather than naïveté. The family also participates in a march organized by Chinatown for the 1939 World's Fair, reconciling with the rest of American society to experience this landmark event. This welcoming land, free of xenophobia, clearly had no need for Exclusion Acts—and perhaps, then, no need for the strict quota restrictions and other scrutinies of the recent past, or the ones on the horizon that would overshadow the next two decades, either.

Lin's description of this harmonious and united extended family, rather than following up the loose threads such as Eva or the runaway Sing Toy, wields the reader's affection for Tom and his family to serve Lin's greater political goal, a diasporic and global world in which national and cultural difference and free movement are celebrated. He frames this not in terms of race but, rather, in terms of antinationalism and a common humanity:

> He did not understand the arrogant sovereignties of nations. . . . You would be surprised how you could get along without a thing called the state if you are a peaceful citizen. If you are a thug or a gangster, your home government can't do anything to protect you anyway. So on this pattern of free-lancing and self-governing individualism, Tom Fong had drifted to New York as hundreds and thousands of his brothers had penetrated Arkansas and Illinois and Lima and Cape Town and Dresden and Marseille. In 1847 a Chinese traveler recorded meetings with his compatriots on the island of St. Helena. It was conclusively proved that government protection was unnecessary. (13–14)

Lin describes the Chinese diaspora around the world, not only within the United States, working peacefully, but hails the values of individualism, perhaps implying their fitness for assimilation in the United States. Tom Sr.'s continual eluding of government help or interference gives him a very peaceful view of America. While this individualist critique is ostensibly aimed at the sovereignties of all nations, it is only in the United States that barriers to "penetration" are recorded and detailed, at least in this novel. The last sentence holds a double meaning in the context of the Fong family's story; government protection was unnecessary not only to protect Chinese abroad in the rest of the world, but also to protect the world against the peacefully migrating Chinese diaspora.

Love or Citizenship

A playful ridiculing of the nuclear family ideal surfaces in the musical play and film *Flower Drum Song*, Rodgers and Hammerstein's adaptations of C. Y. Lee's novel.[32] Love and marriage are, of course, classic topics for a light musical. At the same time, their power is utilized, as in *Chinatown Family*, to contain the possible dangers of illegal immigration, a plot device inserted by Hammerstein and his collaborator Joseph Fields. As befits its heavy focus on assimilation and tradition, the musical play and film offer a look at the tension between American nuclear family ideals and Chinese family structures, presenting that tension in a comic light. Indeed, it is sometimes difficult to tell at whom the ridicule is aimed: Chinese Americans who are unfit for "normal" family life or overly sophisticated American social mores. But for all the laughter and lightness aimed at illegal immigration, the plot cannot resolve the issues that its presence raises. That leaves Chinese Americans, in the end, with unstable family structures and immigration statuses for the future. All they get is love.

Flower Drum Song's splashy, sentimental Chinatown showcases a young, American-born generation in conflict with a few traditional elders, a conflict that is crystallized by the arrival of two migrants. No nuclear families are featured; the main Wang family consists of a widowed father and rebellious sons, with a bossy aunt on the side, while an iron-fisted matriarch terrorizes Sammy Fong, the nightclub owner and reluctant groom to a picture bride, Mei Li, who enters as a stowaway with her father. But as befits the middlebrow politics of Rodgers and Hammerstein, the impetus of the plot is toward the establishment of happy marriages, even more so than in the original novel. The need to suitably pair off Wang Ta and the roguish Sammy Fong drives the entire plot of the musical. It ends with two suitable marriages, the nice Wang Ta properly in love at last with the gentle, traditional Mei Li and Sammy making an honest woman of his "tomato," Linda. While two marriages would seem to promise nuclear families in Chinatown soon, the promise is not fulfilled within the musical except in a truly bizarre fantasy song-and-dance sequence called "Sunday," in which Hammerstein and Fields cast serious doubt on the fitness of Chinese Americans for an assimilatory domesticity. Indeed, rather than a reconciliation plot that would tie Chinese Americans firmly to the nation, the ending divides them into one dubious American couple and one teetering on the edge of deportation.

The two marriages themselves are not wholly promising, undercut as they are by the threat of deportation. The famous ending of *Flower Drum Song* features Mei Li, in full Chinese bridal array, interrupting the tearful sniffles of the powerless Wang Ta, Sammy, and Linda with her confession. At the climax of the wedding ceremony, she rips off her veil, marches to Madam Fong, and says, "I must confess something. I came into this country illegally—across the Pacific Ocean. It is for that reason I cannot marry your son. My back is wet!" Cue the happy ending: the Fongs reject her, Wang Ta offers to step in, and the two couples end matched as they wish. Her illegal entrance has lain fallow during an episodic and entangled plot that sees (for example) Linda ruin her relations with Wang Ta's family by jitterbugging and strip teasing and the Wangs' aunt sing a famous paean to American multiculturalism, "Chop Suey." Only in desperation does Mei Li suddenly return to the power of her illegal entry, reminded by the confession of a TV character. Using the inflammatory word "wetback," Fields and Hammerstein revealed the strength of the association between Chinese Americans and illegal entrance, which they could invoke so easily and fearlessly. Certainly, the musical was exceptional in dealing with the subject openly at all, especially in comparison with the purposeful deception of Jade Snow Wong.

Figure 2.1. A set photo from *Flower Drum Song* similar to the climactic scene of the wedding. The three featured personages (left to right) are Linda Low (Nancy Kwan), Mei Li (Miyoshi Umeki), and Sammy Fong (Jack Soo). Wang Ta (James Shigeta), oddly, is not shown here. In the film, Mei Li rips off her veil and marches over to Madam Fong, who is in the background just to the left of Sammy. (Photograph from the Everett Collection.)

However, in making Mei Li a confessor in line with the government's best efforts to combat illegal immigration, Fields and Hammerstein did their best to foreclose the possibility of any revolutionary change, deploying heterosexual romance in order to normalize and contain the dangers of immigration.

The film of *Flower Drum Song* plays the Lis' illegal entry for laughs, as they stow away in crates on a ship to San Francisco. Mei Li's faint shriek as the crate is unloaded is attributed by befuddled Chinese dock workers to their stomach problems, thus removing the direct implication that she is tricking white Americans. Stowing away also seems more old-fashioned and is certainly more compact for exposition than fraudulent paperwork. The absence of white authority does much to soften the Lis' status. "We are illegal," Mr. Li states baldly, and he fears asking the police for help. But the only government official seen is a comic Chinese American policeman who arrives only to demand to see their license for public performance and then finds himself helpless to assist them because he cannot read Chinese. Sammy Fong's words repeat the illegality in case the audience missed it, as he exclaims at their story, "Smuggled! You mean you got in illegally?!" but he is hardly going to turn in his own picture bride.

It would seem logical to assume that Hammerstein (in particular, who assisted Buck with her work on transnational adoption) was deliberately critiquing immigration policy, especially given Rodgers and Hammerstein's adamant stance against the criticism they received for the depiction of interracial marriage in *South Pacific*. But oddly, they chose to eschew this topic in what is recorded of their discussion about *Flower Drum Song*. "Picture bride" was the publicity team's term of choice, and Rodgers even mashed it up with another term in an editorial promoting the film, calling Mei Li the "mail-order picture bride" with no mention of how she was mailed. The quaintness of the picture bride covered a multitude of sins. One might similarly think that the explicit portrayal of Chinese illegal immigration on Broadway would provoke objections, or at least some kind of comment. Whether it provoked any fears within the Chinese American community, the newspaper notices certainly do not show. However, it did not arouse any in the mainstream theater world. Some reviews, as a part of their plot summation, mentioned Mei Li's illegal entry and the final plot twist by which she manages to get herself the correct bridegroom, though not with any kind of judgment or commentary; most did not mention it at all. Rather, they referred to Mei Li as a "mail-order bride" or a "picture bride," adopting the publicity materials' terminology. But nowhere can I find that there was *any* critical response to the issue of illegal immigration. One particularly negative feature in the *San Francisco Examiner*'s Sunday magazine objected to the neglect of some of a "living community's violence and worries," but the writer made no comment about the *addition* of what was a well-documented concern at the time.[33]

Furthermore, with Mei Li's revision as a romantically motivated character rather than a refugee, as she is in the novel, all reference to communism was gradually winnowed from musical and film. Hammerstein addressed this choice in a kind and surprisingly long letter to a very enthusiastic fan looking forward to the upcoming musical, writing, "We did not deal with political questions, and Communism is of course notmentioned [*sic*] at all since it is not an essential part of the book,—of the original book. The social theme, however, of Western assimilation is very important to our story." Hammerstein's disclaimer of the need to treat communism is at worst disingenuous and at best somewhat inconsistent, considering that the musical departs very far from the novel—not to mention that this was something that the editor, John Farrar, had deemed quite important about the novel. Illegal immigration is not a part of the novel at all, yet it becomes an essential part of the musical. Taking Hammerstein at his word, it seems that the initial mention of communism gradually dropped out because of the creative team's lack of interest in dealing with "political questions." In that case, it would follow that they did not consider immigration a "political question." What seems clear is that they decided not to deal with Chinese politics, focusing instead on the dilemmas of American life for immigrants (regarding assimilation), and the Lis' refugee status dropped out in consequence. Instead, the illegal immigration is impelled solely by arranged marriage entanglements. Perhaps the Refugee Relief Act had dimmed in the public memory by this time, or perhaps the rhetorical confusion was too difficult to navigate. Regardless of their motivations, the artistic statement that they left behind provides a powerful commentary only on the category of "illegal" immigration. In a high-profile Rodgers and Hammerstein musical depicting Chinese Americans on Broadway for the first time, the ultimate decision to make the new entrants part of the "illegal immigrant" category, without even the excuse of communism, rather than the refugee category erases refugees in favor of the more stigmatized category, which then has to be softened and made comedic by mapping illegality strongly and solely onto a sympathetic female character.[34]

Illegal immigration grew in importance over the course of *Flower Drum Song*'s development, as Hammerstein and Fields changed the ending of the musical drastically to find a way to block the marriage of Sammy and Mei Li. Drafts reveal that they actually backed away from a highly confrontational final scene, the politics of which relied on the threat of informing and betrayal rather than the confession that might, according to the promises of the Immigration and Naturalization Service (INS), gain forgiveness. It is difficult to determine the exact order of the various undated draft fragments, some of which are drastically different and even eschew the topic of immigration altogether (one ending surprisingly gives the agency to Linda, who blocks the civil marriage of Sammy and Mei Li by showing up with a little boy and claiming that he is Sammy's son).[35] However, the informant ending lasts through several drafts and probably was in place for some days through the tryout period. Keeping the focus, as it is in the novel, on Wang Ta's maturation, Ta seizes control of the situation by threats based on illegal immigration, threats that are all too believable:

> Ta: I will inform the Immigration Department that Dr. Li and his daughter have entered the country illegally.
>
> Sammy (Coming back to Ta): Look, kid, this involves me. I might be deported with them!

Madam Fong: Deported!
Fong: What nonsense you talk, boy. Thousands of Chinese are in San Francisco illegally. No one ever informs and no one does anything.
Ta: In this case someone will. . . .
Fong: I will teach you, you cannot go on tickling the tiger's nose with a straw. You are facing the most powerful family in San Francisco!
Ta: And you are facing the Immigration Department!
Fong: I cannot believe you wish to bring disgrace on us all.
Ta: That *may* not be necessary! If I marry Mei Li, she will be the wife of an American citizen. Sammy will not be deported and he can marry *his* girl.[36]

What Ta, who has been turned into an American citizen here (he is not one in the novel), proposes is a method to (supposedly) resolve the illegality completely. In a related draft, Ta even disposes of the other illegal entrant, saying, "Her father can return to his family in Hong Kong and know that she is happy and secure."[37] Ta's citizenship will erase Mei Li's entry and give a happy ending to both couples. His blackmail of the Fongs, however, is perhaps too revealing. The Fong patriarch (who disappears in the final version) might jar the middlebrow sensibilities of the Rodgers and Hammerstein faithful by too bluntly stating that thousands of Chinese, such as those they have been watching sing and dance for two hours, are here illegally. Though this ending was retained for some period of time, it eventually vanished in favor of Mei Li's confession.

Hammerstein and Fields were changing the book of the musical extraordinarily swiftly, especially considering that both had been ill and were distracted. It appears that Boston suffered through almost daily changes, as an article marking the end of the musical's "tryout" period there before its Broadway opening commented that "quite a bit" had been changed—notably, "the resolution of the plot has been far better arranged by Joseph Fields." James Hammerstein, Oscar's son, suggested dismissively that these changes occurred because "the Chinese boy was not that good and not that masculine," meaning the actor playing Wang Ta.[38] If he was echoing concerns accurately, that meant diminishing the role of Ta and therefore bolstering that of the other protagonists. The addition of two new songs in Boston would seem to support this to some degree. It is also likely that Miyoshi Umeki, riding a wave of popularity, was favorably received by the audience; it certainly might help to explain the last shift in the ending from Wang Ta threatening to inform on the Lis to Mei Li self-informing. It still does not solve the question of how illegal immigration made it into the musical in the first place or how Hammerstein and Fields decided that it could be made into a *deus ex machina.*

The final version of the ending plays illegal entrance for laughs rather than this intense confrontation, sidestepping both responsibility and scrutiny of the community elsewhere. The night before her wedding to Sammy, after she and Wang Ta have resigned themselves to being separated, Mei Li watches a movie on television featuring a presumably Mexican or Mexican American female character, which we know not only by her accented English but by the loose peasant blouse that signifies Mexican femininity in Golden Age Hollywood: "I must give myself up! I came into this country illegally—across the Rio Grande. I am a wetback. I cannot marry with Rodriguez! He is in love with another woman, and he is a wetback, too! I must give myself up. I am a wetback!" In the film, the camera stays firmly on Mei Li as she germinates her brilliant idea. She "Chinesifies" the Mexican TV character in her charming broken English by saying that her "back is wet," but Sammy's English-speaking mother is properly horrified and exclaims, "My son cannot marry a wetback!" To explain the term and its consequences to viewers, she continues, "She has broken the law and can be deported. The [marriage] contract is not valid."

"Wetback" was by far the most familiar slang term referring to undocumented immigrants and, in the register of the film, becomes part of the torrent of American slang that usually bewilders Master Wang, the all-Chinese elder (other familiar words include "bucks" for dollars and "tomato" for an attractive woman). Thus, Mei Li's ability to pick the term up from television and employ it marks a successful attempt to cross into American culture at the same time she declares herself not part of it. In a way, it simultaneously proclaims and sanitizes her status. At the same time, it is a surprising and novel cross-racial comparison in this wholly Chinese American musical play and film. Chinese immigration was not often compared directly to Mexican or Latin American immigration in U.S. media of the 1950s. By tapping into the dialogue of Mexican immigration, Fields and Hammerstein could appeal to a set of similar dilemmas, but one that was safely removed from communism. "Operation Wetback" had commenced in 1954, a program, like the 1956 Chinese Confession Program, run by the INS and devoted to combating illegal immigration, though without the explicit fears of communism. As Mae Ngai has argued, the wetback was constructed as a "dangerous and criminal social pathogen [that] fed the general racial stereotype 'Mexican,'" much as illegal Chinese immigrants were inseparable from other Chinese Americans, and paired with the bracero program that imported labor from Mexico, it racialized the wetback as male, working class, and undesirable.[39] However, Hammerstein and Fields could then use the cross-racial comparison to sanitize these aspects of the term. Labeling the adorable Mei Li a wetback is so unsuitable in race and gender that it is clearly meant to be laughable and easily dismissed; the beautiful Mexican woman on the television hardly fulfills stereotypes of illegal immigration, either. The term is further sanitized by her Chinese-inflected error in using the word. In the libretto of the musical, Wang Ta jumps in after Madam Fong declares that her son cannot marry a wetback, replying, "I'll gladly marry a wetback." He also slyly says to the Fongs, "As a law student I can tell you that illegal entry breaks a marriage contract. . . . It's at the bottom. You didn't read the small Chinese print," thereby tarring Mei Li with illegality again. The repetition of these labels, which might perhaps have been too jarring, is cut from the film.[40]

But Mei Li's declaration, even if it succeeds in love, leaves her immigration status uncertain and, by extension, Ta's. Rather than keeping everyone in the United States, the happy ending seems to require that Ta be willing to sacrifice his citizenship, as he says, "I would be happy to marry [Mei Li] even if we are *both* deported." It is a shockingly blithe thing for him to say. "You're a brave man, Ta," replies Mr. Li with some understatement. Fields, who wrote the screenplay alone after Hammerstein's death, might here be patching up the hole left in the musical, which in its final stage said nothing about the ultimate citizenship or deportation of the couple. But it seems a curiously pedantic addition to make, perhaps indicating that someone behind the scenes had, Walsh-like, insisted on precision in depicting illegal immigration. To achieve that, Wang Ta has to be willing to sacrifice all for love, too.

The doubt cast on Ta's citizenship here speaks to the generalized paranoia of the immigration sweeps. Historically, male citizenship—or, rather, white male citizenship—was immune from the taint of alien status. Instead, it was female Americans who, until the Cable Act of 1922, could lose their citizenship by marrying any foreign national ineligible for naturalization. Even after the Cable Act, it took nine more years to close the loophole by which women would still lose their citizenship by marrying an Asian alien, since Asians were not eligible for naturalization at this time. Throwing this doubt on a male citizen underscores the precarity of citizenship for Chinese Americans at this time, who were subject to grand jury investigations and deportation at any moment. Likewise, the musical does not take a legalistic approach to resolution. Mei Li confesses, but in contrast to the Confession Program's incentives, there is no path to citizenship for Mei Li, not even through marriage to Wang Ta.

What is more, the film adds an explicit happy ending for Sammy and Linda that is predicated on their shared citizenship, thereby strengthening the impression of Ta and Mei Li's foreignness and possible deportation. As Anne Cheng notes, the concept of citizenship by birth is normalized by

Sammy's final wisecracking declaration as he presents Linda as a suitable bride to his mother: "She came into this country the regular way—through her mother." Is there then no "regular" legal way to immigrate for Chinese? Madam Liang's song "Chop Suey" is undeniably a celebration of the possibilities of cultural blending, but her immigration and pride in her citizenship school, a feature of the musical, are downplayed in the rest of the film script.[41] How citizenship is to be carried out, the musical cannot decide. It is a particularly fraught issue for women, since unlike the source novel, Wang Ta's citizenship is taken for granted, and so is Sammy's. For the two young female leads, it is birth into a seamy Americanness or illegal immigration into a tenuous future. Linda's citizenship redeems her other lack of virtue, as Madam Fong embraces her instantly, both physically and literally. The happy ending for the Fongs comes at the possible price of the Wangs, keeping the threat of immigration hanging over Chinatown.

The American Daydream

The couple who are unaffected by immigration worries, the most thoroughly "Americanized" couple, are also ironically the least suited to respectable domesticity, imperiling Chinatown's future. Sammy and Linda, the nightclub owner and strip-teasing star, serve as counterpoints to Mei Li's traditionalism and Wang Ta's naïveté and ambivalence, but their comic ability to steal the show demands a close examination of their narrative trajectory. Sammy is enjoying his affair with Linda and has no plans for marriage when Mei Li's unwelcome arrival precipitates a series of unfortunate events for him that culminate with the double wedding. Thus, Mei Li's illegal entry precipitates not only her marriage, but the marriage and redemption of this unwilling husband. However, Sammy's character development and his unfitness for domesticity likewise leave serious questions about the supposedly happy ending.

Linda is a clear adaptation of a manipulative playgirl in the original novel, but Sammy is another creation of Hammerstein and Fields, designed to provide the romantic lead of the B plot and a comic foil for Wang Ta. Curiously, Hammerstein and Fields seem to have gone out of their way to create an unsuitable, non-family man for their comic lead, drawing on contemporaneous Chinatown scandals. The most likely model for Sammy, Fong Wan, was a multimillionaire herbalist and owner of multiple nightclubs, and the subject of multiple tax investigations and suits for fraud, damaging his performers' careers, etc., not to mention unspecified immigration mayhem. He had an almost legendarily acrimonious multimillion-dollar divorce from his wife, Helen, full of breathless stories about bags full of thousands of dollars' worth of gold.[42] Fong Wan's club in Chinatown was a longtime bitter competitor of Charlie Low's Forbidden City, on which *Flower Drum Song*'s club is generally said to be based, but Sammy Fong's name suggests otherwise. Club Oakland was even emceed not by a Sammy Fong but a Sammy Tong, "friendly and witty as anything." Though they had closed by the time of *Flower Drum Song*, these Chinatown nightclubs were hugely popular in their heyday in the late 1940s and early 1950s.[43] What is more, there was no lack of *other* scandalous San Francisco Fongs as models. In a separate case, the four-times-married William Fong of Oakland and his wife Helen, a "thrice widowed concubine," were on trial for immigration conspiracy, including suborning a witness. Both were ultimately convicted, and Helen, who had falsified her application, was ordered to be deported. And somewhat incredibly, during *Flower Drum Song*'s composition, a wealthy supermarket owner named Walter Fong pled guilty to immigration conspiracy for bringing a Hong Kong concubine in on false papers, having another Fong pose as her husband. C. Y. Lee supposedly took Rodgers and Hammerstein on a tour of Chinatown, which may have included multiple clubs, and as a columnist at *Chinese World* and a community member, he would have known of all of these cases, which were minutely reported.[44]

By drawing on these scandalous models, whose stories did not reach farther than the Bay area and certainly were not espoused by the U.S. government in any way, as were the stories of Jade Snow Wong and Toy Len Goon, Rodgers and Hammerstein flirted with exposing a seamier, darker Chinatown, one that transgressed every standard, including those of immigration and proper family life. However, Sammy's comic criminality makes him *more* acceptable and familiar to mainstream audiences, as ethnic difference is slipped aside in favor of underworld hijinks. Sammy enters drafts as a facilitator, "a live wire, a young successful politico of Chinatown, known as the Mayor of Chinatown by many, and about thirty seven years of age, well dressed, snappy, an Americanized Chinese, a wise guy," who helps to deliver the Lis to the Wangs.[45] Illegality is thus displaced onto the Americanized Chinese as much as possible and, again, away from government regulations or officials, especially as Sammy rapidly turns into a comic gangster and a major romantic character over the next several drafts. By May 1958, Mei Li is Sammy's picture bride, and he is trying to unload her because he is out of the money, *Guys and Dolls*–style. The effect of all of this, though, is to trivialize the Lis' initial entry by equating it with a shady nightclub deal, as Sammy refers to them as being "hot" and needing to be kept "on ice." It becomes almost an expected piece of Sammy's wheeling and dealing, on par with his car payments for Linda.

Quite late in the film, Sammy and Linda get engaged after five years of a euphemized "friendship." They then perform "Sunday," a daydream number about their future that parodies the mores of nuclear family life. The disastrous ending of their parody, however, suggests that Sammy and Linda are unsuited to this life—and if these two, the most Americanized, are unsuitable for mainstream American life, then the musical leaves open the question of whether any Chinese Americans are at all. Such fantasy numbers were often used in musicals of the time to illuminate psychological dilemmas or to create elaborate dance showpieces; the comic nature of "Sunday" makes it slightly unusual in this genre. Instead, it illuminates a social dilemma particular to this couple and this community.

The apartment setting, rather than a suburban home, might reflect the postwar surge of high-rise apartment buildings in Chinatown favoring young families, as mentioned earlier. Modern conveniences and contemporary furniture dress the white apartment; overdressed post-Victorian neighbors with umbrellas and walking sticks as well as mock Beat poets come to call; and a bouffant-skirted maid sidles around (all played by Asian American actors). Even an imaginary spoiled child makes an appearance, completing the family setting. All of the fantasy characters, including the French maid, are Chinese Americans, whitened by the airy lightness of the fantasy apartment—walls, floor, furniture, and even a San Francisco skyline all white or bright. Visually, it harks back to Linda's earlier number "I Enjoy Being a Girl," in which, Cheng has argued, the whiteness of Linda's dressing room and the enjoyment of femininity that she expresses serves to create a "fantasmatic promise of *substitutive* whiteness" that destabilizes the binary of white and Other at the same time that it lets the spectator have it both ways. *Flower Drum Song* continues and even exposes its pageant of substitution in "Sunday." Linda and Sammy are simultaneously whitened and Othered not merely by the arctic sets but also by the middle-class mores that they are awkwardly performing as they host their guests and parent their child. The excess and theatricality of the daydream seem to say that Sammy and Linda are incapable of properly imagining or performing domesticity, which translates to a misreading of even American stereotype. In "Sunday," their daughter runs amok, overly Americanized and cross-gendered, clad as a little cowboy, and even the all-powerful television, which Lynn Spigel has argued was at the imagined (and physical) center of 1950s family life, bursts its bounds as cowboys and Indians climb out of it and run around the house shooting each other. Indeed, although only Western characters pop out of the black-and-white television set, the intrusion of the television reminds us of the prevalence by this year of black-and-white family sitcoms, which this number clearly is not. Instead, the not-quite-right palette of "Sunday," highlighted with orange and pink instead of black, suggests that there is just a little too much color around.[46]

It is obviously supposed to be funny to watch Sammy and Linda trying to enter into white middle-class domestic life, a ridiculousness that cannot

Figure 2.2. A set photo from the dream number "Sunday" in *Flower Drum Song*. Sammy and Linda are posed on their modern furniture; to the right is their imagined daughter and the cowboy-and-Indian duo that has burst out of the television set. (Photograph from the Everett Collection.)

be attributed solely to their underworld status, considering the lack of Chinese American domestic models in the film as a whole and the script's efforts to present them as quaint but worthy Americans. (One can imagine a similar number for the newly emigrated Mei Li bumbling around a modern apartment, preferring traditional housekeeping methods.) As the chaos dissolves back into "real" life, Linda and Sammy sing "On Sunday, you'll see only me," in a comically ironic refrain, obviously contradicting the visitors and television characters necessary to their pageant of domesticity. Their overly idyllic head-tilted pose suggests that the joke is on Sammy and Linda rather than on domesticity, and the scene casts doubt on inclusion once they step out of their underworld Chinatown sphere.

Only the utterly unfit Sammy and Linda can dream about a silly attempt to substitute a Chinatown of nuclear families for the old Chinatown, as Wang Ta's and Mei Li's fate must languish in the uncertainty accompanying her immigration status. Not even this dream of familyhood is open to them, at least not in America. Thus, the film leaves us without a suitable Chinese American nuclear family at all. The threat of illegal immigration may take away the virtuous, beautiful couple who seem eminently suitable for domesticity but are too foreign—indeed, so foreign that Mei Li has to be normalized by comparative racialization with the Mexican woman on TV. Love has to be enough for both Wang Ta and Mei Li, and a love match may be insufficient for Linda and Sammy. Yet for the audience, love is meant to answer all questions, making us forget the precarity of both couples.

Taken together, the different immigration-focused endings of *Flower Drum Song* set up an ethos in which Americanness means willingness to inform or to confess—notably, an ethos entirely absent in the more comfortable *Chinatown Family*, in which the dilemma never appears. Both Mei Li and Wang Ta are impelled by the individualistic American love marriage to betray their communities and traditions. More comically, Linda and Sammy attempt to give up their wayward lifestyles, and their social success in the United States is no more assured. The sentimental focus on the bonds of love conquering all difference strikes to the very heart of the dilemma facing Chinese Americans, whose family ties were constantly under suspicion; whose marriages were seen as mail-order, deceptive, distant, or unsuitable for suburbia; and who faced the very real possibility of temporary and permanent separation from spouses, parents, children, and other family members. For Rodgers, Hammerstein, and Fields, the unfitness of Sammy and Linda for all-American family life was a source of comedy and entertainment, but for Sing and Grace Sheng and others like them, it was a life-changing and devastating disappointment.

Post-Nuclear Family: The Extended Wongs

Over time, the general shift in social mores and the lifting of these model minority pressures on Chinese Americans allowed Jade Snow Wong to delve into her own alternative family formations in more detail, thereby critiquing her nuclear family. In drafts of *Chinese American* probably written in the 2000s, Wong frees herself from a decades-long self-construction as an extraordinarily hardworking, virtuous young American with an unimpeachable family background and few, if any, complaints about inequity. Adding her mother's and mother-in-law's stories to long descriptions of historical injustices, with frequent quotations from scholarly sources, Wong instead examines the problems of the nuclear family structure and the possibilities of other structures, acknowledging their historical roots in the flows of labor and immigration restriction, and the toll these problems take on women. Her narratorial subjectivity gains even greater significance as a construction shaped with extreme literary care when placed in dialogue with these more candid and fragmented narratives.

While finally revealing her mother's immigration methods, Wong also tentatively ventured on an imagination of her mother's subjectivity and family experience:

> I have the impression that she was a bitter and frustrated bride, stepmother to two teen-age daughters who were critical of her, and having to care for a five-year-old step daughter [*sic*] and eight-year-old stepson, with my father the strict, exacting head of the household. Mother became housekeeper to a family of five. I do not remember seeing my mother smile, but I heard her say, "I didn't marry a husband. I married a tiresome father-in-law." . . . When I accompanied her to rare Sunday afternoon movies, I noticed her rapt attention to dashing love scenes. She loved Errol Flynn flashing his sword, rescuing damsels in distress, passionately kissing them. I gather that she also longed for passionate loving. How many women of her culture and generation have yearned like her?[47]

Even in this moment, Wong ascribes her mother's feelings to her culture and generation, an authoritative narratorial claim on Chinese culture and, as befitting this book that was also to be a diasporic Chinese history, a portrayal of that generational experience. She is no longer just the Fifth Daughter; her historical axis now encompasses her mother's life, generalizing it to its common denominator.

In this last breaking of silence, Wong focuses on her mother's life rather than her father's, attempting to empathize with her experience and remembering some of their shared misery at the hands of these stepchildren/half-siblings. Jettisoning the family portrait of *Fifth Chinese Daughter* and "The Wongs," she focuses instead on the strife within the extended family formations caused by restricted Chinese immigration. She wonders openly how this twenty-two-year-old, falsely documented picture bride felt when faced with an older, distant husband and a pack of grieving, resentful stepchildren, one of whom would, she later describes, deliberately wet her bed for the sheer pleasure of watching her hated stepmother wash her bedding. They also teased and tormented their younger half-sibling Jade Snow but exacted the price of retribution from her mother; she remembers that after she broke her half-sister's glasses, her mother was forced to labor extra hours in order to pay her back for them, a peculiar reversal of authority and responsibility impossible in the nuclear family model.

As mentioned, at least one letter in Wong's archive reveals that she was well aware of these feelings in her mother decades earlier; she did not reveal them then, no doubt partly due to respecting her mother's privacy. Much was also due to her inability in the 1950s to draw comparisons between her family and other families or extended family structures. Both her mother's and Wong's own emotions surface in these *Chinese American* drafts, in the remembrance of her mother saying that she had married a "tiresome father-in-law," certainly an improper familial attitude between wife and husband. Her mother's longing for romantic love and affection could not be expressed in any public-facing document that might suggest that the Wong family structure is lacking, so Wong covers it with a façade of orientalist repression and silence until a later era.

As Wong instinctively linked her mother's experience and identity to "her culture and generation," she suggested in 2003 that her mother had suffered from the effects of economically driven immigration, which particularly affected women across different family structures: "My mother was not born into an urban family wanting her to marry into wealth; she was adopted in the country by my childless grandmother who wanted a female able to work. Was she fortunate or unfortunate? Her father had emigrated to San Francisco, seen the freedom of Western women, and wrote to her mother not to bind her feet." This oddly echoes the remembrance in *Fifth Chinese Daughter* of Wong's own father writing to his (first) wife not to bind their daughters' feet, perhaps a common experience among these men new to the United States. Wong may be seizing on or fictionalizing an anecdote that was perfect to illustrate Westernization and liberation. However, Mama becomes a figure of incomplete liberation. In another draft, Wong wrote, "Instead of being held for a big prize when grown, my mother then became useful to help Grandmother (who hated housework) and wait on her two brothers." Wong notes that not until she was grown up did she see her mother's partly bound and poorly healed feet at doctor's visits, proof of her early servitude. But the two choices seem to be to become a marriage prize or serve as a hardworking servant to her brothers and, as we know, a "tiresome" husband. Mama's suffering and near-captivity, from an adoptive family who used her as a servant to a husband and stepchildren for whom she toiled without thanks, are framed by Wong as part of a long history of economic imbalance and immigration, the clash of cultures as men abroad wrote instructions home, and the paper marriages by Chinese to elude U.S. immigration law.[48]

Wong even ventures on somewhat bemused praise of non-nuclear, non-Christian marriage, as she contrasts Mama's experiences with the range of gender roles available to Chinese American women because of these paper marriages by telling her mother-in-law's story. In class, religion, and family structure, her mother-in-law serves to demonstrate a range of economic and familial experiences that, although non-nuclear, more stereotypically Chinese, and therefore less suitable to Wong's exemplary image, are simply happier:

> Woody's mother, like my mother, had been adopted during hard times in China when the Qing dynastic rule was in its dying days.... Unlike my mother, who was also adopted into a family of boys and had to work like a servant to clean house as well as to attend to their pigs, my mother-in-law was pampered by her adopted family.... This indulgent life ended at sixteen, when she came to San Francisco, betrothed as a "picture bride" to Woody's father, who was unexpectedly much older than represented in his picture sent to her. . . . Moreover, she had not known that she was going to be a concubine. In those days of the Chinese Exclusion Act, the ratio of men to women was about seven to one.[49]

Wong marvels at how different Woody's family is from hers, not least because of the gender difference—Woody being one of four boys—but also from the non-Christian family's adherence to polygamous marriage and the cherishing of their mother, who, despite the initial description that her "indulgent life ended," Wong goes on to note, lived a comparatively pampered existence yet again in the United States. Regardless of the difference in their treatment and affective experience, Wong notes, both women were subject to the vagaries of the Exclusion Act, paper marriage, and its effects on women, both going unknowingly not only to a new country but into marriage with an older stranger, the only option seemingly open to them. Such indulgence as Woody's mother experienced, however, would have had no place in the world of *Fifth Chinese Daughter*, where discipline rather than hardship or mistreatment is the ruling ethic; nor could concubinage or polygamous marriage be mentioned, let alone as a good option for women.

These reflections on immigration-inflected family structures, which come dangerously close to recharacterizing the family story as Mama's picture bride life of servitude, never saw publication, but Wong's late-life musings finally break free from the need to adhere so closely to the nuclear family model and its happy surface. We can only speculate that, in a time with more openly accepted alternative family formations and post-second wave feminism, Wong finally felt that she could speak of her mother's and mother-in-law's experiences, as well as traditional Chinese family structures; her freedom to speak about illegal immigration methods also enables this, as Woody's mother's life could not be described properly otherwise. Regardless of the reason, these drafts make it clear that her concern is no longer with her perfect family image. As I show in the next chapter, it is easy to see why it took so many decades for Wong to feel free, as the particular attacks on the Chinese American family throughout the 1950s left familial ties, as well as family structure, in a particularly vulnerable state.

3

Blood Tells

The Attack on Chinese American Family Ties

The entire narrative of *The Woman Warrior* is framed by the demands of blood ties. "'You must not tell anyone,' my mother said, 'what I am about to tell you,'" the book opens.[1] This warning leads to the story of the No Name Woman, Kingston's aunt, whose sexual infidelity, suicide, and infanticide embroil the family in public shame after her husband has left the village to migrate to the United States in 1924. Years later, this woman bore a child obviously not her husband's. Kingston's father will not hear her name spoken; his demand for silence implies, Kingston believes, that her aunt's shame could follow these immigrants across the ocean.

Kingston interprets this tale as one of sexual shame, a demand for propriety—which we might in turn read in the context of the sexual awakening of the United States in the 1960s and the attempt of Chinese immigrants to control their sons and daughters in America—and a warning of what happens to loose women. "What happened to her could happen to you," Kingston's mother says (3). However, there is more deeply buried context for this story: the paranoia about maternity and paternity caused by immigration investigations. In addition to the extensive interrogations that Chinese immigrants endured, the Hong Kong consulate and other government agencies started to administer blood tests in 1951 in order to check paternity to the extent then medically possible.[2] The illegitimate child of Kingston's aunt, who has "no descent line," lacks the blood and the paperwork ever to be able to leave her village, and her guilt can bleed outward, betraying the entire family. The blood that the vengeful villagers smear on the walls of the family home, swinging a beheaded chicken around and around, represents the public betrayal that bad blood can bring. Silence about this aunt is not exclusively silence about sexual shame or women's independence, rape, or sexuality in China; it silences the subjects of bastardy and false paternity entirely for Chinese Americans, for whom they bore such grave consequences. The aunt must be punished and forgotten, with no grave, no rituals, no offerings: "Always hungry . . . she would have to fight the ghosts massed at crossroads for the buns a few thoughtful *citizens* leave to decoy her away" (14, emphasis added). This sharp, revealing break in terminology (nowhere else is the word "citizen" used in this section, and it is used very rarely in the memoir as a whole) sets Kingston's aunt apart as an alien, a noncitizen; her child's illegitimacy has rendered her, in turn, an illegitimate intruder on this land. Implicitly, the rest of her family, who reject her crime, may become or remain legal *citizens*, including Kingston. The child with the inaccurate bloodline will never be able to become a fully accepted member of either society.

Even as Chinese Americans publicly used the nuclear family structure and exemplary behavior to normalize and Americanize their mainstream image, the blood ties and marriages of Chinese Americans were under an extraordinary amount of pressure and investigation, in which U.S. officials violated legal and social norms of respecting or presuming paternity, familial ties, and family unity. The pressures of these investigations led in many cases, such as that of the unfortunate Ly Shew (see Chapter 1), to tragedy, and the historical accounts and the fictional accounts reflect the constant targeting of marriage and family. Many of these issues, as a U.S. Supreme Court case would argue, specifically targeted the Chinese population, but some, such as interracial marriage laws, broadly affected the terrain of the 1950s through the 1970s. In addition to *The Woman Warrior*, which is valuable for its retrospective look from the post-immigration reform 1970s, Louis Chu's *Eat a Bowl of Tea* (1961), concerned with the social pressures of legitimacy in New York Chinatown, and the novels of C. Y. Lee, written across multiple decades and set in multiracial San Francisco, are particularly important in illuminating the changing politics of mixed-race marriage. These politics were pinpointed by the white-Asian intermarriage case *Naim v. Naim* (1955) and, ultimately, by *Loving v. Virginia* (1967), which settled the question for all interracial marriage in the United States.[3]

For Chinese Americans, the continued inability to narrate and self-determine their families and relationships inevitably intersected with the enforcement of immigration restrictions and the historical gender imbalance, particularly as immigration reform in 1965 served to end most mass-media discussion of Chinese illegal immigration and allowed for freer immigration from the Eastern Hemisphere. These texts also offer a wary look at the exemplary domesticity and private lives required of Chinese Americans, both because of their inefficacy in warding off investigation and stigma and because of the uncertain acceptance of mixed-race marriage. The community policing of family structures and sexual impropriety is not mere cultural conservatism but a system of self-preservation to avoid legal attention and prosecution. Through reconciliation and resistance, different authors protest various aspects of the attacks on family that formed a key part of the government crackdown on Chinese immigration in the 1950s.

The anxiety over bloodlines in Chinese America worked in two directions: one directly related to immigration, and the other with the establishment of nuclear families, which was, as I argue in Chapter 2, a key weapon of acceptance but also tied to immigration methods. While the story of Kingston's aunt often has been read as a claiming of hidden, silenced women's subjectivity and certainly does act in this way, it also can be read in the light of a sacrificial offering of a family member's bad bloodline to the wrath of immigration officials. "I am telling on her," Kingston says, putting the emphasis on betraying her aunt, not giving her a voice or redeeming her. The narrator is informing on her, perhaps to shore up her own claims to American citizenship, against the will of the rest of the family of questionable citizenship status, who fear more than anything the complications of improper blood ties (16). Throughout the memoir and *China Men*, both in final form and drafts, Kingston's anxiety over "telling on" or informing on someone is almost always related to immigration and deportation fears, pushing us to understand her aunt's tragic life in this way, as well. Blood will out, as they say, and the anxiety over blood and narrative authority only creates more confusion about how best to speak for Chinese America.

Bad Blood, Good Family

Bloodlines, especially paternity, drew scrutiny far beyond family scrolls and interrogations about ancestral villages in the 1950s, from far-flung consular sites to the Supreme Court. Using the ABO blood grouping with which most U.S. residents are most familiar today, and later adding the MN typology (a different red blood cell antigen testing system) or Rh+/- testing, the Hong Kong consulate began to try to filter out "paper sons" in 1951. This testing was extended at the consulate's request to U.S.-based individuals, administered by the Immigration and Naturalization Service (INS), in 1952; the Public Health Service tested hundreds of Chinese only, though later in the decade the policy was broadened to include other ethnicities and races. At first, the value of "surprise" made the testing more effective. As it continued, as Everett Drumright described, it resulted in two stratagems for those attempting to enter with paper identities: trying to fake the results by bribing officials or substituting subjects, or pretesting in order to make sure that the people in question would be plausibly compatible. To illustrate, he offered several anecdotes about bribery. Indeed, he suggested that the reason that blood testing still managed to catch anyone was "inaccuracy in the pretesting of blood by the various private laboratories." The investigation was aimed chiefly at biological family claims of citizenship through derivation (i.e., via a parent who was an American citizen), as well as family reunification.[4]

Blood testing gave Drumright a scientific and statistical foundation on which to build the narrative of overwhelmingly fraudulent immigration in his famous report. Notably, it appeared early in the report in order to give more force to his anecdotal assertions of fraud elsewhere. "It could be estimated scientifically from the [blood testing] results that about 80 percent of the applicants then appearing were not related to their alleged parents as claimed," Drumright wrote. This is based on a reported 40 percent rate of failure, then extrapolating from experts that the blood testing could rule out only half of the false cases. (Basic blood tests could not do more than minimal screening, as, for example, a father with an O blood type could plausibly father a child with any but an AB blood type.) For the future, Drumright proposed expanding blood testing even further with new types of testing, mentioning the "Kell, Duffy, P. Kidd, Lewis, or Lutheran" systems—all responding to various sets of antigens—and suggesting that if for financial reasons it was not possible to test using multiple methods, the consulate should adopt a system of random testing so that pretesting would become more arduous for individuals attempting deception. (It does not seem that this battery of methods was ever carried out.) The report acknowledges at one point the invasiveness of blood testing as a defense of the relative inoffensiveness of polygraph testing.[5]

Blood testing to determine legal paternity was only coming into common usage during this decade and faced social and legal reluctance to go against decades of contrary practice. As late as 1945, Charlie Chaplin famously lost a much-debated suit in which the actress Joan Barry named him as the father of her child. Although blood testing had reportedly shown he was not a possible father, the evidence was not admitted to court in California, and Chaplin lost in a retrial, paying support until the child came of age.[6] The Uniform Act on Blood Tests to Determine Paternity, which one waggish legal commenter dubbed the "Un-Uniform Act," went into effect in only a handful of states after 1953 but importantly allowed for the ordering of blood testing by the court or any concerned party *and* for its consideration in finding paternity. Not only could the court now take the test results and expert testimony into consideration, but it could explicitly use them to overturn the "presumption of legitimacy of a child born during wedlock," one of the most important legal assumptions meant to protect the interests of the child and the sanctity of the family unit. The act also finally opened the door for scientific testing to be used to overturn paternity in paternity suits (in addition to the extrajudicial immigration investigations already proceeding). However, many courts were still reluctant to use blood testing as conclusive. Indeed, two states that adopted the act, California and Oregon, omitted this section of it. Chinese blood testing thus was excluded from the still-prevailing legal practice of respecting the family unit above available scientific testing; immigrating family units were suspect rather than sacrosanct.[7]

The practice of using blood tests was contested in multiple Chinese immigration cases in the 1950s on the grounds of discrimination, admissibility, and a number of legal points, such as the lack of permission to cross-examine the technicians who administered the tests—notably, a requirement stipulated by the Uniform Act. The value of an inconclusive, poorly administered test against the persuasion of a documented or sworn family history once again placed the power of individual Chinese American narrators at risk. A key case was *Lue v. Brownell*, a decision upheld by the Court of Appeals in 1955. Three entering sons were shown to have conflicting testimony and inconsistent blood tests. The Lues had filed objections to the administration of the blood tests on the grounds of both racial discrimination (as the tests were only applied to Chinese, which they were unable to prove) and admissibility of a required test. Blood tests, according to the district court judge, were then admissible in New York "for the purpose of excluding paternity, in any proceeding pending in a court of record" (again, a new practice). The appeals court ruled that racial discrimination did not apply and that the tests could always be used to prove nonpaternity, whether or not they were voluntarily offered by the male party in question; it was merely incidental, they wrote, that the tests were usually offered by the male party in a "usual matrimonial or bastardy case."[8] Thus, the exceptional nature of these types of required blood tests was entirely denied by the courts, both as unusual applications of paternity tests and as racially targeted requirements.

Only in 1957 did such a situation reach the Supreme Court case *United States ex rel. Lee Kum Hoy v. Murff*, a case in which the interrogations had been satisfactory; it was only the blood tests that caused a problem, setting the stage for a clear legal decision on narrative power versus the government's science. Mass-media coverage recognized the extreme importance of the case, as the practice affected at least twenty thousand applicants, and the validity of blood tests had previously been upheld. But the issue was not decided by the Supreme Court, as the case was remanded to the District Court for more accurate testing; the Lee children did eventually enter, so the family triumphed over their bad blood. Gabriel J. Chin and other legal scholars suggest that the court was on the brink of requiring race neutrality in immigration law in the case of *Lee Kum Hoy* but was perhaps stopped from doing so not only out of caution in the wake of the *Brown v. Board* desegregation decision, but by the fact that by 1957, when the case was heard, the INS had wisely made paternity blood testing applicable to immigrants of all races. It seemed that the justices had been particularly interested in the equal protection question, since the court had granted certiorari specifically on the issue of unconstitutional racial discrimination. Benjamin Gim, the first Asian American ever to argue a case before the Supreme Court, framed his oral argument specifically around "a question of whether the Immigration Service may lawfully impose blood tests *on Chinese alone* and not on other persons" with similar cases. Chin suggests that in the course of argumentation, Gim had overstressed the problems of accuracy with the blood tests, which may essentially have given the court an out from having to consider the racial issue.[9]

The question of discrimination or justification was inseparable from the cloud of stigma imposed by this era of immigration scrutiny. Once again, the fraudulent nature of Chinese immigration, guilt by association, was advanced as a reason for individualized suspicion and investigation. Gim significantly complains in his argument that the government had changed its line of defense "at this late stage" by appealing to an unspecified "consular report." As a matter of fact, the government lawyers filed the entire Drumright Report as an extra-record memorandum, with some dispute as to its classified status. John F. Davis, arguing for the government, reused the report's historical narrative and statistics heavily, even repeating the entirely irrelevant claim about how post-earthquake claims of citizenship by Chinese Americans were statistically impossible, though he also claimed not to have used the report extensively in the brief. The language of the Drumright Report and other materials, and the undoubted past use of blood testing on Chinese immigration cases alone, gave rise to discussions of equal protection by the justices in private—notably, comparisons to disallowed domestic racial arguments such as "Negroes are prone to commit crime." Although they did not rule on the core issue, their private discussion showed that the narrative of racial discrimination that the government had vehemently argued against did, at last, surface in judicial deliberation.[10]

After *Lee Kum Hoy* and the expansion of potential paternity testing to all immigrants, the spate of legal cases died down, but the repercussions of these blood-based attacks on family remained. In *Eat a Bowl of Tea*, set in New York's fading bachelor Chinatown, the troubled marriage of the young couple Ben Loy and Mei Oi is the result of a rapidly changing ethnic community's demographics and their repercussions for the newly growing nuclear family formation. Ben Loy's impotence with Mei Oi stems from his guilt for patronizing white prostitutes during his bachelor days and leads to Mei Oi's consequent sexual frustration and infidelity. When the community finds out that she is pregnant with her "bachelor" seducer Ah Song's child, it acts to police this bloodline, just as Kingston's ancestral village did, but punishes the man rather than the woman. Ordered by a Chinatown association to leave the city for five years, Ah Song realizes he has no idea where to go, though he has been to several cities in the United States and Canada.[11] The repercussions of illicit sexual relations, even for a man, are all linked to the removal of migratory mobility or choice. Ben Loy and Mei Oi must leave town, as well, starting over in San Francisco Chinatown to escape social embarrassment. Ben Loy "saw on the horizon a chance of a new beginning," where the paternity of the impending baby is not known, and the family ends happily (240).

Eat a Bowl of Tea, published a few years after *Lee Kum Hoy*, notably deals with only legal immigration, which is painstakingly spelled out for the reader, but dramatizes the anxiety around legitimacy and blood ties in a tight-knit community with a less tragic ending. The policing of Chinese immigration hovers in the background, a fact of life that the Chinatown residents now take for granted. When speaking of a police investigation into an assault that forms a pivotal plot point, a character says matter-of-factly, "At first I thought he was from Immigration. You know how those Immigration people work. They hang around out in the streets and all of a sudden they would walk up to you and ask you for your papers" (192). However, in *Tea* it is neither the "Immigration people" nor the regular police, although they at least appear, who enforce order. Policing and concern with blood is reclaimed by the community rather than belonging to a frightening, nameless state; it is drinking partners or employers who interrogate and deliver judgment via the system of family associations, and nobody's business is secret from anyone else in this tight-knit community. Though, as mentioned earlier, this Chinatown is famous as a rare depiction of a bachelor society, the characters nonetheless revere the nuclear family, and almost all of their energy is devoted to policing and preserving its structure from the threat of this tainted bloodline. Bachelor Chinatown assists the family, but it also threatens it through the "lone wolf" predator Ah Song and ultimately pays the price.

In *Tea*, Ben Loy, a drifting veteran working in restaurant service, is in search of his proper role in American society, and with the racial barriers to any kind of career rise practically impossible to overcome, his ambitions take the form of sex, romance, and children. Ben Loy is delighted when his father tells him that he is to marry a Chinese girl and bring his bride to the United States, rather than entering into an overseas family structure, by taking advantage of immigration policies of family reunification. He, too, values conventional marriage, if only (as implied in this scene) because it will fulfill his sexual desires; likewise, he enjoys the privilege of the gender role given to him by a heteronormative 1950s marriage, coming home to a lovely woman and a delicious dinner. Madeline Yuan-yin Hsu has complicated the consideration of homosocial Chinatown's social structures and values, citing early scholars such as Paul Siu, who suggested that the use of prostitutes was normalized during the exclusion era, and suggesting that scholars have reified the heterosexual-homosexual divide in a way that *Tea* continues to foster.[12] (Chu had the freedom to explore more daring topics because he published with Lyle Stuart, his longtime friend and champion who was better known at the time for his magazine *Expose* and as a publisher of quasi-pornographic works.) Though Chu starts by portraying a more complicated attitude toward sex and sexuality, the ability to progress in Ben Loy's life is irretrievably linked to his ability to establish a heteronormative family.

Blood ties are taken for granted as important and provable by the elder generation in the novel until the cherished Mei Oi's pregnancy forces everyone to forge a different kind of future. When Lee Gong, Mei Oi's father, first goes to examine Ben Loy as a potential son-in-law, he looks for proof of paternity: "He noticed the fullness of the lips, the small nose, and the bushy eyebrows. All bore similarity to the elder Wang. When the young man walked, the swinging gait of the ancient model was remarkably there" (32). These qualifications, so easily observed, reassure Lee Gong. Though he is not an immigration official, paternity is no less important for him as a passport into marriage. This attitude, though voiced by Chu as coming from the community itself, is a relic of an older immigration fear, one largely ended by the time of *Tea*, and the concern with blood must give way to the prioritization of the family unit, no matter what the baby's paternity.

The feeling of being enmeshed by blood ties becomes more and more constraining for Ben Loy as he deals with his wife's infidelity and pregnancy. Ben Loy finds himself handicapped by cultural expectations from discussing the problems in his marriage with his own father: "A Chinese would never confide to his own father that he suspected his wife of infidelity" (119). Ben Loy envies American outspokenness, though the reason for that cultural outspokenness is contained in the immigration interrogations that lurk in the novel's background; white Americans are in a position to be open. By taking Mei Oi and escaping from New York and its environs to San Francisco, Ben Loy is able to forget about everyone else's scrutiny of paternity: "It scarcely occurred to him to wonder whether he was the blood relative of this small person who was so dear to him and Mei Oi" (245). Ben Loy has revolutionized his life, not merely by moving away from the regulation of his family and friends, but by leaving behind the obsession over blood ties and legitimacy that ruled the tight-knit Chinatowns even internally at this time.

Through Ben Loy and Mei Oi's happy ending, Chu displaces the anxiety over the bloodlines and legitimacy of Chinese families into a social arena, rather than a legal one, but the legal arena remained the most crucial one for immigrating Chinese. The *Lue* case and the practices of the INS went strongly against the aforementioned legal precedent of preserving the sanctity of the family by presuming paternity within wedlock. As the U.S. District Court ruled in *Lee Kum Hoy*, "The common law, where a child has been born of a woman during wedlock, indulges in one of the strongest presumptions known to the law, the presumption that the child is that of her husband. Perhaps an administrative agency can disregard that rule of law without violating due process but it must, at least, give the parties the fullest opportunity to examine the accuracy of blood grouping tests on which a conclusion of nonpaternity is based." The judge was apparently not even certain that the INS had the power to overrule the presumption of paternity. (The precedents of presumption still exist today, even amid our more complex and flexible legal understanding of family.) The ruling quoted from an American Medical Association committee: "In a number of cases the court has refused to grant a divorce on the basis of the blood tests alone. In uncontested divorce actions, however, when the blood tests exclude paternity, the court has no choice but to grant the decree." The plaintiffs were certainly contesting the action, but in Chinese immigration cases, the INS retained the power to divorce the family, so to speak.[13]

The turbulence caused by Mei Oi's infidelity stands in for the novel's unease about how best to create a nuclear Chinese American family and how that family is supposed to function in Chinatown and in the United States. Most of the "bachelors" are either really married men with wives in China; there are only rare single men such as the rogue Ah Song who seduces Mei Oi, the last in a line of married women with whom he has toyed. The novel reflects many of the social realities of New York and Chinese America as a whole. By the mid-1950s, New York Chinatown was declining as small laundries were put out of business by mechanization and the restaurant business declined; the population, which had been heavily male, dwindled, as well. "New York's Chinese American community actually became poorer and less educated between 1950 and 1960. Its aging population of paper sons, many of them still single or separated from wives in Hong Kong and on the mainland, grappled with falling incomes," notes Charlotte Brooks in her study of Chinatown politics. The male population still outnumbered the female population two to one, but this was largely due to the imbalance in the older generations; the male-to-female ratio among the population age twenty-four and younger was quite even. Kwong also describes a chaotic political and social scene in which the political conservatism that largely took hold in New York Chinatown resulted in the settling of disputes through family associations and tongs—as, indeed, happens in Chu's novel—and that the decline of more liberal social institutions resulted in a male youth "resort[ing] to gambling, drinking, and prostitution."[14] *Tea* closely resembles this description as it juxtaposes a fractured Chinatown with the establishments of suburban Chinatowns populated by younger families; Chu even positions San Francisco as a kind of promised land for the protagonist, who cannot fit into this aging, impoverished Chinatown.

To a lesser extent, C. Y. Lee's novel *The Flower Drum Song* (1957) exhibits some of the same anxieties, as the younger generation faces the problem of getting married and sustaining the older generation of San Francisco Chinatown. (Notably, this is a more diverse and more prosperous Chinatown, though the young protagonist faces similar problems of underemployment.) In both novels, young men seek a proper sexual outlet, experimenting freely before they can find appropriate Chinese wives. The nuclear family formation is important, but not as a vehicle of explicit assimilation, though it certainly serves some of the ends that Alan Nadel notes as typical of the Cold War era,[15] in which sexuality must be contained in the service of the nation-state. In *Tea*, the family also implicitly functions as a means to link Ben Loy more firmly to the nation. Ben Loy is a World War II veteran but has been relegated after the war to Chinatown and a dim future in food service. It is in Washington, DC, while touring the Lincoln Memorial, the White House, and other familiar and important markers of American power, that Ben Loy first briefly "rediscover[s] his manliness" as he forgets his past in the excitement of sightseeing (85). Implicitly, full participation in the nation can restore the veteran to his masculine powers, but a return to New York Chinatown dooms him to impotence. The baby, by reestablishing him as the head of a proper postwar veteran's family, can normalize his experience, regardless of bloodline.

More radically, Chu suggests several variations to the family through which the troubled young male protagonists can properly reconcile their Chineseness and Americanness, heading a nuclear family but preserving Chinese traditions rather than making an ill-fated Sing Sheng–like attempt at an impossibly perfect Americanness. Their marriages are complicated by the gender imbalances and restrictions of immigration, shifting this all-important attempt at family establishment to a transnational one. The extended family and community play important roles but lose out to the new nuclear family. Lee and Chu suggest that Chinatown must come to terms with how to sustain this new family formation and understand the price that some will pay, policing untrammeled male sexuality and prioritizing young couples above bachelors, just as the public discourse did. Like *Tea*, *The Flower Drum Song* constructs social problems around marriage and bloodline. The problems in Wang Ta's love life and his improperly channeled sexual energy can be resolved only when he, too, finds a properly traditional Chinese bride. Both novels suggest that the establishment of solidly Chinese families, not only by blood (I treat the threat of interracial marriage further in the next section) but also by tradition, will create strong, productive, and gender-conforming family units, inherently arguing for strength through a limited assimilation. Wang Ta and Ben Loy find happiness and fulfillment with wives who have come straight from China, but the terms of engagement, so to speak, conform to American expectations of marital felicity, arguing in their own way for the worthiness of Chinese Americans as members of American society if only the virtues of their small cultural differences can be respected. At the same time, their lives placed firmly within Chinatowns suggest a limited reconciliation with the nation rather than a full reconciliatory tableau. Ben Loy's reinvigoration by Washington, DC, is a temporary tourist state, not an actual solution. Chu's choices here perhaps reflect the author's life: Chu, who immigrated to the United States early in his life and married a Chinese woman, stayed mostly within Chinatown in his own work and life, disc jockeying for a Chinese music program, working at a community center, and writing a seminal work of Asian American literature in English. The complex promise of Chinese American families and the argument for an enriching, compatible diversity that surface in these depictions of the nuclear family ultimately came into play in immigration and model minority arguments.

New York Chinatown heavily prioritizes the establishment of a nuclear family in *Eat a Bowl of Tea*, offering what economic and social help it can. Ben Loy's father briefly considers telling his son to leave his bride behind in China to keep his own wife company but discards it as an inappropriate relic of the old days. Although this Chinatown is heavily organized by clan and tongs, their chief function in the novel is to protect the establishment of the nuclear family, not only punishing Ah Song and other seducers of married women (147, 222) but finding suitable jobs, communities, and housing for Ben Loy and Mei Oi. The novel opens with the prioritization of the married couple, as Ben Loy's roommate Chin Yuen—whose apartment it originally was—vacates it for them, saying that "since he was a bachelor, he could find himself a bed anywhere" (10). There is no question of the couple living with his father.

The need for Ben Loy and Wang Ta to get married is ascribed in both novels to Chinese tradition and familial continuation, but in an era in which the average age at marriage had dropped drastically in the United States, it is also inherently American. As with the court cases, the power and presumptions in favor of the nuclear family war with the baby's bloodline and bastardy. Chu normalizes Chinese American family structure as part of the U.S. baby boom, almost nostalgic by 1961. *Tea*'s elders heap scorn on Americans who have embraced the newly socially legitimated usage of birth control for married couples:[16] "Many young couples don't want babies right away. . . . We Chinese are different" (102). Even Ben Loy, suffering from the shame and frustration of his impotence, feels delighted when Mei Oi becomes pregnant: "He was happy because it was the most natural thing for a married couple to do, to have a baby" (118). Chu's phrasing reflects the awkward state of Ben Loy's thoughts. He represses the obvious thought that this is not his child, though it surfaces occasionally despite his efforts. Therefore, he cannot immediately rejoice in the feeling of fatherhood, nor is he traditional enough to reflect on the continuation of the family line, as his father does. Instead, he rejoices because he has been able to enter into his social role as a husband and father, so expected that, despite his circumstances, it has become "natural." In other words, he, too, has accepted the presumption of paternity within wedlock.

In addition to this seeming advocacy of heteronormative nuclear family structure and argument against the purity of family bloodlines, *Tea*'s family politics are further complicated by a decidedly antiassimilationist stance in the explicit discussion of American family ideals. When Mei Oi and Ben Loy initially attempt to leave New York for the suburbs, they enter into a world of competing nuclear families that is brief and comic but merits examination. Mei Oi's cousin by marriage, Eng Shee, refuses to visit her until ordered by her own father-in-law, then arrives with her children in order to passive-aggressively twit Mei Oi about her infidelity by regaling her with tales of wayward wives. Eng Shee, though described as a countrified Chinese woman in origin, is also a parody of a traditional American housewife: she wears badly fitting American clothes, never dreams of asking her husband about his business, and feeds the children quarts upon quarts of milk every day, as well as bread or sandwiches of some kind for lunch (166, 169). In contrast, the beautiful, educated Mei Oi in her Chinese dress is more appealing but socially appears at a huge disadvantage, largely created by nuclear family failures: her well-rumored infidelity and lack of children as yet. Moreover, they occupy confused positions in their attitude toward paternity, with Eng Shee's refusal to ignore Mei Oi's infidelity and Mei Oi's determination to pretend that her baby is her husband's. Their opposition in terms of a Chinese value system is thus confused by their ability to conform to various American familial ideals. But Chinese class cannot be completely erased. Although Eng Shee feels superior, she is grotesque and unsympathetic as narrated through Mei Oi's eyes. All-American suburban housewifeliness does not suit Chinese femininity, Chu seems to say, but nonetheless, Eng Shee walks off in a kind of social triumph, and Mei Oi must heal her family and move to another Chinatown enclave in order to regain her class superiority.

By succeeding in San Francisco Chinatown, Ben Loy and Mei Oi implicitly advance an argument for a new kind of Chinese family: young, fertile, full of hope for the future, and seamlessly uniting the U.S.-born population with the newly immigrating, embracing the American nuclear family structure. Gone is the older generation's concern for the family's pure bloodline, as Ben Loy's acknowledgment of the child is all that matters to the parents and to the community. Indeed, nowhere in the novel does anyone suggest that the child should be rejected or sent away, or even that Ben Loy should disown him. Sentiment triumphs over any legalistic or scientific definition of family. Thus, Ben Loy may embody the community's acceptance of paper sons, picture brides, and other families considered illegitimate by the mainstream.

In the end, the Chinese American nuclear family flourishes in this new Chinatown, keeping Ben Loy and Mei Oi firmly within the bosom of their ethnic community. His underemployment issues are not solved, but at least the threat of his baby's blood is removed so that he may enjoy his status as family man. Rather than the full tableau of the reconciliation plot and a symbolic unity with America, *Tea* ends with the reconciliation of the couple and, thereby, the new family Chinatown with the old bachelor Chinatown. Initially, in San Francisco, the couple enjoy perfect independence from the elders: "The proverbial parental shackle had been cut" (245–246). It is Ben Loy's army friends, men of his own generation (referred to as "wartime buddies"), who welcome him and help him get settled; a friend who was in India, site of some of Ben Loy's dalliances with prostitutes, finds him a promising job that leads up the ladder at a Chinese restaurant. Here Ben Loy and Mei Oi are with peers of their own generation, establishing families together. Mei Oi embraces her identity as wife and mother free from scandal and rumor. They embrace their independence to a cold-hearted and nuclear extreme, not even bothering to inform their two fathers, who are languishing in self-imposed exile after the shame brought on them by Mei Oi's infidelity, of the baby's birth (248). The younger generations' marriages only destabilize the older bachelor Chinatown; immigrations' imbalances and injustices cannot be corrected so easily by the passage of time. Only after Ben Loy regains his sexual vigor does the couple, in the afterglow of successful lovemaking, say that they will invite their fathers to the next haircut (birthday) party for the baby. They have found the successful family structure, away from the stifling atmosphere of New York Chinatown and its now-decaying bachelor society, but still respecting traditions such as the ceremonial cutting of hair. This lifestyle can erase infidelity and bastardy, symbolically triumphing over an unnecessary concern with paternity and blood.

Interracial Intimacy

Chinese American authors of the Cold War era mostly engage in literary depictions of all-Chinese marriage, a seemingly purposeful choice. Among Wong's many omissions from *Fifth Chinese Daughter* and ensuing publications was her younger sister's elopement with an older white divorcé, to everyone's consternation, especially Mama's.[17] In the wider postwar culture, conception of white-Asian intermarriage shifted drastically, thanks not only to war brides and the depiction of many tragic romances between white GIs and (in particular) Japanese women, but also to the images of mixed-race beauties that graced magazines in the lead-up to and aftermath of Hawai'i's statehood. However, most of these cultural productions involve Asian women and white men; a rare cultural forebear is the silent and unconsummated yearning of a Chinese man for a white woman in D. W. Griffith's film *Broken Blossoms* (1919).[18] The pattern of legally contesting interracial marriage as a whole via the unions of white men and women of color lasted through multiple decades and culminated in the well-known Supreme Court case *Loving v. Virginia* in 1967, after a number of state cases featuring white and Asian plaintiffs.

In the attitude toward Chinese American marriages that surfaces in or about the Chinese American literature of the Cold War, I trace deep anxieties about the imbalanced demographics and overseas marriages of Chinese America, casualties of immigration policy—unsurprising, considering that the model minority image was coming into being around a narrative of a happy, self-policing, mono-ethnic U.S. community. As Emma Teng points out, from the very beginning, the presence of interracial marriages and mixed-race children in Chinatown seems to have vanished from depiction. Here, I draw narrative comparisons among the imbalances and difficulties of immigration as a primary issue in fictional depictions and real-life cases of Chinese and Chinese American men in relationships with white American women. These authors link the difficulties of interracial marriage to the policing of Chinese marriages by the U.S. government, a policing that falls chiefly on men as the population that was allowed to immigrate first and then bring in their families. Amid the investigations of the 1950s, in particular, it seemed that there was no correct spouse for a Chinese American man—none that was inoffensive enough, unsuspicious enough, Chinese enough, or American enough. The limited literature on interracial marriage shows how these marriages faced an impossible bind, thanks to the immigration policies that were often ignored in judicial review or mass-media coverage.

The history of Asian interracial marriage, a more prominent dilemma in the literature, stretches back to the nineteenth century and is a complicated and transnational affair. While white-Asian intermarriage in the United States is the best documented, particularly in the twentieth century, there certainly were intermarriages among all races and ethnicities, and these marriages happened across the Chinese diaspora. The "Third Wife" in *The Woman Warrior*, married to Kingston's sojourning grandfather, is from Nicaragua, "black with hair so soft that it would not hang, instead blowing up into a great brown puffball" (82). She brings her barbarian language back to China but eventually falls silent. Kingston's story and Teng's study of attitudes toward white-Asian marriage on both sides of the Pacific remind us that these relationships should encourage us to view the lives of these individuals transnationally, rather than as "Chinese American" or "Chinese," and certainly not by the old labels such as "sojourner."[19] However, Chinese American literature in this era, inasmuch as it focused on these relationships at all, focused on white-Asian marriages in their U.S. setting.

As with attitudes toward Chinese labor and immigration, intermarriage was not always viewed entirely with negative feelings. High percentages of marriages between Chinese men and white women happened quite early in the Chinese presence in the United States, during the nineteenth century, between Chinatown residents and Irish American women. The Mississippi Delta saw several Chinese-black intermarriages in the Reconstruction era, as well. There were also high-profile unions on the other end of the class scale. Louisa May Alcott's *Rose in Bloom* (1876) features a marriage between a white society belle and a Chinese businessman, viewed approvingly but comically by the golden-haired protagonists. Alcott was likely inspired by the marriage the previous year of the Chinese official Yung Wing to a Connecticut society woman, but Yung Wing's Western-style dress and dignified appearance is a far cry from the plump, stereotypical comic Chinese of Alcott's novel. Alcott's characters' jokes and wonderment may have reflected the common discourse of the day—the Wing marriage drew a wide range of reactions.[20]

The high profile of these marriages and the increasing sentiment against Chinese labor and immigration led to the rise of negative—or, at least, uneasy—views about such alliances on both sides of the Pacific, whether overtly hostile and nationalist or pseudoscientific, in the late nineteenth and early twentieth centuries. This occurred as a subset of the rise of antimiscegenation laws in the postbellum and Reconstruction eras in order to enforce separatism and white supremacy. Unsurprisingly, the fierce battles over black-white intermarriage rose to the fore during the political debates over segregation and separatism in the 1920s, a time when advocacy for the right to marry across racial lines had to be politically separated from advocating for intermarriage wholeheartedly. As mentioned in Chapter 2, in this era, female U.S. citizens were still stripped of their citizenship if they married an alien ineligible for naturalization—an Asian man—under the Cable Act. For those born in the United States, the variation in state law and the fluidity of some racial categories profoundly affected Asian Americans seeking marriage licenses. Peggy Pascoe describes the uncertain position of Filipinos, in particular, who were only clearly designated ineligible for citizenship in 1934. This, in turn, changed with the new postwar laws about naturalization and the striking down of antimiscegenation law. In California, antimiscegenation law was overturned by *Perez v. Sharp*, a case involving a Mexican American woman, classified as white, and a black man, in 1948, paving the way for more interracial marriages just as young Chinese were moving out of Chinatown.[21]

The postwar pattern of interracial and even intraracial relationships in cultural works shows a more than common obsession with finding suitable partners, not simply in terms of ethnicity but in terms of values, class, and appearance. There was little precedent for literary depiction by Chinese Americans on this topic. Pardee Lowe wrote in magazine articles in the 1930s, as well as much later in *Father and Glorious Descendant*, about his own interracial marriage and mixed-race child, portraying an entirely happy union from his family's point of view, although his white New Englander wife was jarred by her few encounters with racist hostility, which are detailed in the magazine articles. The couple would later divorce, and Lowe remarried a Chinese American woman, though he retained a lifelong interest in interracial marriage, keeping immense clippings files.[22]

In one of the earliest postwar works comes the sole positive depiction in this era of an interracial marriage between a white woman and a Chinese man, a minor but revolutionary depiction not to be underestimated, though it is not the chief romance of the plot. In *Chinatown Family*, Lin blithely treats interracial marriage as a sign of Chinese acceptance in the United States, though softened by his generally folksy tone and the woman's ethnicity and class status. Of the Fong family's three sons, the eldest, Loy, marries an Italian American; the second, Freddie, marries an unsuitable Chinese American singer; and Tom finds a beautiful, highly educated, perhaps slightly too independent Chinese American girl. Out of the three daughters-in-law, the eldest is the most domestic and most easily fits into the family structure. Flora displays thrift, family values, and respect for her mother-in-law; indeed, her agreement with the family and her focalized narration are of key importance in conveying a positive American attitude toward Chinese immigrants.

This positive depiction benefits greatly from its wartime publication and geographical setting. At a moment when the Chinese were the "good Asians," with propaganda posters proudly proclaiming them "On Our Side," opposition to interracial marriage was likely slightly softened in certain regions. The New York setting also means that no antimiscegenation law need be addressed, merely the social aspects that Lin so easily resolves for the couple. Flora's whiteness is mitigated by her marked Italianness and by her class status; she is a filial, second-generation member of another New York City immigrant population geographically bordering on Chinatown. Their occasional encounters with Mayor Fiorello La Guardia underscore her Italian identity. Similarly, Loy first encounters Flora selling apples and nuts on the street, engaging in an occupation similar enough to his. Her sexual attractiveness is likewise sanitized by her "old world" lifestyle.[23]

This singular interracial marriage also depends strongly on the Fongs' open-mindedness and willingness to accommodate their Italian American daughter-in-law, representative of Lin's determination to describe the assimilatory potential of Chinese Americans. The threat of interracial marriage is thus negated in the novel first by Flora's traditional ethnic identity, and second by the lack of Chinese culture or identity for the child. Indeed, the extent to which the child drops out of the story also further negates the consequences of this mixed marriage; she attracts little notice or attention of any kind. Flora is pleasantly surprised when her in-laws don't mind her children being baptized or given Italian names (162). Nor do any outsiders they come in contact with (which is not often) so much as remark negatively on the interracial union or the mixed-race babies. Instead, La Guardia sends Flora (but not the Fongs) a congratulatory telegram when the newspapers report that a "Sino-Italian" baby has been born in the back of a taxi (154). In short, these two immigrant groups are "simpatico," as Flora's father toasts after the baby's birth, yet are never described with a *Chinese* adjective (160). The Fongs' general social ease in the novel comes largely from the fact that their irregular immigration is so little scrutinized beyond their initial entry, even permitting happy interracial union. Later Chinese American works describe interracial mixing with more fear and foreboding, corresponding to their feeling of continual policing and threat.

Lin's ability to dismiss the consequences or the cost of interracial marriage oddly presages the most notable legal case of white-Asian marriage, in the remembrance of which immigration difficulties have been overlooked in favor of framing it as a case on the road to *Loving*. The only Asian-white marriage case to make it to the U.S. Supreme Court docket (and twice), albeit then reviewed only on technical grounds, was *Naim v. Naim* (1955), a Virginia case now better known as the case that the court refused due to the political pressures of *Brown v. Board of Education* (1954) and *Brown* II. Various scholars have also pointed out that *Naim* was miscegenation the wrong way around, so to speak, with the less acceptable union of a white woman and a husband of color; it was also filed the wrong way around, in that the wife was actually attempting to annul the marriage. The historian Gregory Dorr has further contended that *Naim* fell afoul of eugenics trends due the lower-class status of the couple and the wife's history of "immorality," as she had two children out of wedlock with fathers other than her husband. The history of *Naim* has largely been told through the framework of the Supreme Court's politicized abrogation of duty, and the two protagonists are mostly lost to history. Little is known about their lives before and after the case, and newspaper coverage at the time, such as it was, refers to them with little other than their race and names to identify them. However, Dorr's archival research on what little is available from the original case filed in Virginia shows that the heretofore unemphasized thread of their story was the extraordinary citizenship pressures placed on a Chinese man at this time and how this factor weighed into the dissolution of the marriage.[24]

Ham Say Naim and Ruby Elaine Lamberth met in Norfolk, Virginia, during a shore leave. Ham (as I will call him for clarity, being the name Ruby used for him) was a Chinese sailor, born in Canton, who had worked on British and American ships as a cook and held a legal seaman's visa permitting him shore leaves. Ruby was a white U.S. citizen from Michigan who had moved to Virginia with her two daughters in April 1952. She met Ham soon thereafter, and the two swiftly married on June 26 in North Carolina, where their union was permitted. After the marriage, Ham hired the attorney David Carliner to handle his naturalization case. This was, of course, an extremely difficult moment for Chinese immigration, and Ham's case, although different from the ones previously described due to his seamen's visa and his marriage to a U.S. citizen, undoubtedly fell under the scrutiny of the INS. The marriage was stressed by Ham's absences at sea and likely adultery by both parties.[25]

The issue of Ham's immigration status was perhaps even more critical, as his visa was due to expire on September 27, 1953. A letter by Ruby around June 1953 ran, "I do love you, and tho it has been very hard while your gone . . . it is still you I love with every breath in me. . . . Even if you should leave the U.S. there are ways I can bring you back." Ruby was clearly willing to entertain the possibility of the failure of the naturalization case, perhaps envisioning overseas marriage and a second round of immigration—an unusual reversal of family reunification. However, as the case dragged on, she lost hope. Dorr notes that Ruby visited Ham in New York on September 19, 1953, then stopped at Carliner's office on her way home and wrote Ham one last letter: "Ham, this whole mess is just too much for me to try and contend with. I can't take any more and sincerely feel it best to get completely out of the whole situation. In other words, I would appreciate my freedom." "This whole mess" seems, from the sequence of events, to refer to the citizenship and residency issues that Carliner probably warned her were likely to end badly.[26] Ham's visa would expire in eight days, and Ruby can be forgiven for her downheartedness, given the climate of the times. Their divorce decree was issued in February 1954, but the cases over the legality of their marriage would last into 1956.[27]

In addition to the general suspicion of Chinese immigrants at this time, Ham, as a sailor, fell into yet another particularly suspect category undoubtedly already under scrutiny and later particularly singled out by Drumright. The Drumright report briefly but pointedly mentioned seamen as another class of illegal entrants, suggesting that they averaged more than two hundred a year and that some managed somehow to become naturalized citizens, then sought to bring in wives and children. These were men who "jumped ship," presumably entering without papers at all by overstaying their shore leaves and hiding in Chinatowns.[28] As someone married to a citizen and filing for naturalization, Ham was in a separate category. Nonetheless, the pervasiveness of such ideas in the INS most likely had repercussions even for exceptional cases such as Naim's.

Ham's immigration status proved to be a critical difficulty in his marriage and his divorce. It was, at the time of the divorce case, a complication that even Ham's lawyer would raise but simultaneously attempt to subsume. Although Ham's nationality might have meant that Carliner could move for a change of jurisdiction to federal court, such a court could not have made the constitutional ruling on Virginia's act that Carliner sought.[29] Thus, even at the very moment of his case, Ham's urgent concern about his citizenship and naturalization became secondary. Nor, in the end, do we know whether he protested Ruby's annulment action from love or from practicality; whether he hoped to retain his wife or retain his hope of U.S. residency with the aid of marriage.

While Ham's wishes largely remain lost to history, Chief Justice Earl Warren would not forget the case that his court had refused to hear, citing it in his opinion for the court in *Loving*; so, too, would the lawyers for and against the Lovings cite the case in their briefs and oral argument, inscribing *Naim* firmly in antimiscegenation case law. More recent refigurings of *Naim* still focus on this aspect of the case, though Leslie Bow's study of it introduces the intersectional aspect of the southern location. However, *Naim* also helps us to understand the intimate relationship between interracial marriage and the immigration investigations and precarity of the time for Chinese Americans. While there were Asian-white intermarriage cases out west that were not complicated by citizenship, such as the *Oyama* case in Arizona, *Naim*'s national profile and place in history, including its afterlife in *Loving*, require that its full repercussions, including the intersections with immigration status, be properly noted.[30]

Naim and *Chinatown Family*, although ten years apart and with one unhappy and one happy ending, have important common points in their narratives. Both featured a white woman whose whiteness was diminished by her frank sexuality and class status, as well as Flora's ethnicity and Ruby's illegitimate children; this was the paradigm used in *Broken Blossoms* decades earlier to make an interracial attraction, even an unconsummated one, less offensive. Equally important, both women's desires regarding the marriage loom larger in the narrative—the historical record and the novel—than the racial identity and the individuality of the Chinese husband. Whether in reality or in fiction, only a certain kind of white female-Asian male intermarriage, it seems, could surface in the national consciousness—and notably, neither caused great alarm. *Chinatown Family*'s blithe overleaping of immigration obstacles was impossible in real life and in fiction in the 1950s, as investigations and consular obstacles mounted. However, in both cases the trappings of romance and family life pushed immigration nearly out of sight in the narrative. It is likewise significant that the only national-level white-Asian intermarriage case ended with the desired dissolution of the marriage and that this early novel featuring an interracial marriage was a relative failure in sales, putting this topic literally out of sight.

A Lack of Discipline

Even suitable Chinese-Chinese marriage perpetuates racial hierarchizing rather than social equality; as we have seen, such marriages are more scrutinized and less protected in the legal realm than white marriage. "I enjoy being a girl," sings Linda Low in *Flower Drum Song*, but as Anne Cheng argues, her promiscuity and assumed whiteness in the film are a threat to blood purity and must be tamed by marriage to a similarly improper but Chinese man. Yet in Cheng's reading, Linda's enjoyment is no less a sign of her interpellation than other Chinese women's fear and tension.[31] Chinese Americans are inherently threatened by the systemic racism of the 1950s through which they are socialized, a racism that was heavily framed by the public dialogue about Chinese immigration and the legitimacy of Chinese marriages. Nor can we ignore the natural uncertainty of a newly immigrating population that struggles with its children's very different lives, not only through the promoted values of assimilation, but also through the threat of interracial or interethnic sexual contact and marriage. The difficulty with which the entire subject is fraught, whether in finding suitable Chinese girls to wed or preventing interracial intimacy, reflects the pressure placed on Chinese American family life by the gender imbalances and other injustices of immigration, as well as the extraordinary social pressures placed on the image of proper heteronormative marriage. In this way, immigration stigma fell equally on the sexes.

The few mentions of interracial relationships with white women continued to stress the sexual and illicit nature of these relationships rather than considering them seriously, and even portrayed them as part of the ills of immigration inequities that Chinese American men had to suffer. Well into the Confession era, *The Flower Drum Song*'s patriarch directly blames modernity—and, by extension, the United States, which is identified with the trappings of modernity—for the problems of interracial intimacy. Its presence in Chinatown society is thus attributed to a more universal problem, at least by Old Master Wang. However, he is often wrong, and his refusal to accept modernity, symbolized by Western medicine, is plainly a mistake. His insistence may therefore point us more firmly in the direction of the constantly mentioned immigration barriers that limited Wang Ta's dating pool so severely; the failure of Wang Ta's interracial relationships only serve to show those limits in starker relief, particularly as he ultimately marries (or at least runs after) a refugee. The policing of Asian American men's sexuality, originating in fears of all-male Chinatowns and extending through paternity testing, speaks to mainstream fears of interracial sexual contact, which we can also trace in the lauding of all-Chinese and all-Japanese American families in the instantiation of the model minority.

The action of *The Flower Drum Song* is precipitated by the housekeeper finding a photo of a blond woman in Wang Ta's desk drawer, a discovery that bothers his father greatly when it is reported to him. "Was Wang Ta in bed with that foreign woman in some cheap hotel room now? He thought of it and shivered."[32] Wang Ta experiments with a streetwalker of unknown ethnicity recommended by a Filipino student (14), but in general, during college, he is a rather hapless hero who strikes out with women of all ethnicities, though the novel then focuses on Wang Ta's succession of unhappy romances with Chinese women. Similarly, although *Eat a Bowl of Tea* also focuses on an all-Chinese pairing, Ben Loy's problems in his otherwise suitable and happy marriage with a woman from China stem from the guilt of his use of non-Chinese prostitutes. He sleeps with Hindi women and presumably others while in the military (86) and various blowsy white women in New York City, sharing them with his friend. For both protagonists, these can be only temporary and squalid physical relationships, never taken seriously as marital possibilities.

The antagonism between the dangerous sexuality of single men on the loose and the contained, proper family life that was on the rise spills over from the pages of Lee's novels themselves to a dispute with Jade Snow Wong, who, after all, was the preeminent representative of the Chinese American nuclear family image. In a review of *The Flower Drum Song* for the *Saturday Review*, we see that Wong's insistence on exemplary behavior extended to a fiction writer's work. Her almost uncompromisingly negative review complained about Wang Ta's laziness, some of the main characters' Hunanese ethnicity (rare in heavily Cantonese Chinatown), and the improbable plot. However, her last paragraph, which the *Review* chose not to include, launched her most searing critique of the immorality of the book: "Many incidents in the descriptions of Wang Ta's love affairs are related with their point on sex for sex's sake. This formula may be a mark of 'sophistication' in some types of literature, but as employed in this particular account, serves only to give this reader a bad taste. 'Discipline of the body begins with discipline of the heart' is a familiar and respected Confucian precept of restraint concerning things Chinese which neither the author nor his characters display in this book." It is unsurprising that Wong, renowned by now for her family life and charming Chinese modesty, should publicly flinch from the frank (though hardly explicit) depiction of a young man's sexual activity. Her sweeping condemnation goes much further than this, though, attacking the very authenticity of the novel and restricting true "things Chinese" to those partaking of her ethos of restraint and discipline. Though Wong's memoir and identity are not mentioned in the review—it is merely a short review followed by a byline—she implicitly sets herself up as the true, disciplined, Cantonese, sexually proper voice of Chinatown, the one that knowledgeable *Saturday Review* readers ought to heed.[33] Remembering Wong's own family history, however, this review polices not only exemplarity but the dangers that sexuality poses to all of Chinese America in an era of scrutiny of marriage and immigration, when no family could be good enough.

Instead of Wong's faithful public adherence to the nuclear family model to cover immigration irregularities, Lee instead moves to interracial marriage in order to expose the oddities of immigration investigation and, incidentally, comparative racial histories. Late in *The Flower Drum Song*, Wang Ta's friend and fellow dishwasher Chang, who suffers the same problems of economic opportunity as Wang Ta, resurfaces with a Mexican American wife and an energized, entrepreneurial approach to their job-seeking woes. This marriage is quite exceptional in the literature and serves as an important counterpoint that draws our attention again to the comparative racialization of Chinese and Mexican Americans, though more seriously than in *Flower Drum Song*'s brief mention of "wetbacks" (see Chapter 2). Indeed, this may well have been the inspiration for the musical's beautiful Mexican woman on TV. Chang's new wife, Dolores, is "young and pretty, with large sparkling eyes and a dark complexion . . . 'Born in Mexico City,'" he proudly introduces her (178). He is very clear that the driver behind his hasty marriage, however, is immigration problems rather than love:

> Some Immigration investigators or inspectors . . . completely ignorant of our problems, seem to have the tendency to think that all bachelor aliens over forty are homosexuals. In order to have my immigration status adjusted, I decided to prove to them that I'm a normal human being, just as anxious to get married as they are to get rid of the "undesirables." So I decided to marry anyone who would marry me, no questions asked. . . . You know, the case was getting pretty urgent. I wanted to have my own business and settle down; in order to achieve that you must first have the Immigration officers' blessing, otherwise you're building your castle on sand. (180)

Chang reflects here on the paranoia about all-male Chinatowns described in the previous chapter, explicitly mentioning fears of homosexuality. Astutely, he sees the strong social favoring of young heterosexual couples. How exactly his immigration status is going to be "adjusted" is not clear, but he sees marriage as the key to his life in the United States. The power of the INS extends over marriage and sexuality, as well as Chang's business prospects. Intermarriage with a Mexican American woman is at least legally acceptable. However, while proving his heterosexuality, he chooses a woman from an equally disfavored minority, with its own illegal immigration stigma to overcome. There may also be a hint at the negatively stereotyped sexual attractiveness of Chinese men, as Chang says he vowed to marry the first woman he could get, but Dolores's physical beauty makes her a desirable mate, though she is likewise suffering from racial stigma. While neither character mentions her immigration status, her appearance by the side of the disaffected Chang suggests a certain common immigration and racialization experience, both being from the same socioeconomic level (they met sharing a telephone party line) and both born abroad. While being married boosts Chang's confidence, it does not make him feel more accepted by white America; it merely helps him to avoid deportation. In conversation with Wang Ta's relationships with Chinese American women, interracial marriage seems only a neutral possible outcome, at best, for Chinese men in this novel.

Interracial marriage and sexual relations seem inevitable across these works, a wave of deplorable social freedom to Wong and a natural outcome of immigration imbalances and social mixing to Lee and Chu. But all of these authors see interracial intimacy as less desirable, less suitable, and a sign of the community's peril. As in *Naim*, the history of immigration and the further scrutiny of Chinese status underlies these relationships, enlarging the setting to the stigmatization of Chinese in this era, a broader prejudice that some authors are able to construct as a continuum from international issues of immigration to seemingly domestic issues of interracial marriage.

The Perils of Interethnic Marriage

In his novels set in the United States, Lee reflects on the problems of interracial or interethnic intimacy to a degree rarely seen in the work of any other author of this era. *Lover's Point* (1958; a shorter version was originally serialized in *Chinese World* in 1956) offers extraordinary ambivalence about the interracial intimacy caused by the Asian presence of the U.S. military, and particularly about the entrance of East Asian war brides into U.S. society. *Lover's Point* presents Chiang Fu, a Chinese American man, as a rather dubious savior of Aika Yamamoto, a Japanese war bride whose life has gone off the rails after her divorce. Chiang teaches in an Army Language School in Monterey, California, saving money to bring his wife and children over from Communist China, until she writes that she is ending their marriage. He falls in love with Aika, a waitress at his regular restaurant, who he quickly learns is a divorced mother of three and prostitutes herself on the side to support the children. She in turn falls in love with John Larson, a lieutenant studying at the language school, who idolizes her as a stereotypically modest Japanese girl and cannot bring himself to marry her once he finds out that she has prostituted herself.

Lee uses a Japanese American female protagonist's interracial war bride marriage as the most popular and best-known example of interracial marriage in order to induce familiarity and sympathy for all of the other complicated marriage arrangements for Chinese Americans in this novel. In particular, he suggests that Aika's marriage and the Chinese American male protagonist's overseas marriage are the originary tragedies of immigration for these two lovers. Although Chiang is often angry at Aika in the course of the novel, he cannot blame her. "Aika was a victim of men, heartless men who turned women into torturing devils," he thinks, blaming the white American soldiers who have left her.[34] Nor can he blame his wife, who is obviously under pressure from the Chinese communist authorities, for deserting him and marrying a "young cadre" (46). "He wanted to curse the woman and yet there was no anger in him" (46). "A cow has to graze," agrees one of his friends philosophically (239). These commentaries once again generalize the situation, like Old Master Wang blaming modernity for his son's problems, but this time they are less comic, lifting us from condemnation of the individual. The precise detail of the narration and the setting, placing Aika squarely within the contemporary depictions of Japanese war brides and Chiang within the complicated Chinese immigration situation of the decade, makes their romantic woes politically and ethnically specific rather than character failings or universalized romantic tragedy.

Aika reveals her history only to Chiang. She was a war bride, married in 1950 in Tokyo to a white American GI, Mike. When they arrived in Los

Angeles, Mike found himself torn between his wife and his mother, who bitterly opposed the marriage for unspecified reasons (179). Aika demanded a divorce after Mike deserted her and the children, except for brief visits; after his final visit, she tried to kill herself but failed, then bore her third child. She fell in love with Larson because of his vague resemblance to Mike; there is also an implied erotic preference for tall white men, which Chiang reflects on bitterly. Though Chiang goes back to find Aika by the end, Lee implies possibilities but stops short of showing us a happy marriage, similar to *The Flower Drum Song* and very unlike the decisive ending of Chu's *Eat a Bowl of Tea*.

Aika represents the most frequently depicted type of white man-Asian woman intermarriage: the marriage of a war bride and a white American GI. Beautiful, vulnerable, appealing but not aggressively sexual, the brides also served as foundations for the model minority stereotype, while these portrayals reinforced the heroic images of soldiers already solidified by wartime patriotism and propaganda. The most famous of these cultural products, *Sayonara* (1957), featuring one tragic couple and one happy, defiant one, launched Miyoshi Umeki on her starry Hollywood career. These images, as Caroline Chung Simpson and Naoko Shibusawa have argued, not only served to normalize and recuperate the image of Japan after the war, but they also served as the most favorable image of interracial marriage. The American Civil Liberties Union (ACLU) particularly sought such couples to use as plaintiffs in test cases against antimiscegenation law in the western United States.[35]

As seen in the Americanization and confession of Mei Li in the *Flower Drum Song* adaptations, and the consequent devaluation of Linda Low, the status of the newly immigrated Asian bride was not a straightforward issue. Asian war brides were not even permitted in the first War Brides Act, but racial restrictions were lifted in 1947. Asian war bride entrants, though used by the ACLU and Japanese American Citizens League as idealized images of Asian femininity in the cases against antimiscegenation law, were often spoken of as if there were a taint of illegitimacy about them. Rose Hum Lee, for example, wrote that the acts prompted a rash of marriages with many very young brides, an image that was solidified by popular media. In truth, 77 percent of the war brides had been married for more than ten years, and on average, the Chinese war brides were much older than, for example, the British war brides. While there had been various war bride frauds—in one case, an interrelated set of three fraudulent marriages to Polish women—the Asian war brides were frequently the only ones described in unfavorable language. While the *New York Times* raved about British wives bringing "a dowry of common sense and traditional British ideas of stability," it described "hundreds" of "Chinese, Japanese and Filipino wives" who were about to "escape normal immigration quota restrictions." A similar *Times* piece on German brides, published only ten days earlier, made no mention of immigration restrictions; nor did it use it use terms such as "escape," opting for the sportier description that they would "beat the . . . deadline." White war brides were thus exempted from skepticism of their immigration and painted instead in a romantic light.[36]

There are no depictions of Chinese war brides (a much smaller segment of the total) that I could find in the available Chinese American literature. However, the unhappiness and difficulties faced by war brides were well known within the Chinatown community—ironically, sometimes at the expense of the Chinese bride, who was unfavorably compared to her white counterpart. (Mei Oi in *Eat a Bowl of Tea* is not a war bride but, rather, the bride of a former GI whose army experiences we briefly hear about, metaphorized through his sexual experience. The novel does show that Chinese know about the war and war bride marriages to veterans who have seen action; the matchmaker slaps and examines Ben Loy's legs to make sure he is not wearing prostheses). Lee instead chooses to portray a Japanese war bride, taking the most famous exemplar in order to critique the failure of this type of intermarriage and its downstream consequences.

Aika's odd introduction in the novel—first as a beautiful waitress, then as a prostitute, and finally as a tragic war bride—toys with the reader's possible stereotypes of Japanese women in this era. Her first two personas make explicit both sides of the sexualized image of the geisha in this period; she is even compared to the geisha in *Teahouse of the August Moon*, a popular novel, play, and film in the 1950s dealing with the American occupation of Japan. But Aika's story as a deserted and divorced war bride who then has yet another unhappy affair with a white military man entirely undercuts the narratives of happy war brides and depicts her husband and lover as weak, hypocritical men who idealize and sexualize her but cannot deal with the reality of interracial marriage. Though her sex work might confirm prejudices against war brides, her devotion to her children and domestic life further complicate her character.

All of Aika's exemplary domesticity as she cooks, sews, and cares for the children cannot keep her husband happy. Lee's description of the last Christmas before his desertion dwells on her housekeeping: "Japanese incense and fresh flowers; she had also bought the best fresh salmon steaks, Mike's favorite dish . . . , which she was to fry after Mike had arrived, so it would be fresh and warm" (179). Instead, he fails to show up until several days later, sleeps with her one last time, and then deserts her and the children forever. The domestic scene as the point of failure and improvement for war brides was, unsurprisingly, a 1950s staple. Xiaojian Zhao's archival research has uncovered the extensive discussion of the common problem of tension between husbands and Chinese wives, particularly war brides who were suddenly bereft of a family structure. The burden or blame, writers opined, was often placed unjustly on the wife, who was seen as countrified and embarrassing to her Americanized husband. In some cases, husbands even used the threat of deportation to control their wives, with one man informing the INS of his impending divorce to upset his wife's naturalization process. The pressure on the woman's domesticity was quite similar to mainstream American dialogue; in one case, a woman married to a gambling addict was advised to make her home more attractive to her husband. Once again extolling the white war bride at the Asian war bride's expense, a *Chinese Pacific Weekly* article upheld a German war bride married to a Chinese American man as a model for her cooking, sewing, and refusal to wear cosmetics.[37] Domesticity could be pushed forward as the corrective for personal and even racial differences caused by this sudden immigration and marriage. However, Lee exposes its failure, instead introducing us to a woman who has had to jettison her rejected domestic skills in favor of prostitution. From a respectable wife in Japan, she returns to being a geisha of sorts in the United States, reversing the familiar cultural paradigm.

Chinese American overseas or immigrant marriage, whether overseas wives, picture brides, or local encounters, is no less relentlessly characterized with domestic failure and disappointment. *Lover's Point* is full of lonely or irregularly married Chinese men, all of whom are more or less introspective about their own situation. Chiang has presumably found asylum in the United States via the Displaced Persons Act. In San Francisco, Chiang encounters many more solitary men, gradually finding himself a part of their fellowship as his romance with Aika sours. An acquaintance, Old Chao, jokes about his two wives in Peiping; rather than bring only one over, he brought neither and lives alone. Ling says, "That is the problem of the whole Chinese population in America—loneliness. . . . I doubt if one out of ten has a family here. He is either single or a married man with his wife in Hong Kong or somewhere else in China" (150). The friends go on to muse about why, in spite of this loneliness, Chinese stay in the United States and about the biased and unjust attitude of American officials and the way that Chinese Americans are caught in the political conflict between Communist China and the United States.

Chiang is greatly unnerved when he arrives in San Francisco by the lonely death in hospital of a man who, like himself, has a wife and children in China and works quietly to save money to bring them to the United States (81–83). Thinking of his plight seems to embolden Chiang to use his know-how and English skills to protect himself and to sympathize with those who cannot. At the very moment that he is lost in thought about this man's death, "two large policemen" accost him at the bank and demand to see his identification card. Chiang refuses, "smiling," and says, "I'm afraid I can't show you my identification card. I understand that this is a free and lawful country, you just cannot stop anyone as you please and demand to see his identification card" (82). The policemen, astonished at his resistance, pass on, and Chiang "thought about the plight of many overseas Chinese who couldn't speak English well enough to express themselves and who were intimidated by anyone in a uniform" (83). Chiang is a solitary but intelligent and self-aware man, and Lee uses his interior monologues to reflect wisely on his political plight and on his resulting emotional entanglements. Much of his inner voice in the novel demonstrates his political savvy about the social and legal position of Chinese Americans and how they are interrelated, as in this tragic example that might seem at this point in the novel to foreshadow Chiang's ultimate fate.

The middle portion of the novel briefly diverges, but only to consider other immigration and marriage problems. Chiang's employer, Mr. Yee, frets over bringing in a pretty young woman as a refugee in order to marry her. He is certain that she will have "no immigration trouble" upon her entry (119). Chiang mistakes his anxiety for lawbreaking and asks, "Have you violated any immigration law?" Although the plot makes it apparent that he may well have, Mr. Yee answers, "No, no, no. I wouldn't violate any law. It doesn't pay to violate any law. Besides, I'm pretty grateful to America. The country did plenty for me, and I would be a son-of-a-bitch not to be law-abiding" (112). Rather than a pious attack on the rest of the community, this statement must be read in the light of Mr. Yee's kindheartedness and general naïveté as yet another silly ideal. Mr. Yee's nephew runs off with the pretty bride, precipitating Mr. Yee's proposal to Aika—now also in San Francisco and caring for his mother—who he naïvely thinks is an "angel." Just another sad and lonely Chinese man, in spite of his wealth, Mr. Yee finds that picture bride and interethnic marriage fail him, and his plot thread in the novel ends when he refuses to marry Aika.

Once again, the short supply of Chinese women and the entanglements of immigration law, as well as economic opportunity, create the complex social situation that largely shapes the fates of these characters. Chiang's reflections on how unfortunate *other* immigrants are often position him as far more prosperous and savvy, as in his bold interaction with the San Francisco police. However, to the reader these reflections are little short of tragic. His delight in being able to live in a garage cheaply and sometimes use his landlady's washroom could hardly position him more forcefully as a thrifty, deserving immigrant. Rarely does he complain about immigration directly. Rather, it is the nameless force that never really leaves him, shaping not only his economic and erotic life but that of all the people with whom he comes in contact.

Though Lee is portraying a bachelor Chinatown that is fading away by the time his novels were published, he continues to draw these linkages between migration and marital status across race and ethnicity as lonely Chinese men look for appropriate mates. One Chinatown bachelor, the hearty yet cynical Mr. Liu, lives with and intends to marry a "United Nations" woman. "I have long since stopped wondering what her nationality is," he says. "She speaks English with a Spanish accent, but she has red hair and dark eyes. She was raised in Shanghai by a White Russian couple, but married a Filipino who was killed in the last war" (190). This unnamed mistress, herself a widowed war bride, is a comedic throwaway, but she represents the only U.S.-based option for these men, most of them bachelors or married to women who are still overseas. As with Chiang's longing for Aika, Liu's mistress is his political and social equivalent. A mixed-race refugee (we presume, given Shanghai's wartime history) and the widow of a Filipino soldier who almost certainly fought with or for the U.S. military, she represents a liminal Americanness and immigration status similar to Liu's. But like Chang's marriage to Dolores in *Flower Drum Song*, Lee mentions these interracial marital possibilities as minor, neutral outcomes, not worth the protagonist's while.

There seems to be no such thing as easy marriage for these men, no romantic comedies featuring only the lightest of obstacles and clear happy endings. Instead, Lee substitutes a tableau of the immigrants who exist together in the ethnic ghettoes of San Francisco, a darkly ironic "United Nations" that demonstrates the barriers to inclusion within this particular nation. In an era when the family serves as the vehicle of assimilation and exemplarity, the suspicion cast on single Chinese "bachelors," Asian war brides, and, as I previously discussed, interracial marriage left a small but growing segment of Chinese American nuclear families as the sole acceptable social formation. Furthermore, as I discuss next, the fate of the next generation in this society was far from clear.

Think of the Children

The child is rare in Chinese American literature of this era, perhaps reflecting the demographics. Prosperity from Heaven in *Fifth Chinese Daughter* is a memorable but very minor character. Even the product of a happy interracial marriage, Flora and Loy's child in *Chinatown Family*, is virtually invisible after her birth. The liminal Americanness and uncertain acceptance of these unions is contained in the body of the child, as in Kingston's story of the No Name Woman. However *Loving* might rearrange laws, it could not so swiftly change perceptions and, indeed, across these decades we see a constant stress on the peril of the child—*any* child of the community, whether wholly Chinese or of mixed race, as the figure of the child is unusually rare in these works. Indeed, aside from Sui Sin Far's frequent depictions of children, very few young children appear in Chinese American literature to this point, and far fewer are happy, reflecting the constant peril of immigrating minors whose parentage was being questioned.

Family also functioned to bring Asians into the American nation in this time via the high-profile adoptions of Asian and mixed-race orphans (not, in this era, primarily from China). While obviously a wildly different construction that, if anything, served to abrogate the rights and the very existence of Asian parents, transnational adoption powerfully linked the social acceptance of Asians to their inclusion in a white heteronormative U.S. family. As Christina Klein has described, the Asian orphan, working at this time in tandem with the flow of refugees, bolstered the image of the white mother devoted to the home and family and served to metaphorize the inferiority and helplessness of Asian nations.[38] The infiltration of these images into popular culture, such as Rodgers and Hammerstein's runaway hit *South Pacific*, served to promote the suitability of Asian children for U.S. family life. It is all the more striking, then, that Chinese American literature positions children in such precarious states, mirroring the precarity of Asian orphans but lacking the optimism about their ability to unite with the nation via a Chinese American family.

An unusual immigrating child is found in Lin's *Chinatown Family*, set before the most exigent investigations and deportations. Yet even this child passes through perilous migration at the hands of the government. In a scene early in *Chinatown Family*, while enjoying a quiet evening with the family on the roof of their building in New York, young Tom Fong remembers his Chinese home. He remembers it fondly but with an unnatural clarity that the reader soon learns was induced by "almost a matter of life and death. . . . He had had to memorize these details when he was coming to America, to meet the test of the immigration authorities. In fact, he had had to write them down and memorize them on the ship. . . . If his father should have told the authorities that there were ten windows in their house and he should tell the immigration authorities there were twelve . . . , he might be shipped back across the Pacific" (105–106). From an affective child character's point of view, the exclusion becomes frightening and senseless. We know that Tom actually is his father's son (despite Lin's elastic timeline), but the idea that he could be separated from his family for forgetting such ridiculous details subtly critiques the Exclusion Act. From the beginning, Lin presents immigration restriction and interrogation as an attack on this loving family and this child who grows into an exemplary American.

This political stance begins immediately as a sentimental critique of the harshness of immigration policies that divide parent and child. Tom applies a child's logic and tells his little sister, who cannot remember these details, "You'd better find out when you go to China. We wouldn't let you land in China if you guessed wrong" (106). He innocently assumes that this is a process that always occurs with entry into a new nation rather than a barrier to Chinese immigration to the United States only. Tom further assumes that Eva can be left behind easily, just as they were left behind when his father and brothers went to the United States. Tom's heartless, childish teasing of his sister, as he becomes the questioning authority, perhaps heightens Lin's critique of the cruelty of the government, especially the naïve assumption that other countries must have the same interrogations and barriers to entry. Even the Confession Program had to be designed around this issue of child immigrants and family separation. However, the stated goal of the Confession Program was the closing of slots, not family reunion.

The 1950s, as already mentioned, saw a flurry of legal cases about Chinese immigration to the United States as had not been seen since the post-exclusion cases in the late nineteenth century, policing the growth of Chinese families and threatening these strong and stabilizing family bonds. However, not all of these cases were filings for reunification with a citizen parent. Many of the Chinese plaintiffs or defendants shared the status of Tom Fong, children of Chinese American merchants who had failed earlier to cover some aspect of the complicated immigration procedure and had been ruled ineligible for residency or naturalization. In 1951, the Second and Eighth Circuit Court of Appeals upheld the petitions of five and three cases, respectively, of Chinese "minor children of domiciled Chinese merchants" for naturalization, a different legal class from those applying for citizenship by derivation. The INS had been objected on thin technical grounds, one key reason being that the children's certificates of arrival had been marked for entry as the children of "treaty merchants," based on the 1880 treaty, rather than for permanent residence, and then amended. The court opinions overrode these objections clearly and forcefully.[39] It was a decision based on the relative prioritization of treaties and congressional acts, but nonetheless, the courts' refusal to uphold the government's position was striking. If anything, it might seem amazing that the federal government bothered to contest such obviously clear-cut cases based on nothing more than technical grounds (in complete opposition to the other stream of cases in the 1950s, which were at least based on questions about the legitimacy of children or the falsification of slots); it reflects the overall aggression with which Chinese family structures were policed in the 1950s.

These cases focused on men in this odd in-between position, one of the suspect areas of scrutiny similar to seamen such as Ham Say Naim: Chinese merchants' minor children who had entered after 1924 and, not surprising, given the Chinese political situation, between 1926 and 1932. All of these young men, therefore, were in exactly the same seemingly dubious position as Tom Fong (his father's false merchant status notwithstanding) or Wang Ta in *The Flower Drum Song.* Having entered as children, they had grown up in America—given the wartime conditions, likely exclusively in America—and then applied for naturalization not very long after the passage of the Magnuson Act and the end of World War II. What is most striking is that in *none* of the cases were the young men's actual entries, their paternity, or the merchant status of their fathers being contested, so that they were associated with illegal immigration only by overwhelming social context and a climate of suspicion about communist infiltration. What is more, the scrutiny falling so hard on this second generation threatened the continuation of Chinese America, once again lending an air of urgency to their marriages.

The portrayal of Tom Fong in *Chinatown Family* thus enters American literature at a critical moment, when the full acceptance and happy endings of these newly naturalizable Chinese Americans were by no means assured. Though legally permitted to immigrate under both the old laws and the new, these minors found themselves in a legally precarious state that is perhaps reflected in their relative disappearance in literature. Lin is able to imagine a fulfilling life for Tom, a clever, Benjamin Franklin–like figure, as he grows up in America after his somewhat dubious and frightening entrance, and, as already mentioned, the novel largely dismisses the continual threat of immigration scrutiny for the Fongs. But Tom's vivid memories of his frightening entry serve as a reminder for readers how easily this child might have been excluded.

In *Lover's Point*, the children are barely even given names; they are merely burdens, the visual proof of racial mixing and the exigencies of immigration, leaving nothing but misery in their wake for their mother and her suitors. The specter and economic burden of the mixed-race children, fruit of a war bride marriage and a liaison with a military man unprepared to face harsh realities, suggests the ultimate failure of this particular form of immigration. Chiang sees Aika's children from her marriage only once, when he drives her to visit them. They are happy with the jolly white couple who care for them and barely recognize her, suggesting that white adoption is the way for mixed-race children to enter U.S. society, a reflection of much transnational adoption work then in progress. Chiang never sees the fourth child, fathered by John Larson. Initially, he assumes that the child is his and refuses to help Aika abort the pregnancy in order to marry their rich employer, Mr. Yee. When Chiang tells Mr. Yee about the pregnancy, Mr. Yee initially offers Chiang money to let him and Aika raise the child as theirs, his privilege and his faith in the system allowing him to overlook the dangers of illegitimacy. After the birth, however, Mr. Yee refuses to marry Aika when he sees a blond, blue-eyed baby, whose appearance represents one step too far for him. The fact that the children's white fathers are absent, unknowing, or both suggests that the misery of the mixed-race child will redound primarily to the unfortunate Asian mother, whose marginal position as an immigrant and minority has already driven her to a life of prostitution.

The novel ends when Aika and Chiang return to Monterey and their old jobs. Aika has somehow brought her children to live with her and given up prostitution, taking up sewing instead in a return to domesticity. Chiang goes to the restaurant where Aika is working once again and orders his usual, a message that he has decided to pick their relationship up as it might have been back when they first met. Despite the ostensibly happy ending, Aika's four mixed-race children remain a shadowy threat to their happiness. Chiang resolves his feelings about Aika by reflecting on her alone, but just before he decides to see her again, "John Larson's baby was a dark shadow weighing heavily on his mind and straining their relationship" (246). His lack of firm decision about the children, particularly the extramarital child, leaves this thread unresolved, papering it over with the rosy promise of sexual attraction and romantic love.

In the original (shorter) serialized form, the story of *Lover's Point* ends with Larson and Aika together, and Larson explicitly takes on the parenting of her first three children, joyfully writing, "Damn it, I'll be a father of four!" Chiang himself brings about the reconciliation, and the story ends with him alone at Lover's Point, looking out to sea, but "to his own surprise, the great load on his mind had disappeared. He was finally free."[40] The mixed-race children are with a racially appropriate father, at least, and Chiang may be alone, but he has been relieved of the responsibility of trying to parent half-white children, which he feels unfit to do, or to accept an illegitimate child, whose bloodline (once again) feels threatening somehow. Paradoxically, his inability to accept mixed race children is relieved by another interracial white-Asian marriage, but in the more complex novel, which deepens racist confrontation, the repulsed Larson will not swoop in to solve Chiang's problem of acceptance. Neither ending is unequivocally happy, but the status of the children seems shakier in the novel's plotline, which does not offer them an enthusiastic father figure of any race. There is no family, then—either mixed-race or monoracial—to bring the children into better unity with the nation.

In a way, the ambivalence and inconclusiveness of *Lover's Point* echo the lack of a Supreme Court decision in *Naim*; U.S. society as a whole simply did not develop a clear stance in the 1950s on the issue of Asian intermarriage, particularly as all cases labored in the shadow of white-black (and primarily domestic) interracial marriage. The manifold complications of Asian intermarriage, including war brides, generation gaps, and the gender imbalance of immigration, surface in the threats to these characters and their imperiled children.

Loving Post-*Loving*

Through these novels, we have seen primarily dark or ambivalent visions of interracial and interethnic intimacy, reflecting the immigration pressures and inequities of the past and necessitating or rupturing the (proto-)model minority image. As the flow of immigration from East Asia increased, the reforms of 1965 opened the door even wider for family reunification and would eventually enable a huge surge in Asian migration to the United States. In 1967, the decision of *Loving v. Virginia* struck down antimiscegenation laws across the country. These two events, legal landmarks highly significant to the Chinese American community, enable a tentative vision of optimism in the works of two major writers. *Land of the Golden Mountain* (1967) is a now-forgotten comic novel and the most clearly focused on white-Chinese interracial intimacy of all of C. Y. Lee's novels, resolving that intimacy with a reconciliatory ending. Interracial intimacy, as so often happens in literature, becomes the means for a bridge between cultures, foreclosing discussion of political unease with a happier trajectory. Kingston, though also looking for a hopeful ending, progresses from a dark vision of infanticide to a vision of migration figured as translation and cultural understanding, slightly more ambiguous and certainly lacking in erotic reconciliation.

In the year of *Loving*, Lee offers a stereotypical and utopian vision of interracial intimacy set *before* the exclusion era. A girl who dresses as a boy to sign on as a coolie laborer and journey to the United States falls in love over time with her white employer, and vice versa. *Land of the Golden Mountain* offers a romantic story of triumph over past immigration and interracial barriers, implicitly suggesting that such difficulties are all literally in the past. Though the novel stops short at the couple's reunion once again, this lighter and more humorous novel promises a happier interracial union than his novels in the 1950s. In its use of a deep historical setting and partly in its aims (though the similarity stops there), *Land of the Golden Mountain* can be compared to Toni Morrison's *A Mercy* (2008), which seeks to reimagine race relations in the early colonial era, when indentured servitude, early slavery, different European ethnicities, and a strong indigenous presence all create a wildly different racial landscape, with a much more confused hierarchy than in our modern understanding. By selecting a time well before the era of exclusion, Lee creates a different origin story, centered on a female Chinese migrant, that suggests an alternative history leading to a world in which interracial marriage is permissible.

The relationship in *Land of the Golden Mountain* constructs a strong bond of sympathy between the white romantic hero, Mr. Carnahan, and all of the Chinese American workers, but particularly Mai Mai, the disguised protagonist. Carnahan takes an interest in Mai Mai after her brother dies aboard the coolie ship and agrees to send any deceased Chinese back home for burial. Their bond overcomes all of the barriers and discrimination that the Chinese workers face. The cartoonish but atmospheric Gold Rush setting serves to soften any discussion of immigration and racism. Mai Mai is described erroneously as "the first Chinese woman ever to set foot in America," and her friend Miss Randall, a white American missionary, suggests that she should "marry one of the handsome Chinese bachelors and produce the first-born Chinese-American."[41] However, this is not the direction that Lee takes for establishing Chinese American presence in the United States, opting instead for the usual erotic racial reconciliation. Instead, although Mai Mai is initially attracted to the handsomest of the Chinese workers, she turns her attention to Carnahan because her vanity is piqued by his racist dismissal of her as a dirty little boy.

The flatness of almost all of the characters makes it difficult to read their relationship in any but a symbolic fashion; it is a bland declaration of love that makes Mai Mai choose to stay with Carnahan rather than return to China with her best friend, suggesting not only a happy interracial union but a happy life in America for Mai Mai, who "for the first time . . . felt she belonged" (248). Her happiness washes away her brother's death and all the hardships of the past, and the construction of the first Chinatown in San Francisco at the same time promises a happy future for all Chinese Americans. Lee uses Mai Mai and Carnahan's union as such a hasty reconciliatory device that it actually troubles the ability of romance and sentimental writing to erase the past. Mai Mai cries with happiness at the end of the novel to be reunited with her lover, but her Chinese friend is erasing the past of suffering by returning home to China with his father's body.

What is more, the romance is so unevenly written and characterized (at one point, Mai Mai and Carnahan have their first kiss and then, with no explanation, she sneaks away with her friend) that it is only a vehicle for Lee's true narrative interest, which is a historical account centered on the Chinese experience in the rough-and-tumble Gold Rush and building up of San Francisco. Beginning in a famine-stricken region of China and taking the reader through the details of crossing the Pacific, panning for gold, and walking through early San Francisco, Lee employs a great deal of orientalism and Mark Twain–imitating local color both within and countering racist stereotypes, but he consistently celebrates the experience and importance of Chinese in the American west.

Mai-Mai's fictional happy ending resolves everything for her, and it recenters history on the experience of Chinese and the construction of Chinatown and Chinese culture in America. Indeed, *Land of the Golden Mountain* arguably serves as a speculative historical novel, since it offers such a fictional early starting point for white and Chinese mixing and understanding. The parameters of the marriage even suggest a different power dynamic, since by the end of the novel Mai Mai and her friends have hit an enormous gold strike, and Carnahan's mining venture has failed, leaving him working as a stevedore. At a moment of optimism for the acceptance of interracial marriage, Lee's novel brims over with the joyful possibilities that it offers for the nation and the complete revision of race relations.

A decade after *Loving*, Kingston takes these symbolic uses of interracial union even further, not just creating an alternative narrative but self-reflexively thinking about the utility of intercultural narrative. Like Lee, she goes into an alternative past to conclude her memoir on a hopeful note about Chinese American artistic expression, creating a progression from the No Name Woman left behind in 1924 and her child, the literary descendant of the imperiled children in 1950s literature. Kingston touches only briefly on interracial marriage in *The Woman Warrior*, at first inevitably associating it with silence, illness, bigamy/polygamy, and all other woes associated previously with immigration and marriage in combination. Similarly, a crazy, childless Chinese American neighbor in Stockton adopts her husband's half-white, half-Chinese illegitimate son from the Midwest: "She was very happy to have a son to raise in her old age, although I saw that the boy hit her to get candy and toys" (184). These frightening outliers signal the migratory disorder of the world. The "little village" of Stockton Chinatown, safe and circumscribed though it may seem, is still constantly under attack by Others.

Other mixed-race individuals exist as threats, the "fool half ghosts" who won't be quite fool enough to marry someone like Kingston (190). Indeed, returning to the No Name Woman, Kingston's potential marriage or sexual relationships are another impetus behind this book of secrets. It is not only the deceased aunt's sexuality at stake, it is Kingston's budding sexuality and independence, which she fears may end with familial rejection, exposure, and disaster. The untrammeled sexuality of her aunt "translates" into fears about interracial sexuality, which implicitly symbolize Kingston's comfort with her Chinese American identity. Speculating on how her aunt managed to find someone not within the kinship network to have an affair with, Kingston secretly wonders about her own unsuccessful love life, viewing boys at school as "brotherly" as a defense mechanism against their complete lack of sexual interest in her. Yet, she says, if she stood up and shouted, "Hey, you! Love me back," she was afraid not only that the Chinese American boys in the class would fall in love with her but that everyone else—"Caucasian, Negro, and Japanese"—would, too. That interracial or interethnic contact is so clearly forbidden that she opts for sisterliness instead.

This section also tells of the perilous fate of children caught in the web of migration and imperiled family, including the fate of Kingston herself, an angry child grown slightly wiser. No Name Woman throws herself and the child down a well, an action that Kingston wants to interpret as love. The destruction of families via immigration was metaphorized and, in at least one documented Chinatown case, tragically carried out in infanticide, the death of children in a socioeconomic structure that strained the marriages and relationships of their parents and often resulted in children's lives as half-orphans or renamed into other families. As in Toni Morrison's *Beloved*, infanticide is the horrible but inevitable conclusion of the social death of the parents, whose marriages, kinship ties, and parental rights are abrogated by the structures of immigration and the strictures of the state. The extreme abjection of the mother pushes her to the final destruction of the child's already compromised life, a paradigm in Chinese American literature as early as Sui Sin Far's short story "The Wisdom of the New."[42]

This introductory infanticide in *The Woman Warrior* is a shocking opening, but it introduces us to a memoir full of children gone, children left, children hidden or far away or emotionally distant, suffering in their own ways from the ruptures of travel and immigration. The Mulan-inspired figure in the memoir has to send her child away in order to achieve her vengeance and enact her perfect filiality (41), and Kingston's mother speaks affectionately of her two children who died young and the slave girl she purchased to serve as her nurse, left behind in China (82). Kingston's narrator feels herself to be such a child, fascinated with other children who are strangely isolated or abandoned. The aunt "take[s] the child with her into the wastes," the only place she could possibly take such a daughter (Kingston assumes, thinking that there might be forgiveness for a boy) (15). But taking her daughter with her is singular enough that Kingston remarks on it wonderingly, attempting to see it as love rather than a lack of choice. The threat of the illegitimate child is contained in *Tea* because the community decides to police the improper sexual behavior of the seducer in order to preserve the family, but Kingston's aunt, already suffering from an overseas marriage, becomes instead the dispensable sacrifice, along with her infant.

Kingston substitutes infanticide for a direct political critique of the laws and regulations, and even the economic flows, that impel these tragic situations. However, rather than relying on gothic or fantastic horror or a mere clash of culture, her aunt's story contains just enough information about the exclusion-era separation of families to hint at the immigration realities beneath them. Maternal infanticide captures the trauma of parenthood and familial separation in the rupture of the most idealized familial bond.

In keeping with this stark beginning, with its dark warnings about violated families and fears of interracial intimacy, Kingston ends her memoir with a loose historical anecdote about forced migration and interracial sexual violence, yet manages to find a positive artistic inspiration. "Song for a Barbarian Reed Pipe" reimagines artist Ts'ai Yen, kidnapped and raped by a barbarian, whose mixed-race children laugh at her language. She eventually goes home, leaving the children behind, and also bears "Han" Chinese descendants. This border-crossing artist, the named and long-ago historical counterpart of Maxine's suicidal aunt, communicates in both places through the universal medium of a music that transcends linguistic and cultural barriers as she is continually separated from one family or another. Perpetually singing about the past, the place she has left, Ts'ai Yen expresses the "sadness and anger" that plagues her literary descendant: a historical line broken, families separated, anger unrecognized. If her music has "translated well," then perhaps Kingston's work can also draw from this deep past to "translate" across cultures to express the anger and outrage of her own time.

This translation, not quite a reconciliation, leaves many questions unanswered about the immigration history that Kingston has sought to reconstruct. In this ending, the optimistic take on historical story or myth obliterates the sadder subcurrents of Ts'ai Yen's story, as well as the more recent stories of Kingston's family. No Name Woman is informed on, not given a voice. We never learn the fate or about the later life of Third Wife, the black woman brought back to China, who stops talking because nobody understands her even as she learns more about history. Nor, for that matter, do we learn about Ts'ai Yen's second marriage or her separation from her half-barbarian children, which seems not nearly as heart-wrenching as No Name Woman's refusal to leave her child. Instead, her rape and kidnapping prove the need for the artist to keep singing, to allow the possibility of transmitting a narrative even when all communication across culture and language seems impossible.

"Song for a Barbarian Reed Pipe" was not the original ending. As Kingston's manuscripts show, she originally ended with a myth about a king whose son was born with cat ears. The king hides the secret of his otherwise perfect son until he can no longer contain it. He goes out into the fields, digs a hole, and shouts his secret into it. But when the grass grows over it, the wind picks up his cry: "The king's son has cat ears!"[43] The two endings are radically different, not only because Ts'ai Yen's anecdote, ironically, further occludes the voices of outsiders. Both are preceded by Kingston's reflections on sending money to relatives back in China and the stories that they are told in letters—in particular, the youngest grandson of the grandfather's third wife, the silenced "black" wife, who wants a bicycle. Dubious stories and truths linking interracial family members suggest that there are, as ever, gaps and misunderstandings caused by this strange marriage. Framed by this, the tale of the king's son suggests not only that family secrets will out regardless of the measures taken to protect them, but that when they emerge, they may be harmless—an idea hard to square with the rest of the book.

It seems, then, that Kingston had to change the last anecdote because the story of the king's son did not suit her ontology of storytelling. Ts'ai Yen's story of crossings, by contrast, focuses not on family secrets but on family migration, misunderstandings, and a linguistically limited amount of revelation. Kingston's focus in *The Woman Warrior* on mother-daughter relationships is itself diametrically opposed to the focus on paternity, chiefly fathers and sons, that dominated immigration discussion. Paternity, with the exception of her own father, who plays very little role in the memoir, is left shadowy and ambiguous, like the unnamed father of No Name Woman's child and the barbarian father of Ts'ai Yen's children. Kingston introduces the story of Ts'ai Yen through her own cross-racially linked family's love of theater and stories. She "like[s] to think" that they watched a performance of Ts'ai Yen's story, preparing them for their own journeys. "It translated well," she concludes simply, implying that her story may do the same. Interracial intimacy—even one marked by violence, misunderstanding, and mockery—metaphorically becomes the vehicle for better cultural understanding and a voice for Chinese America. Like Lee and his figuration of historical erotic intimacy as a vehicle for an alternative and better future, Kingston ultimately ends on a note of imagined possibility, but one in which the cultural product itself, content unknown, substitutes for the usual tableau it depicts.

These tableaux and Ts'ai Yen's songs seek to convince or comfort the audience that blood purity is irrelevant, replacing investigation and violent separation with understanding and historical models of migratory disorder. The disorder of bloodlines reflects the disorder of the Chinese American world, which must be reconciled in particular by the struggling protagonists, who cannot solve all of society's ills but whose symbolic reconciliation in these largely sentimental novels can give us some temporary comfort. The harshness of reality—Ruby and Ham Say Naim's divorce, the families threatened with deportation—lurks in the background, however, making us wonder whether Ben Loy and Mei Oi will be happy; Aika and Chiang can raise Aika's children harmoniously; and Carnahan and Mai Mai will prosper in this alternative, Chinese-centered west. The weight under which authors labor in trying to imagine and build happy families in the United States despite the immigration-rooted attacks on paternity and marriage, was not, as is evident in these works, viewed in the same light by all. Nor, in their search for reconciliation, can they all find an optimistic ending. It is a weight that they all acknowledge, whether with anger or philosophy. In the next and final chapter, I look at how Kingston and other authors reckon with the weight of history writ large, attempting to reshape it into a source of strength.

4

History, through Literature

Rewriting the Past after the Confession Era

The 1970s brought profound changes in Chinese American politics, demographics, and artistic expression as a new generation came of age and an older generation, including authors such as Jade Snow Wong, found themselves newly willing and able to address the topic of illegal immigration. These authors narrate themselves into authorial and artistic being and, simultaneously, attempt to bring Chinese America, past and present, into unity with the nation—if not the nation-state. As Rocío Davis writes, "The idea of a family memoir's process, structure, and information being supported by 'official' documents leads us to consider the relationship between personal stories and narratives of nation." In this chapter, I focus on the progression of Wong's and Maxine Hong Kingston's memoirs, in particular, into a deeper engagement with the archive: the institutional and legal history of Chinese America and the documentation against which their families struggled. They and other activists aimed to educate a wide audience in the 1970s and, in so doing, reclaim authority over history. Musings and debates took place with a new emphasis on the "mutually challenging" negotiation between the personal and the officially documented, with struggles for narrative control among Chinese Americans and in dispute, as ever, with officialdom.[1]

As Estelle Lau has written about the era of heavily restricted and interrogated immigration, "Fiction, once officially documented, could overcome fact, turning fact into fiction" (fiction here meaning fabricated family histories).[2] Chinese American writers adapt documentary history plentifully in many strategic ways: as education, as authentication, or as a kind of belated confession, to name a few. But literary writing serves to rewrite the facts, endowing the author, rather than the government, with the power to judge. For that reason, when attempting to elucidate the relationship between history and personal narrative for Asian Americans, the political setting and the change in the author's voice over time must be put into dialogue in order to look at the reclamation of a testimony and confession that was co-opted by immigration authorities for so many decades.

Demographically, Chinese America changed greatly in size, age and gender distribution, and employment over the course of the 1960s. War brides, family members, refugees, and specialized professional workers had swelled the ranks of immigration before 1965, in addition to "regular" national-quota immigrants. Over the course of the 1960s, about 110,000 Chinese entered, though the full impact of the 1965 reforms, which lifted all restrictions on national origins, was not felt on the population until the 1970s. New Chinatowns sprang up, many of them suburban, with an increasingly educated population from different parts of the Chinese diaspora: mainland China, Taiwan, Hong Kong, and other countries. Binary gender distribution had become nearly equal at this point, with men and boys still a slight majority, and a striking 37 percent of the total population age nineteen or younger, demonstrating how family reunification and the postwar baby boom had changed the population. In the 1970 census, California's Chinese population (encompassing numerous Chinatowns) remained primarily urban, with a total population of slightly more than 170,000. In California, 36 percent of the population older than twenty-five had had some or a complete college education, and 21 percent of the employed labor force (men and women) age sixteen and older were in the field of professional, technical, and kindred workers. The West Coast continued to receive the bulk of professional immigrants in this decade. (New York was undergoing its own economic and demographic transformation through the garment industry and an influx of families.) In 1979, only 3.2 percent of professional and technical immigrants, according to a report by the U.S. Immigration and Naturalization Service (INS), were planning to settle in New York, which thus continued to fall behind. Studies of San Francisco Chinatown in this era, such as Victor Nee and Brett de Bary Nee's *Longtime Californ'*, describe a society rapidly shifting and, although growing and prosperous, still uncertain of its future and acutely conscious of discrimination and confinement.[3]

Chinese America was newly politicized and refigured publicly after 1965 with the birth of pan-Asian American political consciousness at the end of the 1960s and the Third World student strike of 1968. New York Chinatown and San Francisco Chinatown had gotten more politically engaged in the mainstream in different ways during the 1950s and 1960s. However, a great shift in the late 1960s and 1970s was the Asian American movement, which paired a cross-racial, cross-ethnic solidarity in addressing domestic civil rights issues with a sense of global solidarity with those affected by U.S. imperialism, particularly focusing on the Vietnam War. Chinese American authors could thus appeal to an invigorated audience that they had not previously been able to rely on, framing themselves within a larger and more visible political identity.[4]

The landscape of U.S. relations with mainland China was also rapidly shifting for the better, which relieved some of the negative perceptions through which Chinese Americans had suffered during the Confession era and made it easier for authors who had embraced the proto-model minority image to now voice critiques and hard truths. The so-called ping pong diplomacy of the U.S. men's table tennis team's trip to China in 1971 paved the way for President Richard Nixon's weeklong visit to China in 1972, which ended the quarter-century of diplomatic estrangement between the two nations. The strong media coverage of Nixon's trip ensured positive reactions back in the United States. By the end of the decade, the United States and China had once again established formal diplomatic relations. Peter Kwong describes this as leading to a halcyon time, when Chinese Americans were viewed with less suspicion before economic competition and renewed scrutiny of Communist China in the 1990s.[5]

In this new climate, with a larger, more diverse, and more politically active community, as well as a more favorable mainstream climate, Chinese American writers neither embraced a utopian future nor joyfully shed the fears and stigma of the past. Instead, the ethnic nationalism of the 1970s provided a platform for them to speak openly—or more openly, still cautious about the legal status of individual family members—about the past of illegal immigration, which was now working against the model minority image. The works of this period managed to incorporate the documentary history and testimony of Chinese American experience as both an uncovered truth and an impossibly mediated past; whether nonfiction writers or novelists, they not only "circumvent[ed] authoritarian narration and signif[ied] the instability of 'truth' and 'history,'" as King-kok Cheung has powerfully argued, but they were also able to reflect publicly on an unstable "truth" about Chinese America.[6] They were thus able to employ their signifying on documentary and legislative history to deliver a persuasive narrative to a mainstream American audience that might never have known that history. Looking specifically at these authors' relationship with an unstable and contested (as I described in Chapter 1) narrative of illegal immigration permits us to understand the political origins of their historical and archival interests. Whether a family's faked immigration papers or newly discovered citizenship papers, the delivery of the documentary history exposes a "truth" that the author then can undercut and complicate, playing on it to renarrate Chinese American history and the current, complex landscape of identity construction and national subjecthood.

Though, as I discussed in Chapter 1, Kingston's *The Woman Warrior* is grounded in immigration history, *China Men* (1980) was her overt effort to tell history in this new, more favorable landscape. The binary division between *The Woman Warrior* and *China Men*, as fostered by Kingston herself—whose plethora of beautifully spoken interviews long exerted influence over criticism of her work—led to the interpretation of *China Men* (and not *The Woman Warrior*) as a history. She said, "The sense of mission in *China Men* is that I was responsible for history. *China Men* was written in order to give us a history and to educate everyone as to our Chinese American history."[7] Such declarations may well have been fueled by the public disputes over *The Woman Warrior*'s use of myth and its reception. Whether in a tone of protest or optimistic celebration, Kingston retains a stated focus on reclaiming the history of her family, and thereby of Chinese America, as told through government acts of exclusion and prejudice in *China Men*. However, following her personal quest for family history and documentation through her archive, Kingston's complex narrative revision over time reveals the manifold versions of history that even one author may construct for different political ends. Most prominently, her effort is to reserve ownership of Chinese American history for the community, perhaps even more than for herself, as her sense of "responsibility" for history moves beyond discussing her own relationship to history.

Much less discussed than Kingston's overt effort at bending the arc in *China Men* is Jade Snow Wong's attempt at historical education in *No Chinese Stranger* (1975) and, eventually, her unpublished last work, *Chinese American*. Wong, too, reminisced in this post-reform landscape about the hardships that her parents and other Chinese had suffered through early immigration, even finally reflecting on the prejudices of the 1950s. These detailed accounts of their suffering are an extraordinary about-face from her adherence to the proto-model minority image in her scarce portrayal of immigration in *Fifth Chinese Daughter* a quarter-century earlier—a much more politically fraught time, before even the 1952 reforms, and at a moment when Wong's claim on the public attention was through her exemplarity, with racism a minor personal challenge serenely transcended by the individual rather than a systemic injustice. While she continues the obfuscation of her father's wives in *No Chinese Stranger*, she takes a radically new stance on the injustices of immigration, symbolized by Angel Island and by the common practice of paper sons. This shift in Wong's narrative voice marks a shift over time from the anxious young proto-model minority to, if not an activist, at least a strong proponent of the strength and survivorship of Chinese Americans.

Whose History?

The attacks on the family detailed in the preceding chapter and the fears and silences caused by immigration investigation and the Confession Program resulted in a generational rift that was portrayed at least by some as an ignorance of history on the part of the younger generation. Healing families, then, also meant reconstructing and relearning history in order to undo all of the narrative ills caused by the community's persecution. The plausibility of Kingston's ignorance of names and immigration methods was hotly debated at the time of *The Woman Warrior*'s release, betraying a deep anxiety in the Chinese American community over a long-buried history and its consequences for mainstream perceptions of the community. From members of her own family, including her father and mother, to the boy at school who shares her confusion, Kingston constructs a community with a secretive past that must be learned by the younger generation. In the larger debate over her use of history and other Chinese Americans' public history work, this would prove to be the historical narrative that most embraced.

However, even as a memoirist Kingston occasionally slips and reveals greater knowledge, layering her actual narrative with silences and secrets hinting at another, still secreted narrative. She offers one telling anecdote of childhood: "But when I saw Father's occupations [listed] I exclaimed, 'Hey, he wasn't a farmer, he was a . . . ' He had been a gambler. My throat cut off the word—silence in front of the most understanding teacher. There were secrets never to be said in front of the ghosts, immigration secrets whose telling could get us sent back to China."[8] She must maintain her silence because, obviously, at no time were gamblers or undesirables of any country technically permitted to immigrate—but Chinese in particular, as Kingston's father would have immigrated just as the 1924 act was set in place restricting national origins and all but barring Chinese. Silenced story within public story within memoir: Kingston unveils her family secrets only in the last layer. Yet this anecdote is exceptional within the text, as the child narrator actually knows her father's true occupation. Normally, Kingston presents her narrating self with a vacuum of information and resents it. This anecdote and other, similar slippages in her texts suggest that her total lack of knowledge of history is a deliberate literary construct, a purposeful dramatization of Chinese America's loss of narrative authority.

In the 1970s, the demands of ethnic activism and nationalism created two main competing channels of thought about ethnic historical knowledge—namely, the desire to bring to light a long-overlooked and oppressed history and to recover a history that had been oppressed and occluded sheer out of knowledge. Though these might seem to be only different degrees of the same problem, such was not at all the case in the high-profile conflict over Chinese American epistemology. This process can best be seen in the literary history of a specific debate within the reception of *The Woman Warrior*: not the famous debate over gender, myth, and Christianization with Frank Chin that has already been so thoroughly discussed as an anxious fracture in Asian American literary history, but one specifically over immigration history. Though Chin asked whether art could "restore" Asian American history and culture, he also insisted that there was nothing *to* restore: "Losing touch with China did not result in Chinese Americans losing touch with 'The Ballad of Mulan.'" His own historical emphasis on a long presence in the Americas turned away from the issue of more recent immigration, whether legal or not—an ironic stance in the post-1965 era.[9]

Conversely, in Diane Johnson's highly positive review of Kingston in the *New York Review of Books*, she explicated—or, rather, further orientalized—the Chinese American community as a mysterious, mistrustful group, particularly using one aspect of Kingston's plaints as historical truth. "Their own parents have given them fake names to say," wrote Johnson, with absolutely no mention of why, though Kingston herself does give a reason when, as already mentioned, she reveals that her father was a gambler: "There were secrets never to be said in front of the ghosts, immigration secrets whose telling could get us sent back to China." Along the same lines as her own novels, Johnson's main desire is to discuss autobiography/memoir of American women's experience. In describing Kingston, then, she focuses on her gendered battles and "the universal qualities of female condition and female anger." Yet sawing wildly back and forth between Kingston's universality and particularity, Johnson returns to the specifics (such as disgusting foods) of her "notably unassimilated culture," treating it as static and immutable. When she refers to the episode of the boy at school who cannot tell the teacher his father's name (see Chapter 1), Johnson says sweepingly and without explanation, "A Chinese child does not know his father's name," treating it as a cultural practice.[10]

Jeffery Paul Chan, then the chair of Asian American studies at San Francisco State University and one of Chin's coeditors on the foundational Asian American literary anthology *Aiiieeeee!*, wrote a scathing response to Johnson that outlines a literary history focused on the trauma of illegal immigration and immigration policing. One of his main grievances was Johnson's dehistoricization of cultural practices. In hailing Kingston's feminism, Chan charges, Johnson "can conveniently ignore what are key historical themes in Kingston's book, themes that help shape that mongrel sensibility

Johnson admires and incidentally touch on the major currents of Chinese-American literary development since Sui Sin Far." He expounds on illegal immigration and its consequent and frightening policing: "Mass deportation was a distinct possibility in the minds of my parents' generation. . . . There is an explicit sociology in the development of Chinese American writings, and they can be gleaned from a cursory examination of public records, a matter of public law." However, other aspects of his critique were aimed at Kingston, which Johnson used as an opportunity to dismiss his critique in her brief reply, in which she also willfully misunderstood several telling points Chan made about her characterization of Chinese American society.

Kingston's opacity around the reasons for the boy's ignorance or her own ignorance, which I discussed in Chapter 1, provokes disparate responses reflecting the two main community attitudes toward history in this period. When Chan doubts Kingston's veracity, saying, "The Chinese-American custom of being an illegal entry, a paper descendant of Hom when you are really a Wong, was simple and commonplace. . . . If Kingston did not know her father's name as a child, her experience is unique," he offers instead a view of Chinese American history as a simple, straightforward narrative easily transmitted among families. Chan was not alone in this critique of a historical ignorance or secret keeping. Another early critic, Katheryn Fong, complained of Kingston's line about immigration secrets: "Your attempt to explain this 'secretiveness' raises more questions than it answers." Fong addresses the immigration issues at length in her article, explaining "paper sons" and the extensive interrogation process at Angel Island for Chinese immigrants, but Johnson ignores them entirely. For her, the notable aspect is the exotic and unassimilated culture, not the race-restricted policies of immigration and their impact on a minority community.[11]

Chan objects to Kingston's translations and her supposed ignorance of her family history, but the bulk of his ire is directed at Johnson, who, he points out by way of condemning by affiliation, was then teaching at the University of California, Davis, which was in the process of dismantling its Asian American Studies program. Similarly, Fong takes aim at several reviewers in addition to Kingston, objecting to some of Kingston's emphasis on poor, sexist treatment by her parents (which Fong compares to *Fifth Chinese Daughter*) at the expense of other moments of clearly loving treatment, but for the most part concludes that her "greatest criticism is directed at those who believe" *The Woman Warrior* as a representative, factual Chinese American text, something that Kingston has also publicly bemoaned.[12]

The overarching narrative of Kingston's oeuvre, as already noted, which slowly reveals more details about her family's immigration as she learns them, maintains the historiographical pattern of this type of silence and revelation, positioning her narratorial self as moving from ignorance to understanding in her artistic process. Such a pattern predominates in the post-1965 era as the narrative of illegal immigration is transformed by the next generation. The structure of this new narrative reflects the continual oscillation between the persistent legal vulnerability of those who immigrated "illegally" and the desire of artists and activists to tell the story publicly. Most accounts of Angel Island at this time, for example, speak of "rediscovery." Genny Lim and Judy Yung wrote one of the earliest mainstream pieces on this by Chinese American authors in 1977, a source that Kingston cited as an important influence in initial drafts of *China Men* (1980). Entitled "Our Parents Never Told Us," their article strongly focuses on the same generation gap that so painfully affected Kingston in *The Woman Warrior*. "The most difficult part of our research was in unlocking and ferreting out the many painful facts the older generation kept secretly buried," Lim and Yung write. "Our parents never talked about their past. To them, these were dark years better forgotten." Even within the community, "[It] was not easy finding willing subjects. [They] had only agreed to be interviewed if they knew one of us or if someone they knew well had arranged the interview for us." Lim and Yung's account sounds similar to George Sessions Perry's flippant words in 1948 about his inability to find Chinese American subjects, all afraid of public exposure. Despite the drastic change in immigration, now equitably open to Chinese, the peril and caution of the community had not diminished.[13]

Lim and Yung noted that the older generation of immigrants were content not only to be silent, but for that silence to extend to the larger narrative: "'It's a chapter better left out of America's history books,' they say" (9). However, the younger generation would gradually become more and more vocal, emboldened by immigration reform and the waning of Cold War anti-Chinese sentiment. The stakes of such reclamation of history were high, not only to continue the work of 1950s public figures in offering their own versions of the narratives of Chinese American history, but in the debates within families and within the community. Even in 2006, Lau noted in her study that she had had to forego family interviews as a research method because "family members who had any experience related to the creation of paper kin were reluctant to speak . . . or could not remember any details. Younger family members were often eager to talk about their family history but could only repeat vague stories they had heard."[14]

In the 1970s, writers sought to bring the understanding of a supposedly past era of racial exclusion and illegal immigration to a new, post-1965 America. However, all faced the difficulty of touting progress to a community still suffering the aftereffects of the Confession era, when the attempt to discover secret histories was fraught with such danger. Though Lim and Yung do not belabor the feelings of the younger generation, instead straightforwardly offering the accounts of the few immigrants they interviewed, they note that the "bleak memories" of "humiliation," "fear," and "degradation" (7) have created a rift between the generations: "Although only a generation separates us from our parents, we have come to feel that a vast chasm exists between us that is impenetrable by words" (6–7). The article thus seeks to break this silence through public history and oral history. The aim of Lim and Yung's piece is to bring these stories to light, to pay tribute along with Angel Island, the restoration of which they mention at the end of the article, to "the thousands upon thousands of Chinese who with their sweat helped to create America" (9).

Yung extended this theme of rediscovery to her own family history, taking a rhetorical tone even stronger as she spoke for her ignorance of the past. Around the same time that Kingston's *The Woman Warrior* was published, Yung narrated a strikingly similar autobiographical story about discovering her parents' immigration stories. In her regular column in the newspaper *East/West*, Yung's roundup of community anecdotes featured, halfway through, her personal discovery not only of the immigration story but of her grandfather: "My father finally broke down and *told me that I had a grandfather* and that he came to America at an early age in order to send remittances home to a starving family." Although Yung's grandfather had been killed in a biking accident in his thirties, her phrasing clearly plays up the extent of her ignorance of his existence, rhetorically reinforcing the suddenness of the discovery of the information. Notably, Jade Snow Wong clipped this article for her scrapbook, underscoring the commonality of interests among these memoirists and historians.[15]

Ultimately, the empowering narrative of rediscovering history, from the "rediscovery" of Angel Island to the individualized discovery of family histories, dominated the characterization of the pre-1965 immigration. Kingston's historiography thus seemed to win the day, leaving critics to decide whether this was yet another model-minoritizing view of Chinese America as so thoroughly assimilated that the new generation had forgotten its own history or a radical recapturing of history by a community scarred by immigration scrutiny. With her imaginative and fragmented narrative, Kingston, as one who bore the responsibility of great success, offended those who preferred to confront the mainstream with a proud but overlooked history. Yet she herself would adopt a tone of historical authority in *China Men*, a profound shift drawing on a new generation of community history work. Considering the high stakes of telling (and retelling) Chinese American history during the era of investigation and confession, the desire to claim an enduring transmission and narrative authority is equally understandable. In terms of narrative ownership, these historiographies share a need to assert the community's ownership; one could argue that they find common ground as the community as a whole never loses the history. Even more important, they share the goals of politicizing and celebrating a history not of fraudulence but of discrimination and triumph, moving away from a superficial model minority status to one that embraces an entire historical trajectory.

Reentering Angel Island

New literary narratives emerged in conversation with the wave of public history work in the 1970s. As Dai-ming Lee's mentions of it in the 1950s showed (see Chapter 1), Angel Island was not forgotten in the community, but its memory had not been preserved or publicized. The "rediscovery" of Angel Island happened in 1970, after it had been out of use as an immigration station for thirty years. Alexander Weiss, a seasonal park ranger, found Chinese calligraphy over every inch of an abandoned building. Knowing that the building was scheduled to be torn down so the site could be redeveloped for recreational use, Weiss brought the writings to the attention of faculty at San Francisco State University, where the Third World strike had just established ethnic studies. In the next few years, a large network of activists and scholars came together to restore and commemorate the site, which was officially launched in 1976. A second wave of activism would bring its National Historic Landmark designation in 1997.[16]

Both Kingston and Wong used this well-known public history and anchor for Chinese and Asian American community formation in the 1970s to authenticate their accounts of rediscovering family history. It serves not only to politicize their family history anew by putting it in a context of racially based incarceration, as well as modern activism, but also to position the younger narrator alternatively as either a historical authority or an audience. Wong's narrative takes us on a transition of sentiment from a triumphant model minority to critique and perhaps a side-slipped protest regarding Angel Island, whereas for Kingston, incarceration is from first to last an enduring pain imaginatively connected to the present. As they navigate retelling their parents' experience, they make different choices about how to present their own knowledge or ignorance but importantly make the decision to demonstrate intergenerational experience rather than yielding the stage entirely to their fathers. These decisions, while producing some inconsistencies in Wong's memoir and drastic revisions in Kingston's, create politicized family stories to educate.

The mention of Angel Island in *No Chinese Stranger* was the first time that Wong discussed her parents' immigration experience in any detail; *China Men* continued the exploration of and speculation about Kingston's family stories that had begun in *The Woman Warrior*, but with the reinforcement of historical grounding. As with Wong, Angel Island is not mentioned at all in Kingston's first book, though Ellis Island is referenced erroneously through Brave Orchid's recollections. This marks a shift in storytelling within the Chinese American community, as well as, most likely, a shift in the mass audience; Angel Island's preservation reached mainstream political and media audiences in the mid-1970s, as had other minority ethnic histories and literature.

In the end, Kingston said very little about her own previous knowledge, or lack thereof, about Angel Island in *China Men*, preferring in the end to focus attention on "The Laws" and other aspects of racialized violence. Instead, her section on Angel Island blends history and imagination, focalized through the experience of the "legal father," one of the many ways that Kingston imagines his epic journey to the Gold Mountain. She retells the travails and tragedies of the men held in captivity there, using many of the historical details that had been newly retold in the previous decade: the poetry all over the walls, heart-wrenching methods of suicide, interrogations and examinations, bad food, and crowded conditions and an oft-described episode in which a note, possibly a "coaching document" to help someone pass the interrogations, was snatched back from a matron by the angry prisoners. (She draws these stories from many of the sources that she cites in her papers of the original version of "The Laws," such as Lim and Yung's article.) The "legal father" is not individuated; he serves as a vehicle for the story of an island full of suffering Chinese immigrants trapped in captivity that resonates with the struggles of Kingston's male family members across time.

Initially, Kingston had framed the section by emphasizing just how little she knew about Angel Island and how recently its history had resurfaced. This can be seen in the initial draft of *China Men*:

> Just lately I have heard that some fathers and mothers who came to the Gold Mountain between 1910 and 1941 came through Angel Island, which is an island in San Francisco Bay, flatter than Alcatraz. Now only in the last few years have I heard about this island. I had even landed on it for picnics, feeding the deer and the raccoons on the lawns the navy keeps mowed, and no one said, "This is the island where people hung themselves or jumped off and drowned trying to swim to San Francisco, or that there were abandoned buildings where you could look at where the literate ones had written poems on the walls about being lonely and afraid."[17]

Kingston had been living in Hawai'i throughout the composition of *The Woman Warrior* in the early to mid-1970s, and her lack of direct involvement in the campaign to preserve the buildings may surface here instead as her ignorance of the island's history altogether. Regardless of the truth of her ignorance, Kingston once again maintains a tone of sudden discovery, creating a black-and-white contrast between the before and after of historical knowledge. Notably—and surely controversially, had this paragraph appeared as originally written—Kingston does not discuss the community activism and lobbying or the establishment of Angel Island as a memorial that happened at this time, focusing merely on what the lone artist "heard" on the wind and on her own ignorance.

The sense of naïveté and historical discovery in the draft keeps the focus on the narrator's experience rather than the family members' or even the community's as a whole. Nor does it particularly connect history to a politicized present. The draft offers a more self-reflexive narrative, in which we follow some of the history via the narrator's discovery of the history. The shift to a fuller historical discussion of Angel Island and away from herself is consistent with the revisions elsewhere in the manuscript; another imagined father's experience as a stowaway, for example, was revised to eliminate an original short passage purporting to describe Kingston's recurring dream of a stowaway emigration. A line that remains in the final version, "A white demon . . . poked him in the ass and genitals. . . . [T]his was not the way a father ought to have been greeted" was originally followed by, "This was not what [*sic*] fathers should be seen by children. So they did not tell us about Angel Island." She further excuses her ignorance in a crossed-out line, "I didn't know about it because my parents did not go that way but through the Panama Canal, to New York."[18] The revisions focus the reader instead on compassion for the multiplicity of experience in this generation, as Kingston imagines legal and illegal entrances of multiple kinds. In the final version of *China Men*, Kingston roots the diverse trajectories of Chinese Americans not in her personal experience or yet even her family's story, but in the concrete site of Angel Island and its newly established public history.

Angel Island sits within a highly fractured, almost pastiche-like chapter in Jade Snow Wong's memoir, which is mostly devoted to her married life and State Department–sponsored trips to Asia. It is a somewhat unusual episode; on its surface, it seems to continue the proto-model minority (and now perhaps explicitly model minority) presentation from *Fifth Chinese Daughter*. Early in the memoir, Wong describes a visit from her parents to the newly married Wong and her husband in their apartment in Tiburon, which they found only after a search in which they encountered many white landlords unwilling to rent to them. Wong delivers the information here through her father's voice. Setting up the scene, she writes about the view: "Angel Island faced them across narrow Raccoon Straights [*sic*]. In clear view were 'China Cove,' a boat landing, and a small cluster of buildings, details Jade Snow had seen and dismissed, since Angel Island was no longer inhabited."[19] Her prior easy dismissal of the buildings and her surprise at her father's reaction to the view imply an admittedly unlikely lack of knowledge about her family's immigration. This initially sets up a trajectory similar to that of *The Woman Warrior*, moving from zero knowledge to historical expertise, a novel move for Wong.

From a literary standpoint, Wong (perhaps tellingly) misses a grand narrative opportunity here, as she does not foreground any personal emotional reaction or sense of discovery at this supposedly new information. Instead, she slips into a dispassionate tone in which she narrates her father's words and then gives some larger historical context, an even firmer factual basis than that of Kingston's imagined "legal father." Wong's father, on waking up to see the view of Angel Island from their apartment, starts "pacing back and forth in excitement" and orders everyone down on their knees for prayer:

> King of ten thousand kings, we have deep thoughts as we gather here and face Angel Island. Thirty-one years ago, Mama was detained there at United States immigration quarantine facilities. As a prisoner, she looked from her window to this very spot. In isolation, she was terrified. She could not understand a word of English. How could she foretell that some day we would be gathered here in happiness, where my son-in-law placed me at the head of the table, and declared me to be master of the home? . . . Thank You again for Your generous gifts. Our children born here can only have one view of those buildings on Angel Island: from the outside, forever free. (43)

This moving prayer, demonstrating unusual emotion and openness about their immigration experience, is driven by the displaced trauma of Mama's experience (rather than his own) and gratitude for his children's freedom. It is an emotional crack in Daddy's strict façade similar to the moment when he takes Mama's hand during her difficult delivery of their youngest child in *Fifth Chinese Daughter*. Daddy phrases triumph, gratitude, and religious devotion once again in terms of the family; Mama's triumph over her incarceration results in Daddy as the head of the household. His delight in his children's freedom and perfect filiality is then followed by prayers for their continued happiness, and particularly for Jade Snow to have her own children. The family says nothing except "Amen," conveniently restricting any possible indiscreet discussion, and indeed, Wong's reconstruction or recollection of her father's prayer may already be redacting key details. The nuclear family tableau triumphs over the trauma of immigration, almost sealing it off from the possibility of wreaking further damage.

Rather than offering her own emotions, Wong then slips into third-person narration that disjointedly offers historical expertise despite her supposed ignorance of Angel Island. As the implicit expert, she avoids mentioning her mother's experience by substituting a very brief summary of laws and conditions on Angel Island, once again drawing on the common descriptions of experience on the island that were circulating at the time: "Jade Snow's mother had come over before the 1924 Immigration act that prevented the entry of Chinese wives and for the following five years, no Chinese alien woman was admitted, after the passing of the Exclusion Act. Unkind immigration authorities operated under the theory that all Chinese were guilty and ineligible for entry until conclusively proven innocent. Some immigrants waited three months on Angel Island, while their qualifications were debated. Their mail was censored, their food was poor, sometimes eaten on their feet" (58). This shift also allows Wong to gloss over Mama's unusual silence at the dinner table. Over the course of her revisions, she expanded this section still more, perhaps as she became more aware of the community and general public interest in Angel Island. Though it declines to detail Mama's individual experiences, Wong's recounting of the history of the island starts to contradict the tone of Papa's joyful prayer, unusually going against the patriarch to offer her own version of the community's history.

Mama is peculiarly silent on this topic presumably because, once again, what she says cannot be told to the reader. Her reminiscences of Angel Island might go into too much detail and become unsafe. With the benefit of our retroactive knowledge of Mama's illegal immigration as another man's paper wife, the silenced and shifting depiction of Mama's immigration and even Wong's supposed ignorance here suddenly become clear; indeed, it pragmatically explains Wong's overwhelming focus on her father's triumph and her desire to speak generally of the community rather than specifically for her mother. Even at the moment of her openness, she continues to protect her mother's immigration status, and so it would continue until her mother's death and a new millennium—an excess of caution that shows the vulnerability of falsely documented entrants even after the 1965 reforms. Looking at the decade that followed the publication of the *Saturday Evening Post* feature and *Fifth Chinese Daughter*, Wong's past silence looks not only prudent but essential. Indeed, her silence may well have saved her family from investigation and jail or deportation during the investigations of the 1950s.

Returning to the Angel Island scene, though Wong does not openly contradict her father's triumphant characterization of history, she turns to different speakers to represent the community's experience and the darker side of Chinese American experience. Wong highlights the voice of an anonymous sufferer and a foundational piece of Asian American literature. She describes the poetry famously carved into the walls by detainees (with a classist observation that only a scholar, "no ordinary laborer," could have written such poetry [43]) and inserts one of the most famous Angel Island poems, one by an anonymous immigrant:

> *Wooden house detained me scores of days*
> *Because rules in ink involve me*
> *A pity that it's useless for a hero to be violent*
> *Only await the word for the whip to spur him back to the old country*
> *From now I leave this house for a long distance*
> *All of my village gentlemen, rejoice with me*
> *Never mind that everything here is Western style*
> *Even if walls were jade, they have become a cage.* (44)

This poem, particularly in Wong's translation, dwells on the detention and the hopes and fears of a man waiting for freedom, but freedom via deportation. In direct contrast to the freedom and bounty described by Daddy, this anonymous sufferer can rejoice only that he is likely to leave this "cage" to go back to China; he has been entirely unsuccessful in this Western-style world. The Wongs' freedom and success in America thus become exceptional, a move that might seem complimentary only to them, again burnishing their model minority status. However, this moving poem and Daddy's unusual emotion radicalize their success by finally stressing the high price paid by the whole community.

No special credit is given in the copyright information of *No Chinese Stranger*, from which I conclude that this may be Wong's own translation (perhaps with her father's aid), a somewhat archaically phrased and literal version. In particular, the translation makes no mention of the "Mexican exclusion laws," a famous misnomer contained in this poem as translated and published at the time by Genny Lim, and one that Kingston cites in her description of Angel Island in *China Men*.[20] Instead, Wong translates the character in question via its literal meaning of "ink," an interpretation that appeals rather to the idea of the inflexibility of law. (This seems a reasonable translation choice and, considering the rest of the memoir, cannot be interpreted solely as an avoidance of mentioning the exclusion laws or the history of legal exclusion.) For Wong, this is as direct a critique as she ever makes.

It is Kingston who uses the Angel Island poems less as protest than as a vivid detail to add to the historical account. Kingston cites little snippets of poems, including the "Mexican exclusion laws," as a metaphorical way to address the elder generation's experience and a legacy of Chinese American artistry. This is one of the few ways that she adds some actual family resonance and vivid, original imagery to her description of Angel Island, making her father a secret, silent poet, writing poems with his tears and spit at night and modestly failing to claim his contributions in the morning. Although she would write more about her father's poetic abilities in Chinese in *The Fifth Book of Peace* decades later, she makes no claim to his poetic contributions or any of the poems here. His contributions are not written out; they are merely described. The Angel Island poems become fodder for her imagination of her father's experience rather than proof or protest of his presence.

Though Wong eschews describing her own emotions about Angel Island, she further politicizes her Angel Island discussion through a personal framing narrative in which she reveals a more aggressive, aggrieved political stance, which, unlike Kingston's choice to eliminate the personal, grew sharper over the course of her revision. Indeed, in one very early draft of the chapter, Wong blunts the political import of Angel Island by describing in detail the dinner that the family sits down to eat, continuing the emphasis on the family that ends her father's prayer and returning to the popular mode of her first memoir.[21] In the final version, however, Wong frames the Angel Island episode with the contemporary prelude and aftermath, describing how she and her husband encounter prejudice from landlords and real estate agents. She thus sets up a continuum of racism, a departure from her usual self-portrayal that befits the political moment. At their previous residence, she recounts, a "white drunk" once came to the house in the night and "asked where [her husband] kept the girls." Woody calmly beats him up and equally calmly hoses the blood off the steps in the morning (39–40). Wong voices no critique, perhaps showing some admiration of his competence, but frames this as a startling departure from her own family's Christian rule of turning the other cheek. The mere juxtaposition suggests that Wong might be willing to punch back now against racism or, at least, accept it as a method of resistance. The anonymous Angel Island poem she translates includes the line, "A pity that it's useless for a hero to be violent," suggesting the impotence and political disenfranchisement not only of this incarcerated immigrant but also of the generation he represents. Instead, for the modern Chinese American, Woody's knowledge of fisticuffs and his tutelage of Wong's beloved younger brother demonstrate, in Wong's gentle, domestic way, that the new generation can and may use more aggressive measures.

When concluding this description of Angel Island in *No Chinese Stranger*, Wong still hides her mother's story but surprisingly reveals a new piece of family immigration history that is certainly illegal: her father had sponsored a "nephew" for immigration "every year." She writes, "All but one entered successfully. This nephew, detained at Angel Island, become [*sic*] so nervous that he had answered incorrectly the date of his grandfather's birth. Consequently, he was returned to China" (44). However, there is no provision in the Exclusion Act for bringing in nephews, even nephews of merchants. Instead, we must conjecture that her father sponsored these men as paper sons or partners, and the nephew who got his grandfather's birthdate wrong was reciting his paper family's information. These "nephews" are nowhere to be seen in the family story of *Fifth Chinese Daughter*; nor do they make more of an appearance in Wong's later memoir. Still, this mention, though somewhat elliptical, points at the history of Chinese immigration and fraudulence, shattering Wong's model minority façade and even expanding the nuclear family structure for those who have the knowledge to interpret it.

Kingston and Wong use the newly popularized history of Angel Island to put not only themselves but, more importantly, their families into the communitarian context of a violent and disenfranchised immigrant history, writing against a model minority identity. Attaching their family histories to a newly iconic aspect of Chinese American history, the poems written and carved on the walls at Angel Island, also inserts both writers into the lineage of protest literature. *China Men* inscribes Kingston's family into the long and checkered history of Chinese feeling alienated in America, stretching from its earliest days to her brother's experiences in Vietnam, and Angel Island serves as one anchor. For Wong, it is an even more significant shift: Angel Island serves as the springboard with which to rewrite her happy family history in the context of an ethnic history marked by systemic legal and physical violence.

Drafting a Pure History

The urge to reclaim and disseminate Chinese American and other ethnic history in the 1970s served to reconnect the violence of personal experience, long silenced and kept secret, to government acts and laws that had likewise been forgotten in mainstream histories. It was Kingston, more than any other author, who was able to transform the narrative struggles of the postwar immigration era and incorporate it into her postmodern meditation on the struggle for historical knowledge that hovers just out of reach. Though she frames it so strongly as a struggle between parents and children, the presence of the state—more explicitly outlined in *China Men*—looms over them, a root cause of parental silence and childish curiosity. Her deep concern with the rifts within Chinese America caused by postwar immigration policy, as well as her constant search for history, uniquely positions her to retell and reshape Chinese American history in forms that fascinatingly navigate her deep personal connection to an illegal immigrant consciousness.

The desire to discuss the unending search for history goes hand in hand with a desire to educate others about history. Kingston later stated that she had evacuated the history too completely from her first memoir, then filled it in with *China Men* only five years later, this time with a title emphasizing not only gender but country of origin. In an oft-discussed musing during a *New York Times* interview, she said:

> The mainstream culture doesn't know the history of Chinese-Americans, which has been written and written well. That ignorance makes a tension for me, and in the new book I just couldn't take it anymore. So all of a sudden, right in the middle of the stories, plunk—there is an eight-page section of pure history. It starts with the Gold Rush and then goes right through the various exclusion acts, year by year. There are no characters in it. It really affects the shape of the book, and it might look quite clumsy. But on the other hand, maybe it will affect the shape of the novel in the future. Now maybe another Chinese-American writer won't have to write that history.[22]

History is dependent on family story rather than official record in *The Woman Warrior*, and the absence of the official echoes through Kingston's frustration. She has progressed, however, from an ostensible narrator's desire to discover the history herself to an explicit goal of educating others. Here, she declares that she would like to free future Chinese American writers from tension, educating the audience of *China Men* in order to set them free from the burdens of historical narration. She carefully tailors the history to that end, providing a narrative that is not only detailed but also liberating, an arc of progression and triumph over discrimination. Yet in her drafts, we see the drastic political shift she made in the construction of her "pure history," as she chose to excise much of her overt anxiety about illegal immigration and her enduring fears of deportation.

To understand the revisions of *China Men* and the essay that split from it during composition, which I discuss in the next section, it is essential to understand Kingston's concern with the usage of historical detail to highlight her narrator's quest. Kingston sparingly uses facts and dates in *The Woman Warrior*, which only serves to impel more questioning and doubt: "My mother left China in the winter of 1939, almost six months after the stoning, and arrived in New York Harbor in January, 1940. . . . On Ellis Island the officials asked her, 'What year did your husband cut off his pigtail?' . . . [W]hat if they were trying to trap him politically?" (96). This location may strike some readers as instantly questionable—and, indeed, Kingston never stops trying to solve the factual problems that she presents, carrying out an investigation of her own that impels her toward her artistry. Unlike Wong's narrative discrepancies, which often hide an elision or silence, Kingston's tend to be a site of confusion for both narrator and reader.

Kingston's authorial quest for historical accuracy to counterpoint her narrator's ignorance and curiosity, particularly surfacing in dates important to immigration history, is apparent in her composition. She notes to herself in early drafts about her father's early teaching career, "How long does he teach? He has to leave by 1924." Later drafts spell out the connection even more clearly, as her father's departure is marked by the commentary, "So, in 1924, when it was virtually impossible for a Chinese to enter the United States, the United States having just passed two more Exclusion Acts to make sure there were no loopholes a Chinaman could crawl through, when the Chinese plus Chinese-American population in the United States had been reduced by lynching, burnings, and laws to its lowest point since the beginnings of Chinese immigration, my father and his male relatives walked to Canton and looked for ships that would take them to the Gold Mountain."[23] This was condensed in the final version, which nonetheless clearly noted 1924 as the date of departure for her male relatives and elsewhere repeatedly mentions the 1924 Immigration Act (43, 154–155).

By comparison, as David Li notes in one of the few critical analyses of the history behind *The Woman Warrior*, the mention of 1924 is not analyzed within the text; nor has it been footnoted in any of the anthologies Li has checked (or in any I have seen, though, to be fair, many of them do not do any footnoting at all).[24] The narrator notes the year of male villagers' departure at the commencement of the narrative, but it is left to the reader or critic to explicate the larger historical significance—or not, as it has largely not been for *The Woman Warrior*, a lack that Kingston compensates for in *China Men*. However, she also paid careful attention to this date, which appears first as 1930 in drafts of *The Woman Warrior*, and must have been corrected quite late in the memoir's composition.

Even in *China Men*, which focuses on her male relatives, Kingston professes to be unable to elucidate how her father entered, and it is not entirely obvious considering the entry requirements at this time. In *The Fifth Book of Peace*, she writes that her mother has finally told her of her father's illegal entrance, stowing away three times and returning the last time from his deportation to Cuba—a dimension of immigration little talked about, though the Mexican border was frequently discussed. However, stowing away, Cuban entrance, and visas are some of the immigration methods stressed in *China Men*, which again suggests not a factual recounting of her slow discovery over time but the desire to return to how she (and others) look for and feel unsatisfied by a "truth." As with Wong, the oeuvre creates layered narratives that can be read back onto earlier texts not as corrective, but as history itself: a history of Kingston's reclamation of immigration narrative.

In the plunked-down "section of pure history," entitled "The Laws," Kingston famously lists several acts, court cases, treaties, and laws targeting Asians, each with a short description. They are introduced by year—for example, "*1946:* Congress passed the War Bride Act" (157). She covers many of the most famous laws and cases, including discriminatory local taxes and statutes, the Burlingame Treaty, the War Bride Act, and the various immigration acts. Although this is often referred to as a "catalog" or "list" by critics, Kingston's highly focused list and her pointed descriptions have narrative power. In immigration numbers, at least, Kingston is able to show a steady increase from law to amended law. Slowly, the laws and acts describe gradual inclusion and rights for Chinese Americans, ending, "In the last decade, the ethnic Chinese population of the United States has doubled. The 1980 census may show a million or more." The power structure remains clear as she continually uses the words "allowed," "reallocated," "limits" to emphasize the government's role. "The Laws" is preceded by Kingston's humorous anecdote of the effect of the San Francisco earthquake of 1906 on the Chinese American community: "Every paper a China Man wanted for citizenship and legality burned in that fire. An authentic citizen, then, had no more papers than an alien. . . . Every China Man was reborn out of that fire a citizen" (150). Only through natural disaster on an epic scale can the power of the government be undercut, an event that constantly chafes in governmental accounts of the earthquake, such as Everett Drumright's. But Kingston's presentation of it, so visually different from the other sections of the book, helps her to compete with the government for control in this section.

"The Laws" did not originally exist in Kingston's conception of *China Men*; her original notes show a very tight family history structure.[25] Gradually, she clearly felt the need for more and more context for their experiences, editing "The Laws" heavily until it assumed a chronological form and a powerfully optimistic historical trajectory. The evolution of this material commences with a small historical section incorporated into the introduction of the section "The Grandfather of the Sandalwood Mountains" and ends with the published version of "The Laws" as a chronology. It serves to doubly endow U.S. literature and Chinese America with an optimistic, progressive narrative; not only can literature and the literary audience progress from ignorance to knowledge, responsibility to freedom, tension to release, but America itself can move forward from exclusion to inclusion. While the historical progression that Kingston creates moves away from exclusion, it also glosses over the existence of systemic racism and enduring need for social movements such as the ones in which Kingston herself has participated (being famously antiwar), selectively using the official documentation to construct a happy trajectory. So, too, does her belief that perhaps future writers will find that the work of historical education is done. Indeed, Kingston's need to include "The Laws" and its progressive spirit wars with her impulse, structurally, to confine it away from the rest of her more imaginative, individual-driven narrative. As critics immediately pointed out, and as Kingston herself would surely never debate, *China Men* is not a history, but rather, a new nation's Odyssean epic of wandering men, borne out by the fact that her initial title was *Gold Mountain Heroes*.[26] The "pure history" seems to cast the entire epic within the arc of the United States forever bending toward knowledge and justice. Just as *China Men* ends with "young men who listen," the history of "The Laws" reaches those who will read and learn.

However, "The Laws" wars with the ambivalence of the other sections of the book. The vexed question of U.S. citizenship runs throughout, even as the book ranges worldwide over adventures in Cuba, Vietnam, American territories, and other places. Kingston's attention to historical detail shows how she views her family's history as shaped by U.S. political events. China Men encounter corrupt and venal Citizenship Judges, who offer more or less fraudulent papers, in Alaska and the American west. They beat the Exclusion Act by getting to Hawai'i earlier to work the plantations (a dubious gift). Sojourners first, they change nationality slowly, even unwillingly at times, but inevitably piled with papers: "visas, passports, re-entry permits, American birth certificates, American citizenship papers" (44). The history itself supposedly shapes Kingston's interest in documents and immigration.

Kingston's drafts of *China Men* show a progression away from a heavy and overt emphasis on the history of immigration and racism and a continuing worry over immigration status, told in prose narrative form; for unspecified reasons, she excised many of the most passionate passages, personal anecdotes, and brief historical expositions she initially composed in favor of segregating the history into "The Laws," the birth of which was neither so sudden nor so confined as Kingston's interview suggests. These excisions are consistent with the types of revisions she made to her account of Angel Island, but on a larger scale.

Only in very late revision did "The Laws" turn into a point-by-point general history rather than a more sweeping and activist essay, vehemently protesting the continued persecution of immigrating Chinese Americans and offering an extensive bibliography for further reading. First, the revision process excised the more radical and statement-making digressions in Kingston's writing. The sojourners, in particular, detail the violent history of anti-Asian sentiment and warn newcomers: "Carry a knife. When you can afford it, buy a gun. Fight to the death" and "They blew up the air shafts in the mine tunnels where the uncles were working." She does not excise all interest in these topics, but she removes the more radical expressions of them, for reasons on which we can only speculate.[27] Second, her initial emphasis in early versions of "The Laws" is to illuminate explicitly the continuing injustices of immigration scrutiny and the government's continued campaign against illegal immigration. The earliest full draft (as far as I can determine, since they are undated) begins with the fear that "another wave of persecution" might start at any time, prefaced by the "U.S. Immigration Service announcing that 'illegal immigrants' are entering the country in large numbers, and these 'aliens' are taking jobs away from citizens." This naturally leads to a discussion of past persecution and labeling as illegal or illegitimate. Kingston ends on an oddly exemplary note that a true Chinaman is one who, despite persecution and discrimination, "has never lost sight of the Gold Mountain," a very American dream–style appeal for sympathy. These emphases are quite different and offer a pointed critique of personal safety.[28]

Kingston's drafts give a clearer sense of her twinned motivations for discussing legislative history, as the omitted material hews clearly to very personal fears and questions of identity and, unsurprisingly, a much bleaker view of history than ultimately appears in *China Men*. She enlarges the concept of illegal immigrant from a legal category to a consciousness, similar to the recent term "refugitude" used by scholars to redefine refugee experience. "It didn't really matter that the laws became easier. They still felt illegal," she wrote of her migrating relatives, and so did she. In her handwritten earliest version is the heart of her dilemma: "Immigration laws ought to have nothing to do with me, not concern me whatsoever, an American born here, with a great-grandfather and grandfather who had come here before the Exclusion Acts of 1882. . . . I am nothing like an FOB, ~~And yet~~ America insists on lumping all us Chinamen together."[29] Her anxiety about being lumped in with these others, similar to her fear of being married off to the "idiot" of *The Woman Warrior*, represents the peril that all Chinese Americans face because of the hunt for those who immigrated with fake papers or stowed away in the older, more adventurous storyline that she also imagines. Although Kingston positions herself here legally as a pure and validated American, the model minority in opposition to the illegal immigrant, it is a singular moment that belies the difficult immigration history that she struggles to uncover and understand throughout her writerly life, a state of consciousness that takes immigration status beyond something defined solely by a government.

Originally, Kingston uses herself to connect personal grievance to systemic injustice, a long history of continued racism and persecution. The excessive taxes, restrictive laws on employment and landownership, and, most important, the restrictions on immigration appear consistently in Kingston's many drafts, maintaining the legalistic definition of an "illegal immigrant." Like the published version, the drafts of "The Laws" (once it coalesces in that form) focus on the judicial cases and immigration acts that restricted Chinese citizenship and even right to live in the United States, but unlike that final form, they use more emotional language and relate them more strongly to herself. *United States v. Wong Kim Ark* (which Kingston perhaps purposefully reversed for emphasis), a landmark Supreme Court case, is the case of a man who sued to establish not simply his right of citizenship by birth, but also "the law that gives me my own citizenship, my own American-ness." In a description of the Displaced Persons Act, Kingston highlights that "Chinamen were reluctant to come forth, suspecting the United States Immigration and Naturalization Service of setting traps. . . . Also, many of *us* were confused by conflicting laws, valid and invalid papers, also the Chinamen who resorted to stowing away, the slot system, the paper sons." The 1924 act was passed "to ensure the end of the Chinaman." The laws not only shape but seek to destroy Chinese America, including Kingston herself, American-born but still a member of this group.[30]

Peril, not triumph, is the end of the draft history. Kingston variously begins or ends different versions with a long discussion of the then current (i.e., late 1970s) dialogue about illegal immigration. She cites recent news coverage of INS studies of illegal immigration, estimating 500,000 "fraudulent entries" in 1975, and a second phase of investigation that will involve literal native informancy, as a contractor will "go out into ethnic communities in the spring of 1977 to select and train leaders whose job it will be to convince members of their own ethnic groups that hey [*sic*] ought to 'cooperate with the INS and report themselves.'"[31] Ongoing revisions update the status of this study, which Kingston was clearly following closely, and give her draft a tone of ongoing struggle and illegal immigrant consciousness, not a triumphant swelling of the population.

In addition, Kingston originally reintroduces her contemporary personal fears into the narrative by citing the INS's profiling practices detailed in the American Civil Liberties Union (ACLU) handbook *The Rights of Aliens*, the first edition of which came out in 1977. Based on foreign-looking appearance such as the cut of their clothing or carrying their lunch in a brown paper bag, the INS stops and questions "those who 'look like orientals' or who are of 'obvious Mexican descent.'" Fear of deportation once again silences the artist and afflicts her body. "What I find most regrettable,"

Kingston writes in what might seem a somewhat self-centered passage, "is that I can't tell the good stories because not to endanger people who might get deported. all those lost stories. This thread of deportation, temprs actions, limits freedom, makes me want to be insconsipicuous, not take stand out in political activities, not to get arrested for any reason [*sic*]." It even gives her a sore throat, as she continues that "cancer of the throat is common among Chinese Americans" from all this silence. Instead, "I listen and am warned when the Chinamen say 'Don't tell.' Otherwise, what stories. what lost stories. therefore, anonymous heroes, therefore omitted stories."[32] The stifling of freedom extends, as always with Kingston, to her artistic freedom and freedom of speech, but she originally links that stifling directly to the investigation and deportation of undocumented or falsely documented Chinese Americans.

Most significant, in these early drafts, rather than ending "The Laws" with a factual time point at 1978, singling out the impressive number of Chinese Americans—"a million or more" in the final version—she ends with a condemnation of the INS and foreboding about what immigration scrutiny means for all Chinese Americans. Through several revisions Kingston's drafts conclude, "It is still not a safe time to apply for food stamps or protest the bomb and the draft or to tell your real pastor use your real name or to give it to your child." The jeopardy that Chinese Americans face from the INS, equivalent to the risk of arrest for civil disobedience, silences them politically and personally. Nor is there any hope of an end; her penultimate sentence quotes the INS Commissioner Colonel J. Castillo, as saying, "I think you can slow illegal immigration, and you can regulate it, and you can manage it a lot better, but I don't think you can stop it."[33] This more searing original version of "The Laws" insists that illegal immigration even in the era of "reformed" immigration will always be accompanied by racial profiling and persecution, a vicious circle that will produce yet more immigration strategies.

"The Laws" ended up terse and numerically progressive, leading to a feeling of racial progress. But as these drafts help us to recognize, even in its restrained and optimistic final form "The Laws" is haunted throughout by illegal immigration, as Kingston details immigration restrictions, scrutiny, deportations, and fights for citizenship, but does not detail the paper sons, stowaways, and others who worked around the laws. Their stories are told in the rest of the book, separate from this narrative of governmental acts. Nor does she date and detail any individual immigration cases, the Chinatown association subpoenas, or even the instantiation of the Chinese Confession Program in her chronology, instead choosing to emphasize the case *Mao v. Brownell*, which she erroneously dates to 1954 and says restricted

Chinese Americans (or any) from sending money to people in Communist China. This topic, regardless of the errata, oddly ruptures her mostly immigration- and civil rights–focused chronology.[34] Knowing Kingston's revisions helps to draw our attention to these gaps left in the final history. The ending of the published version of "The Laws" may not contain her musings on the INS, the ACLU's advice, or forebodings about a current investigation, but it is nonetheless haunted by illegal immigration. Kingston notes, "About 22,000 Chinese enter *legally* every year, and the rate is increasing" (157, emphasis added). In addition to this careful adverb, a meticulous reader will read through Kingston's gradually increasing, triumphant numbers, which progress through immigration quotas of as little as one hundred and two hundred in earlier years to note that the final numbers that she offers suggest quite a few undocumented entries. Even in the "pure history" section, carefully shorn of much personal and political commentary, Kingston hides resistance and other, less-told histories.

Documenting Chinatown

The frustration to which Kingston alludes in her interview with Timothy Pfaff grew not only out of a frustration with Americans' ignorance of Chinese American history, but specifically with one American artist's elision of that history. Commissioned to write an essay in 1978 for *American Heritage* on Arnold Genthe's important turn-of-the-century photographs of Chinatown, Kingston found herself creating a rather sprawling history, which occasionally alluded to the photographs in telling a story of oppression and violence. While she ended up rewriting and refocusing the Genthe piece separately, drafts seem to indicate that this essay split off from or perhaps evolved in parallel with "The Laws." In the essay, "San Francisco's Chinatown," she retained her explicit focus on illegal immigration, a highly interesting and little-studied piece that, even more clearly than "The Laws" in *China Men*, places immigration history and the legal history of racial discrimination at the heart of understanding Chinese American experience. In the opposite of what she tries to construct in the supposedly purely documentary and actually optimistic "The Laws," Kingston bitterly critiques Genthe's seemingly neutral documentary history of Chinatown and the exotic culture presented in text by Will Irwin. Genthe's famous black-and-white candid photos of Chinatown are important because they are one of the very few visual records of Chinatown before the great earthquake of 1904. This collection, acquired by the Library of Congress in 1943, was not forgotten by historians, but Genthe's books were entirely out of print in the 1970s before renewed interest in Chinese American history, new exhibits in various cities across the country, and coverage such as Kingston's essay brought them back into prominence. Jack Tchen edited a new book of the photographs in 1984.[35]

As her subheading, "A View from the Other Side of Arnold Genthe's Camera," promises, Kingston offers a look at the omissions from Genthe's historical record, assuming an unquestioned insider identity even as she describes herself as an outsider, someone who sees *San Francisco's* Chinatown—reminding us that it is not the only one—as "foreign territory." She takes issue not only with the seemingly neutral eye of the camera, but also with Genthe's orientalist assertions about the reasons for his "candid" documentary approach, which hide the sound reasons for caution and skepticism. Instead, she embeds his work in American history—specifically, the history of immigration and deportation of Chinese. While Genthe claims that Chinese did not want their pictures taken, attributing it to some primitive superstition (no doubt along the lines of the spirit being stolen), Kingston points out that portrait photography was instantly popular among Chinese, as in many other cultures, but that Genthe's fearful subjects probably "were afraid of incurring trouble from the white authorities with their Exclusion Acts and deportation laws."

Indeed, as proof of how easy it was to get into trouble with the authorities, she notes that Genthe photographed a man carrying two baskets on the ends of a pole across his shoulders (47). The use of poles had been banned in San Francisco as a discriminatory measure, as Kingston mentions prominently in "The Laws": "At this time San Francisco supplemented the anti-Chinese state laws with some of its own[, including] a pole law prohibiting the use of carrying baskets on poles" (152). Kingston emphasizes this line of thinking in *American Heritage* to expand on the multitudinous forms of employment discrimination Chinese faced in the United States, as well as some details about citizenship that she repeats in *China Men*: the rush for citizenship after the San Francisco earthquake or the descriptions of Chinese America provided by Ng Poon Chew, editor of the *Chinese Western Daily* at the turn of the century (38). This, however, is again far more than straightforward information delivery. Because of the correction of Genthe and her more energetic emphasis on discrimination and prejudice, Kingston's essay offers a direct and defensive portrait of a community under siege, though it still omits her most searing fears about contemporary illegal immigration.

Once again, immigration history is the central and essential piece of knowledge that Kingston requires readers (or, in this case, photographers) to have in order to fully understand Chinese Americans, though limited to one Chinatown in this instance. The other deceptive quality of Genthe's pictures on which Kingston focuses is the restriction of his subjects, once

Figure 4.1. "The Vegetable Peddler," photograph taken by Arnold Genthe in San Francisco Chinatown around 1900. Kingston singles out this photo to discuss the discriminatory laws against Chinese, which included an ordinance against carrying baskets on poles. (Library of Congress, Prints and Photographs Division, Arnold Genthe Collection, LC-G4033 0119.)

again touching on her deep interest in immigration and its effect on families. Genthe's portraiture focuses heavily on children, both with parents and alone. "This gives the impression that Chinatown was a healthy community of flourishing families when exactly the opposite was the actual, lonely situation" (46), Kingston notes. It is largely an essay of proof by individual experience, however, as Kingston does not pause to give statistics, instead discussing the bachelor society that to this day leaves residences in Chinatown full of lonely old men. Explaining the Chinese Exclusion Act and its restriction on bringing in family members, Kingston points out how beautifully the women and children are dressed in the photos, most likely because they may be wives of merchants or ambassadors and because "women and children were valued, specially treated because they were so rare" (46).

Figure 4.2. "A Slave Girl in Holiday Attire," photograph taken by Arnold Genthe in San Francisco Chinatown around 1900. As Maxine Hong Kingston and John Kuo Wei Tchen note, Genthe often photographed on holidays and focused on women and children in formal dress, giving a somewhat skewed view of Chinatown. Kingston suggests that these women are unlikely to be slaves, as well. (Library of Congress, Prints and Photographs Division, Arnold Genthe Collection, LC-G4085-0185.)

Tchen notes that Genthe also seems to have photographed a great deal on holidays, when everyone would be dressed in their best (which does not necessarily contradict Kingston's hypothesis). Kingston further notes that amid this exotic landscape are no white Americans or even any Chinese dressed in Western style, which was being heavily promoted by certain community members by that time. Noting this improbable omission, as well as the undoubted market for white business contacts, clients, and gamblers, Kingston suggests that Genthe aimed his candid camera selectively to preserve "the spell of a self-contained, mythical Cathay" (39). Not only is this Cathay self-contained, but it is free from the laws, restrictions, fears, and prejudices of the time. Kingston serves as the close reader who is able to see past Genthe's omissions and gaps to retrace a more complete historical record. Tchen's examination of Genthe's unpublished plates, before retouching, shows that Genthe erased and edited white subjects in his prints, indeed creating images of a more hermetically sealed Chinatown.[36]

In spite of her newly assumed authority, Kingston's critique, as always, dwells on the difficulty of retracing history; she speculates on her own childhood encounter with Genthe's photographs, recalling the black-and-white images that she used to see in a Chinatown restaurant. "As an adult, I have looked for this restaurant on my own rare trips to San Francisco Chinatown but have not found it again" (38), she notes, before returning to the difficulty of reading the past and reclaiming it through her writing. (Earlier drafts merely note that you can find Genthe's photographs in a Chinatown restaurant; perhaps she tried to find them and failed.[37]) This not only reappropriates Genthe's photographs in their original site but erases and replaces them with her own narrative, much like Fae-Myenne Ng's citation of one of his photos in her novel *Bone* (1993).[38] In the end, Kingston frames the past injustices of Chinatown around her own "tightly knit" family, who went to San Francisco's Chinatown to shop together and who, she concludes, would have restricted Genthe's photography to the streets of Chinatown. "Homes are for families and for friends who are almost family" (47), she says firmly, not for outsiders like Genthe who objectify their subjects. Her reclamation conflates home and history as sources of belonging and identity, two sources that Genthe entirely fails to access.

Kingston's essay omits the family strife of *The Woman Warrior* but showcases the pain and rupture of history, as well as the past orientalism and exoticism even at the hands of documentarians that hid darker aspects of Chinese American treatment. In *China Men*, Kingston opted in the end for a pastiche of chronology and family history against a backdrop of slow and triumphant progression in America, perhaps refusing to make the overt critique in a family memoir. However, her narrative style makes a political point similar to that in the essay about Genthe, as the fragmented narratives and exposure of the difficulty of reconstructing a family's immigration history suggest the gaps and wounds of institutional violence. Kingston's struggles in her drafts with constructing and reconstructing history, as well as the reclamation of authority from writers such as Genthe, make the complicated nature of her historical narrative more evident. Not simply the celebratory and progressive historian of "The Laws," Kingston attempts to reclaim and correct a community history, the same one that she earlier was accused of falsifying.

Post-Confession: A World after Documentation

In the 2000s, both Wong and Kingston ostensibly search in their books—*Chinese American* and *The Fifth Book of Peace*, respectively—for the final link, the papers that, Estelle Lau suggests, can turn their family "fiction into fact" and place their family stories into the context of documentary history. These narratives, both composed across the 1990s and early 2000s, initially present these two authors as children of the Cold War attempting to grapple with their perilous past, still dwelling on the events, documents, and fears of the era of investigation and confession. This ironically places the narrator—as Kingston openly reflects—in the same position as government officials, who think that the true answers to their questions can be found in secret documents. Kingston's interest in the documents can only mean exposure and betrayal to her mother, even at so late a date; Wong's discussion of the documentation she finds comes only after her parents' deaths. Both authors end by moving beyond interrogation and documentation, downplaying the information of these supposedly all-powerful papers and realizing that the more elusive nature of family histories is their true concern. "Pure" history does not exist; they embrace the constructedness and speculative nature of stories and family histories at long last, jettisoning the legalistic search for documentation and truth. For Wong, this means embracing some of the personal speculation and curiosity that Kingston, who began there in *The Woman Warrior*, moves away from in order to accept a larger history.

Chinese American immigration documents were both a target of government investigation, as in the subpoenas I discussed in Chapter 1, and, paradoxically, as Mae Ngai points out, the *creation* of "documentation of native-birth citizenship where none had previously existed . . . a paper trail derived from the state's efforts to enforce exclusion."[39] She persuasively argues that the INS depended on the validation of the masses of paperwork its agents had created; the agency was thus in the somewhat ridiculous position of looking for documents that would undercut the documents that it had created in an effort to eliminate false documents. Wong and Kingston, however, have already created multiple narratives themselves and only late do they come to documentation that uncovers the long history of their parents' struggle. By the time they reflect on the documents, both are too wise to think that history is something that can be easily found. These late works thus serve as an afterword for my study of each author, showing how they find themselves coming back to the archive not for authentication, but for freedom. This embrace of a postmodern notion of a fragmented, constructed history certainly speaks to the shift in historiography, as well as literary form—though whether Wong's late work is deliberate pastiche or unfinished construction is hard to say—but my emphasis here will be on their negotiation with the personal, an abrogation of investigative authority but not their own narrative authority.

The probing of family documents became a paradigm very early for Chinese American life writing. "I strongly suspect that my father's life is a fraud," baldly opens *Father and Glorious Descendant* (1943). From childhood, it seems, Pardee Lowe, Chinese American social scientist, writer, and federal employee, doubted that his father was born in the United States as he claimed to have been. But when Lowe finally confronted his father at age seven, having heard (from whom?) that he had arrived in San Francisco as a "ragged, illiterate peasant boy of twelve," his father "opened his creaky iron safe and pulled out two very musty yellow legal documents, marked formidably *Writ of Habeas Corpus* and *Judgment*. . . . In the very heat of the Hayes-Tilden Presidential campaign, with both parties insisting that 'the Chinese must go!' the court had proclaimed Father an American citizen, thus snatching him from the clutches of the immigration officials."[40] This documentation, foregrounded as it is at the commencement of the narrative, is essential to the foundation of Lowe's construction of his identity. It serves as a historical benchmark for the modern struggles he will describe.

Lowe's memoir, which serves as a useful time point and stylistic template since it inaugurates the midcentury wave of Chinese American memoir, opens by acknowledging that members of the American-born generation question their own legitimacy via the legality of their parents' residency status. After the astonishing beginning, Lowe, without further ado, embarks on a narrative of his father's life that culminates in a typical reconciliation plot, as his father celebrates his longevity festival in a Western-style suit. The issue of the conflicting stories of citizenship by birth and classic immigrant rags-to-riches and citizenship, however, is dropped entirely. And it is his father who grows so reconciled to American ways that he refuses to critique the immigration laws of his country. Lowe's openness about immigration details and engagement with his father's documents sets up decades in which Chinese Americans had to negotiate the desire to flourish their documents and the need to hide them.[41]

Though writing in very different political climates in their initial memoirs, Wong and Kingston engage in a pattern of silence and elusion with which these young narrators make sense of Chinese American ways of communication. Yoon Sun Lee has persuasively argued that Wong and Kingston, in their first books, engage in a construction of Lukácsian realism, an impression of typical patterns rather than an accurate reflection of reality.[42] Her reading serves to draw our attention to the significant shift in style that takes place when these authors engage with historical documents and specific laws and acts. Narrative emphasis shifts to the narrator's own thoughts and doubts instead, a much more introspective and stream-of-consciousness style that once again attempts the impossible of wordily filling in the gaps of history. Wong and Kingston return to the hard realism of family documentation, only to elevate it to a meditation on the impossibility of retrieving family history from the archive. Indeed, it becomes unnecessary.

In a broad examination of Wong's oeuvre, there is just a little reason to doubt her father's immigration story—or, at least, there seems to be in Wong's own mind. The circumstances of her father's immigration are returned to and elaborated time after time, evincing some doubt and curiosity on Wong's part, though she expresses this much more circumspectly than does Kingston. Wong's first essay, "Daddy," which appeared in *Common Ground*, may well be the most revealing. Describing her father, Wong Hong, as "just another one of twenty-four thousand Chinese who had been encouraged to immigration by reports of fabulous riches," Wong says: "He was by turns a cook, a bookkeeper, a confectioner, a minister, and finally a manufacturer of overalls" ("candy-making" is also eliminated from a list of professions in drafts of *No Chinese Stranger*).[43] Two of these professions, cook and confectioner, will be unfamiliar to readers of *Fifth Chinese Daughter*, while the others (bookkeeper, minister, manufacturer) do follow the chronology of the memoir and, in doing so, might raise some questions. If the more manual professions, cook and confectioner, were inserted chronologically rather than for poetic effect—the nice rhyme of cook and bookkeeper being particularly appealing—then they would betray Wong Hong. In particular, entry in order to become a cook—that is, a laborer—would undoubtedly be illegal. Later accounts, including the *Saturday Evening Post* profile and *Fifth Chinese Daughter*, clearly state that he came in as a bookkeeper to audit his firm's San Francisco branch: legal merchant status. This may have been an excess of caution and clarity as the family gained publicity and investigations increased or a prideful clinging to a more exemplary, middle-class status.

For the restrained Wong, who demonstrably always knew more than she was letting on to her readers about her family's secrets, the documentation she finally investigates in *Chinese America* does seem to reveal not only new details but, more important, new insights into her father's life and the difficulty he had in navigating life in America. That is, it is uncharacteristically more an emotional discovery than a historical one, and it gradually expands from immigration to consider immigration travails on a continuum with racial prejudice in America. Wong turns to her father's diaries for details of his first entry in 1903: "According to a notebook which my father kept, he boarded the Pacific Mail's *S.S. Peking* in Hong Kong on March 21, 1903 and arrived in San Francisco on May 13 when he entered 'the wooden building' and was detained for translated questioning until June 3 when he 'climbed on the mainland shore.'"[44] This plain statement of facts offers some certainty, though his detainment and questioning are passed over; whether or not he wrote of detention and interrogation in his notebook is not revealed in Wong's summary. His extreme excitement at seeing Angel Island in *No Chinese Stranger* hints at a grueling time for himself as well as his wife; even the easiest questioning amid the conditions often described at Angel Island in this period would likely be worthy of comment.

Though Wong is never what most would call imaginative or speculative, she then pieces out the statement from the diary with childhood overhearing and historical knowledge: "Since 'merchant' was one of the few occupations qualifying for entry, he must have produced enough proof of capitalization. (From remarks I overheard when growing up, my father was actually twenty-four years old but he reported his age as twenty-nine for fear immigration officials would think he was too young to be a merchant.)"[45] This reconstruction constructs the desired effect: a plain narrative of entry and documentation, with the only lie or difficulty being a little white lie, told only for fear of the "immigration officials." Her father's dignity and integrity remain intact, his only lies being those of precaution, but Wong betrays her lifelong doubts.

After this introduction, Wong finds the real trove: legal and government-sealed documents that attest to her father's fears for his position and safety in the United States, and perhaps even to her own. In a curious echo of Lowe's account written fifty years earlier, Wong finds her father's documents in a box and reflects for the reader on their revelations. Unlike Lowe's direct confrontation with his father, Wong's discovery is posthumous, but both draw on their own knowledge of life in America, confirming feelings about racial discrimination rather than a father's biography. Wong wrote in her unpublished manuscript, "I can now understand why among my father's papers left in his black lacquered trunk, I have found three affidavits testifying to his legitimate entry and proving his merchant status in this unfriendly land. The Geary Act of 1892 required any Chinese person, not a laborer, to carry a certificate as evidence of 'having a right to be and remaining in the United States.'"[46] Her historical knowledge provides some context for herself and for the reader that, it seems, she can "now understand . . . this unfriendly land" but might not always have understood in the past. Given the various legal challenges to returnees, including the requirement to carry documentation, one could not in any way complain about paranoia over establishing residency. Being a fellow Wong, it seems likely that Wong Hong was keenly aware of the Supreme Court cases of Wong Kim Ark and others about reentry, including the requirement to carry reentry and residency permits. Once again, Wong positions her family member as a fully legitimate, fully vested inhabitant, but this time stressing how he must combat a hostile and skeptical immigration service.

For Wong, these documents mark not only her later-in-life public admission of systemic racism, but the acknowledgment of how her father changes and adjusts to life in America over time, this time venturing on some direct commentary on his actions. Far from the emphasis on enduring Chinese traditions and American modernity that clash only in the children, the subtle shift in Wong's 1990s–2000s framing of her father's modernity finally confronts U.S. laws and prejudices. After looking at the newly found documents, Wong does not "correct" her narrative of her father but is pushed to articulate different vantage points on his life in America. Wong Hong's notarized papers (his name is spelled Wong Hang in the papers) show his foresight in establishing his residency and his American bona fides. The diasporic nature of his business, a facet of life not normally reflected in Wong's Chinatown-centric published writings, might make it even more doubtful. Out of the fifteen listed officers on the 1904 affidavit who have an interest in the company, the residence of four is listed as China, and one as Panama. Likewise, the passage of time shows Wong Hong's transition to life in America, as his photograph on the 1904 affidavit shows him with queue and in traditional Chinese shirt and cap, but the 1906 affidavit shows a newly bearded man in Western suit and a homburg. A second affidavit from 1906 notes that he is about to go on a short trip to China and provides the authenticating signatures of several witnesses, mostly white, who attest to his residency *and* his merchant status. Such signatures attest to Wong Hong's embeddedness in U.S. life, another aspect rarely seen in Wong's Chinatown-centered accounts of her childhood and self-portrayal as the family's lone adventurer into the white mainstream. Wong reflects on the change in her father's appearance, rather than his business dealings, as proof of his increasing Americanness: "The Chinese Exclusion Act made it mandatory for a Chinese immigrant to verify his residency here prior to departure, in order to gain re-entry upon his return. But what a change in the picture! He has cut his queue and is hatless. His hair is in the style of the conventional Western man's cut. The revolution to establish the new republic in China has not yet succeeded, and he has already cut his queue in anticipation of the imminent collapse of the Qing dynasty!" Rather than viewing this through the lens of Chinese history, however, we might also speculate that this haircut had been chosen in view of U.S. events, since Wong Kim Ark's Chinese dress had been unfavorably remarked on when he sought to reenter the United States. After her brief expostulation about an unfriendly United States, Wong falls back, a little disjointedly, on positioning her father's motivations as stemming from a Chinese political identity. She has not developed a consistent political voice, but this dive into the archive finally brings other facets of Chinese American experience to light.[47]

Kingston, too, returns to her sense of ignorance about her parents' actions and motivations in *The Fifth Book of Peace*, noting that she has learned in the intervening years that her mother entered the United States through Angel Island, not Ellis Island, as she states in *The Woman Warrior*. "Hong" is her father's true name but simultaneously her mother's fake married name, as her father, while gambling, won the visa for a different Hong's wife

(361). Such moments might lead us to believe that *The Fifth Book of Peace* returns us to the personal, questing mode of *The Woman Warrior*, but if so, it is a quest this time for something beyond the history she craved initially. Kingston's estrangement from her parents' experience is not softened by the passage of time; nor can a document, however exciting, bridge the gap. *The Fifth Book of Peace* is a book haunted by lost and found documents, from the original manuscript of Kingston's fourth book, lost in a house fire, to the turtles with "poems and laws" carved on their backs (46) and the lost books of peace for which she quests throughout the narrative. Her own lost manuscript is compared to her lost father (14), who used to write tomes of poems in China but lost the ability in America, an artist severed from his voice (15). Among these lost and found papers is the one that finally answers so many of Kingston's questions from *The Woman Warrior* and *China Men*, a find in one of her father's hiding places, even more obscure a posthumous find than Wong's: "A scroll about the size and shape of half a roll of toilet paper. The cheat sheet for Immigration. Fake paper village of MaMa's fake paper husband. . . . Sneaking this paper in and out of hiding, she studied it while seasick on the USS *President Taft*. She came through Angel Island, not Ellis Island; she has corrected that story since my father's dying," keeping the scroll hidden in the "false bottom underneath the cupboard in the pantry" (54–55).

Lies and reality converge around this fetishized scroll, which offers the visual proof of falsehood. Kingston proposes to give the scroll to the library at Berkeley or the museum at Angel Island, archiving and preserving it to elucidate the false and the real history and perhaps to memorialize the entire experience, but her mother refuses, accusing her of wrecking immigration routes and destroying Chinese families. She claims to have burned the scroll, but Kingston later finds it hidden and takes it, only for it to be burned in her great house fire. Kingston's mother's inability to destroy it and Kingston's inability to preserve it suggest the essential slipperiness of papers and true history. Though the documentary history seems such a reliable goal for narrative investigation, the artist—even a powerful, famous artist—*has* to invent it, as all of her efforts at preservation are doomed to failure. *The Fifth Book of Peace* represents her artistic triumph over the need for documents and documentation, a book reinvented on the ashes of the past.

The writers of the U.S-born generation have far fewer concerns about documentation, and thus Kingston rarely reflects on documents for herself, though her protagonist Wittman Ah Sing often does during his travels in the novel *Tripmaster Monkey* (1989). Still, she is far from immune from anxieties and fears of prosecution and even deportation. Wong, however, is forced to confront the reality of her own need for documentation in retrospect:

> Those papers in Dad's lacquer trunk included other surprises, including identification No. 1783 with my name, signed by myself and C. T. Feng, Chinese Consul General on December 27, 1941. It certified that I was a member of the Chinese race. My picture and my father's are side-by-side. The number of my birth registration with the San Francisco Department of Health is included and the whole is duly notarized. I have no recollection of having to produce this document when I was then a senior at Mills College, but my father's care in arranging for this record testifies to the defense which he thought was needed against California hysteria concerning the Japanese race after December 7, 1941. Innocent persons who didn't choose their race, time, or place of birth were condemned by those circumstances. They lost hard-earned properties and were incarcerated like criminals without the benefit of trial, without knowing if the nightmare would ever end. Sixty years after the Chinese Exclusion Act, the same factors of ignorance, jealousy and greed again motivated the American government to ignore the constitution-guaranteed birth rights of citizens.[48]

Remarkably, Wong not only understands and implicitly approves of this long-forgotten precautionary document but puts it into the cross-ethnic context of the Japanese American incarceration. Her "forgetting" of it in her 1950 or 1975 memoir demonstrates the political reawakening that documents in the archive can provide; the mixed history and memoir format of her final manuscript indicates her own embrace of this form. Discovering this document in her narrative can serve no purpose other than a kind of protest by showing her father's great care to safeguard his family from racial prejudice; it is not as if Wong's ethnic identity is unknown to either her or her reader. In a now familiar narrative style, she side-slips any emotional reaction other than surprise into the recitation of historical context. But as is equally typical in this late manuscript, she uses much stronger and harsher language, not abstaining from a direct critique of the government's "ignorance, jealousy and greed." Documentation such as this does not need to answer questions for Wong, but it can still help to generate new feelings and new language for her. For both Wong and Kingston, even if the archive has lost its authority, it can still impel a new artistry.

Kingston establishes an epistemological chronology for Chinese America of searching for lost family knowledge at the age of maturity, but more than that, she offers a model for transforming historical knowledge into an artist's voice, art that represents a community experience. She evinces an enduring concern with the fraught issues in her family history, which appears even in *The Fifth Book of Peace*. It takes knowledge and the destruction of her family history to come to peace, at last, with her personal past before she can seek to write about peace in the world, her ongoing cause. Just as San Francisco's fire figures as a cleansing, redefining political power in *China Men*, allowing men to claim citizenship, it cleanses Kingston, launching her on a new type of quest, not to create new documentation, but to move away from the need for it entirely. Even Wong, whose anxiety is so little professed in her earlier memoirs, arrives at a point of historical contemplation and some critique in her final book, at a time when she is freed of concern about her parents' immigration status and papers and looks back nostalgically at the relics, speaking instead for an entire community (as the title of her unpublished last work declares).

Concealment, in the era of immigration restriction and exclusion, was a protective strategy. Public speech became necessary in order to create and sustain a positive image of Chinese America, but it could also threaten the speaker or the community with exposure and deportation. Likewise, we face the question of where the silence lies: it was chiefly an outward-facing silence that preserved certain secrets for the community, but as the Asian American movement grew in the 1970s and the immigration reforms of 1965 relieved many (but not all) anxieties, silence was recast by many as an evil that had resulted in a lack of public recognition and political agency and produced profound familial and community rifts. To see Kingston and Wong break free of the desire to investigate documents and the pressures to be silent about them suggests that the lingering fears of the Confession era took decades to erode. When one looks back at the mid-2000s and their last works, it may seem that they again had a halcyon political moment in which to embrace the deceptive nature of documentation, as the topic enlarges from their own concerns to an entire ethnic history and even to cross-ethnic and cross-racial concerns. Still, ironically but not surprisingly, despite the earlier dependence on the reconciliation plot, there was no reconciliation on the complicated subject of illegal immigration and its place in the nation.

Epilogue

The Failure of the Model Minority Narrative?

There is no conclusion to be written to a study such as this. Instead, *Illegal Immigrants/Model Minorities* serves as a single temporally and ethnically specific case study in the long construction of the category of the "illegal immigrant" and the fight against its stigma that continues to seethe in contemporary U.S. politics. The limited efficacy that some Chinese Americans found in the model minority image has been severely curtailed by further attacks on immigrants of all kind, including fully documented ones, in a globalized labor market and a decade of increased nationalism and populism. While the model minority is still wielded as a tool of antiblackness in U.S. court cases against affirmative action, which have divided the Asian American community (a different kind of failure and one beyond my reach to expound here), exemplarity and achievement look feeble indeed against the surge of xenophobia. When narratives of exemplarity and social norms cease to have force in combating brutal or restrictive immigration policies, we must consider whether new narratives are needed both privately and publicly.

No better proof could be found of the powerlessness of the model minority image to ward off racist and xenophobic discourse in our own time than the "birther" attacks on President Barack Obama throughout his candidacy and presidency, some of which were leveled by the man who succeeded him as president. Obama's stellar academic pedigree and brilliant political rise to become the first black president of the United States as a relatively young senator were nonetheless insufficient to ward off a ceaseless stream of questions, rumors, and outright lies about his race, religion, and citizenship. Birther attacks sought to bring into play a number of unusual—for presidential politics—aspects of Obama's life and parentage, such as his birth in Hawai'i, his Kenyan father and other relatives, his Indonesian stepfather, and his non-Anglo name. Such biographical aspects and his ability to connect with the Asian American community led some to postulate him as the first Asian American president, in the same way that Toni Morrison dubbed Bill Clinton the first African American president. Unsurprisingly, this connection extended to the stigma attached to migration, immigration, and questionable citizenship.[1]

The heart of the birther conspiracy focused on Obama's birth, claiming that the evidence of his birth in Hawai'i was suspicious or nonexistent and that he therefore had been born in Kenya and was ineligible for the presidency. While not directly positioning Obama as an illegal immigrant—as his mother was a U.S. citizen by birth and white, to boot—these attacks questioned his *type* of citizenship and, thereby, the legitimacy of his presidency. His Americanness was targeted more overtly via Islamophobic attacks on his religion and racist attacks on his Kenyan family. News of his aunt's immigration status was leaked by a hostile U.S. Immigration and Customs Enforcement (ICE) official four days before the 2008 election, to predictable effect, with hostile commentators seeking to tar Obama with the brush of illegal immigration. Even Hawai'i's ever-liminal status came into play, as the documentation required in Hawai'i at the time of Obama's birth looked different and unofficial to voters in the 2000s. Rumors that the opposing vice-presidential candidate, Sarah Palin, transferred away from college in Hawai'i because there were too many Asians only exacerbated the perception of Hawai'i as a land alien to white Americans.[2]

In a fashion highly reminiscent of the Cold War dialogue, Obama's extended and complicated transnational family fed attacks while his heteronormative American-born nuclear family formed the basis for his most potent defense. Senator John McCain, when running against Obama in 2008, famously used Obama's family life as a non sequitur defense against a supporter who said he was Arab: "He's a decent family man, citizen."[3] McCain's well-meant if somewhat incoherent defense missed an opportunity to defend the idea that someone of Arab descent could be a legitimate president (or a decent family man) in favor of defending Obama the individual via the most mainstream and all-American aspect of his image. Much like Sing Sheng or immigrating war brides of the 1950s, Obama's Americanness (and even his blackness) was shored up by his marriage to Michelle Robinson, a South Side Chicago descendant of enslaved African Americans, equally model minority but without the complicated linkages to Africa and Asia that enfolded Obama's own identity. Their strong marriage and two cute daughters completed a perfect nuclear family image that made any of the more conventional scandalous attacks on Obama impossible.

But the "family man" defense did not protect Obama from the racism filtered through attacks on his citizenship that were only regenerated by the election of Donald J. Trump to succeed him. As president, Trump ceaselessly attacked Obama in numerous ways. Though he did not openly renew the precise birther discourse, he drew from the same playbook to attack congressional opponents known in the media as "The Squad." Representative Ayanna Pressley, Representative Ilhan Omar, Representative Rashida Tlaib, and Representative Alexandria Ocasio-Cortez, four women of color of different races and ethnicities—and again, by the measure of political success, four model minorities—were all nonetheless tweeted by Trump to go back where they came from, quite literally. Echoing his reported comment earlier in his administration about immigration from "shithole countries," he tweeted, "Why don't they go back and help fix the totally broken and crime infested places from which they came." Notwithstanding the fact that three of these congresswomen were born in the United States and one is a naturalized citizen, Trump's tweet was designed to illegitimate them and, increasingly, to illegitimate all immigrants, particularly people of color, who do not perfectly toe the line. The line, of course, is an ever-moving barrier that can be designated only by people in power.[4]

Thus, through the might of the narrative of illegal, illegitimate, or imperfect citizenship to tarnish someone who otherwise fulfills many of the so-called model minority strictures, we see the model minority narrative's failure to fully accomplish political and social acceptance in the United States, particularly when it clashes with immigration. The strictures of the Obama-era Deferred Action for Childhood Arrivals (DACA) policy memorandum explicitly outline forgiveness only for the model minority: in school, graduated, honorably discharged veteran, or holding a general education certificate, not convicted of any serious crime. Yet even these requirements were no longer enough by 2016 to be politically efficacious, as the support for DACA recipients eroded under the Trump administration. During the 2017–2018 debate leading up to the court-ordered continuation of the renewal of immigration status under DACA, the publicity surrounding exemplary young DACA recipients, including two Texas high school students who revealed their undocumented status publicly during their valedictory addresses, led one Arizona congressman to remark, "The picture that's given to us is you've got a valedictorian—these are all valedictorians, they're all highly performing, highly achieving, but we don't know that." Implicit in his statement is the idea that perhaps we *ought* to require all DACA recipients to be valedictorians, that perhaps the goalposts should be moved again to require extreme model minority status. Furthermore, the backlash that the two Texas valedictorians received from some white community members, many of whom drew on their own disappointment about college admissions and the rhetoric of attacks on affirmative action, suggests that we have reached the limits of the political efficacy of this type of discourse.[5]

Likewise, the ideal of nuclear family unity and family reunification has failed to protect or even, in some quarters, garner sympathy for migrant families whose children were taken from them by U.S. government agents, died crossing the border, or died for want of medical care in U.S. custody at the U.S.-Mexico border in 2018–2019. The nuclear family ideal's utter failure to protect at this political moment, as the number of refugees worldwide skyrockets, demonstrates that the discourse of illegality and illegitimacy is ascendant. It only further confirms what many activists and scholars have postulated: that the model minority image was not a positive but a negative, a racist love rather than a racist hate, a wedge to separate Asian Americans from African Americans to further anti-black policies and legislation, and a means of repression and discipline via a very limited economic acceptance rather than a full acceptance to civil rights and national belonging.

It needs hardly be said that under the Trump administration the constant threat of new immigration restrictions based on a combination of religion and national origin, as well as the devaluing of family reunification as a priority (as announced in August 2017) and the forcible separation of migrant parents and children on the U.S.-Mexico border, has not only revived but normalized an aggressive anti-immigrant narrative within the United States. The fight to build a "wall" along the U.S.-Mexico border prioritizes and makes explicit the exclusions that always existed in the Statue of Liberty's rhetoric of a lamp uplifted beside a golden door—a door that, by definition, must be set in a wall. The great, unintended boom in ethnic Asian population that resulted from the 1965 immigration reform prioritizing family reunification cannot be undone by any established processes, but the community can be attacked anew by policies and policy makers inflamed by the ugly rhetoric surfacing in the stigmatization and deportation of immigrants of all kinds that brings back other memories of the past. As always, those who are especially vulnerable in racialized immigration and socioeconomic status feel its effects first. Among Asian Americans, they have recently included the deportation of Southeast Asian refugees and Asian adoptees not properly naturalized as children.[6]

Worldwide, the increasing debate over refugee entrance and asylum, as well as the impending flood of climate refugees over the next fifty or one hundred years, raises the question of how a nation-state in a globalized world can stop migrant flows and what then becomes of stateless refugees and migrants, however exemplary. An archipelagic system of refugee and migrant encampments and jails have come into prominence around the world, from the Greek islands receiving Syrian refugees across the Mediterranean to Nauru and Papua New Guinea serving as holding centers for refugees headed to Australia. Angel Island may stand today as a National Historic Landmark no longer in use, but it is one in a long chain of detention and incarceration centers around the United States and the world.

New Directions in Chinese American Writing

Though the racialization of illegal immigration has turned greatly to the stigmatization of Latin Americans, particularly Mexicans and Chicano/a Americans, and Muslim Americans and away from the fear of communist infiltration, it continues to be a factual and fictional concern for Chinese Americans. As of the production of this book, statistics show that overall immigration to the United States from Asia has risen, with more new immigrants now coming from Asia than from Latin America; likewise, though undocumented or unauthorized immigration has held relatively steady in recent years, Asians now make up a larger percentage of the total, with China the second highest country of origin (behind India).[7] At the same time, the numbers of highly educated students and workers entering from Asia have also continued the class stratification experienced by Chinese Americans in the 1970s.

Regular breathless media features on the topic of undocumented or loophole Chinese immigration once again cover othered or demonized family formations and lives ranging from the crowded and dangerous conditions in New York Chinatown to the newly named pattern of "birth tourism," in which Chinese women in late pregnancy enter the United States to give birth and obtain birthright U.S. citizenship for their children. What is more, the same presumed narratives of fraudulence and stigma still plague would-be immigrants in government policy and the judicial system. Jeffrey Chase, an immigration court judge in New York City, was famously removed from the bench in 2007 after he became nearly unbalanced in his hostility and skepticism toward asylum seekers. Chase accused applicants in the courtroom, many of whom were Chinese, of being coached by "snakeheads" and lying to their lawyers and further used "combative and insulting language," a federal court found. This case was all the more extraordinary as Chase had previously been an advocate for asylum who scolded judges with preconceived notions, and he greeted his own removal with something resembling relief. At the other end of immigration complaints are remarks such as the ones made in 2016 by Steve Bannon, then a Trump administration official, about "too many Asians" in Silicon Valley. Calls such as this led to renewed restrictions on H-1B visas, an indirect method of restricting

Asian immigration, this time again demonstrating that the model minority image is insufficient to ward off immigration stigma and, as ever, the economic yellow peril.[8]

Such events, in combination with trade tensions with China similar to the economic competition with Japan that provoked such hostility toward Japanese Americans and east Asian Americans in the 1980s, may well be pointing us to another era of the public demonization of Chinese immigration, this time in conversation with the stigmatization of other ethnic and racial groups, which, in turn, will evoke another flood of literary responses. The transnational Nobel laureate Ha Jin's story collection *A Good Fall* (2009), set in Chinatown in Flushing, Queens, offers a matter-of-fact look at the omnipresence of immigration awareness and weaponization in the daily lives and businesses of this community, focusing on individuals rather than the nation-state. Jin occupies a position perhaps reminiscent of that of Lin Yutang: a privileged transnational adult writer attempting to lovingly describe a community in the United States. What both emphasize heavily is the desire for freedom—the need to wrestle free of the fear that one's life may be destroyed by immigration secrets at any moment—and the pragmatic recognition of immigration scrutiny for new waves of immigrants. But in direct contrast to Lin, the earliest writer examined in this book, Jin, the latest, does not find hope in the model minority image to plead for acceptance, and his darkly comic resolutions turn reconciliation on its head, ridiculing it as a form of escape.[9]

Jin's chief illegal immigrant protagonist ends optimistically, with ironic reversals of fortune in which the modern media machine, not the model minority image, helps to fix immigration woes. The titular story, "A Good Fall," is the only one to focus on the life of an illegal immigrant, Ganchin, a monk abused and cheated by the corrupt temple master who refuses to renew his visa or to pay him. Ganchin's wanderings through a friendly Chinatown as he navigates his powerlessness and despair culminate when his leap off a building (the "good fall") goes wrong. His situation is resolved not with suicide but with publicity that brings him champions and help with his immigration situation. His happy ending includes an American-born girlfriend, so he leaves his life and his identity as an exotic kung fu master behind. He turns into a hapless, penniless immigrant just like any other in the United States. His illegal status may be erased, but with it so is his exemplarity.

A lack of freedom characterizes the confined lives of *A Good Fall*, whose characters find themselves continually plagued by the migration of people who entangle them in legal and emotional complications, breaking up happy families and precipitating everything from inconvenience to disaster. In "The Beauty," the handsome and successful protagonist, Dan, a seeming model minority, suffers some of the same anxieties as Ben Loy in *Eat a Bowl of Tea*. He wonders whether his surprisingly homely baby proves that his beautiful wife, Gina, has had an affair, but, faithful to the nuclear family ideal, he remains steadfast in acknowledging the child. He learns that Gina is being blackmailed by Fooming, a man from her hometown in China. Ultimately, Dan forces Fooming to leave Gina alone by threatening him, in turn, with exposure of his Communist Party membership, which would invalidate his visa. While immigration status changes the course of the three characters' lives, it is merely a tool, something to demonstrate the protagonist's perception but nothing exceptional or horrifying. Indeed, it is put on equal footing with Gina's secret, which is that her beauty is the result of plastic surgery. That is not to say that immigration is trivialized as an issue; the story unusually reimagines immigration secrets as an intraethnic weapon and a means of personal retribution and positions Dan, a naturalized citizen, as not only secure in his socioeconomic and citizenship status but savvy about the intricacies of immigration law.

Jin posits a continuing concern with how secrets about immigration status both bind and fracture families and intimate relationships, so necessary not only to personal happiness but to the positive images of assimilable and model minorities, under the threat of the state. Jin enlarges this concern to think about transnational families, as well. Fooming only caves in to Dan's threats because he cannot repudiate his Communist Party membership out of fear of what will happen to his siblings in China. Huong, a prostitute smuggled to the United States by obscured Asian mafia trafficking in "The House behind a Weeping Cherry," is persuaded by her lover to run away and forget about sending money to her parents, since they have effectively sold her into sexual slavery. In "Shame," a professor defects, thinking he can earn more money in the United States to help his ill wife, but his fate is unknown as he disappears into the underground network of undocumented migrants working in Chinese restaurants, presumably never to return home to his wife. Here Jin illustrates the inability for education and qualifications to cross national borders to establish a model minority life, a well-known dilemma and the reverse of the much more publicized H-1B, or "specialized skills," immigrant. What is more, the loneliness of Jin's characters, even the elite and financially stable ones, suggests an isolation peculiar to the stress of immigration that crosses class lines. Rather than providing happy endings, the love of family crosses and impels crossings across borders. To negotiate and forge personal relationships is the chief concern of these characters, not the laws and government acts that seek to define an "illegal immigrant." Such an attitude also informs critical refugee studies and other similar fields that, while still critiquing the nation-state, seek to foreground the consciousness and experiences of the individual rather than the definitions of the state. The literature and scholarship may thus continue to help us to new considerations of "illegal immigrant" status or identity (perhaps without that moniker) as Kingston began to do.

The narratives of the Cold War era offered us an imaginative response to the political climate of their time, a climate of threat, inhospitality, and surveillance. Some hopefully imagined a narration of self and state into a harmonious whole that would demonstrate the worth of Chinese Americans to be American, and others examined the unease and impossibility of that, trying (and sometimes failing) to imagine other ways to be Chinese in America. For the most part, those speaking for specific political purposes adhered to the narrative of patriotism and exemplarity, a stance that is now often condemned by later, U.S.-born generations. Certainly, many Asian Americans have politically eschewed this narrative, though it arises yet again in attacks on affirmative action that position Asian Americans as offended and virtuous minorities. Offering us a new response for a new political era, Jin undercuts and reimagines model minority discourse in the melancholy lives of his immigrant characters. In addition to its apparent political inefficacy to extricate these characters from their immigration tangles, he appeals to the damaging effects of this disconnect between the false exterior and the fraught interior. Gina, in "The Beauty," physically demonstrates the superficiality of perfection, which can be bought and sold. Dan, likewise, ends the story with a hollow victory, chasing away the blackmailer so he can resume his seemingly perfect family life, but, repulsed by the knowledge of his wife's natural appearance and his disappointment in his ugly child, he turns away from his family emotionally, seeking refuge in massage parlors that seem to deliberately pun on Dan's need for a "happy ending." Jin importantly turns the consideration of the hollowness of the model minority image inward, thinking about the consequences for the individuals.

It may seem that, on the political front, I am concluding that this book tells a tale of two narratives in which one, the illegal immigration strand, has triumphed. However, this is also a story of the negotiation of these two identities and categories by a community. The changing attitudes of Chinese American writers over time also remind us that historical and political events and narratives can be openly and publicly debated and given new definition and direction as writers learn new strategies to confront the injustices of the past and gain a stronger mainstream footing to explore their family histories. Angel Island's establishment as a memorial and the growth of oral history provided a more cohesive community narrative and openness about the illegal immigration and hardships of the past. However, as the reception of *The Woman Warrior* showed, this did not mean that there was perfect agreement on a political attitude toward the past, any more than there had been agreement on confession or informing. Ironically but not surprisingly, despite successful public history projects and the dependence on the reconciliation plot, there has been no reconciliation on the complicated subject of illegal immigration and its remembrance. But amid its ever more turbulent discussion, the literature of illegal immigration may provide us with an empathetic understanding of the strategies that individuals in the public eye seek to use in order to withstand and redirect the winds of change.

Notes

INTRODUCTION

1. Henry Koster, dir., *Flower Drum Song*, film, 133 min., Universal Pictures, 1961.

2. William Petersen, "Success Story, Japanese-American Style," *New York Times Magazine*, January 9, 1966. The article that used similar language about Chinese Americans, though it did not employ the term "model minority," was "Success Story of One Minority Group in U.S.," *U.S. News and World Report*, December 26, 1966, 73–76. For a fuller discussion, see Chapter 2. Ellen D. Wu, *The Color of Success: Asian Americans and the Origins of the Model Minority* (Princeton, NJ: Princeton University Press, 2014), 56. K. Scott Wong, *Americans First: Chinese Americans and the Second World War* (Cambridge, MA: Harvard University Press, 2005). Madeline Yuan-yin Hsu, *The Good Immigrants: How the Yellow Peril Became the Model Minority* (Princeton, NJ: Princeton University Press, 2015). Mae M. Ngai, *Impossible Subjects: Illegal Aliens and the Making of Modern America* (Princeton, NJ: Princeton University Press, 2004), 223.

3. Bonnie Honig, *Democracy and the Foreigner* (Princeton, NJ: Princeton University Press, 2001); Ngai, *Impossible Subjects*, 5, 13.

4. Maxine Hong Kingston, *China Men* (New York: Vintage International, [1980] 1989).

5. Cindy I-fen Cheng, *Citizens of Asian America: Democracy and Race during the Cold War* (New York: New York University Press, 2013); Wu, *The Color of Success*, 28–38, 115; Charlotte Brooks, *Between Mao and McCarthy: Chinese American Politics in the Cold War Years* (Chicago: University of Chicago Press, 2015), 123; Peter Kwong and Dušanka Miščević, *Chinese America: The Untold Story of America's Oldest New Community* (New York: New Press, 2005), 226.

6. Hiroshi Motomura, *Immigration outside the Law* (Oxford: Oxford University Press, 2014), 14. See Ngai, *Impossible Subjects*; Elliott Young, *Alien Nation: Chinese Migration in the Americas from the Coolie Era through World War II* (Chapel Hill: University of

North Carolina Press, 2014); Ian Haney López, *White by Law: The Legal Construction of Race* (New York: New York University Press, 2006), 152–153.

7. Kunal Parker, *Making Foreigners: Immigration and Citizenship Law in America, 1600–2000* (New York: Cambridge University Press, 2015), 7–8, 151. See also Neil Gotanda, "'Other Non-Whites' in American Legal History: A Review Essay on *Justice at War*," *Journal of Gender, Race, and Justice* 13, no. 2 (Winter 2010): 358–369; Torrie Hester, *Deportation: The Origins of U.S. Policy* (Philadelphia: University of Pennsylvania Press, 2017); Hsu, *The Good Immigrants*, chap. 1.

8. Beth Lew-Williams, *The Chinese Must Go: Violence, Exclusion, and the Making of the Alien in America* (Cambridge, MA: Harvard University Press, 2018), 33, 47–52; Nayan Shah, *Contagious Divides: Epidemics and Race in San Francisco's Chinatown* (Berkeley: University of California Press, 2001), 77.

9. *Wong Kim Ark v. United States*, 169 U.S. 649 (1898). See, e.g., the case *Chae Chan Ping*, in Robert S. Chang, *Disoriented: Asian Americans, Law, and the Nation-State* (New York: New York University Press, 1999), 38; the case *In re Low Yam*, in Lew-Williams, *The Chinese Must Go*, 61; and the case *Chew Heong v. U.S.*, in Bill Ong Hing, *Making and Remaking Asian America through Immigration Policy, 1850–1990* (Stanford, CA: Stanford University Press, 1993).

10. See, e.g., Izumi Hirobe, *Japanese Pride, American Prejudice: Modifying the Exclusion Clause of the 1924 Immigration Act* (Stanford, CA: Stanford University Press, 2001); *Takao Ozawa v. United States*, 260 U.S. 178 (1922); *United States v. Thind*, 261 U.S. 204 (1923); Immigration and Nationality Act, Public Law 82-414, 66 Stat. 163 (1952).

11. Erika Lee, *At America's Gates: The Exclusion Era, 1882–1943* (Chapel Hill: University of North Carolina Press, 2003), 42, 63–74. *Fong Yue Ting v. United States*, 149 U.S. 698 (1893); Hester, *Deportation*, 5–19, 30–34, 68–81; Hyung-chan Kim, *A Legal History of Asian Americans, 1790–1990* (Westport, CT: Greenwood, 1994), 118, 155–156.

12. Maxine Hong Kingston, *The Fifth Book of Peace* (New York: Vintage, 2003); Lee, *At America's Gates*, 116.

13. Kwong and Miščević, *Chinese America*, 225. They explain in a footnote that these numbers differ from those cited by Ngai in *Impossible Subjects* because they use a later Department of Justice report, which revises the numbers from INS reports upward: Chen, cited in Lee, *At America's Gates*, 95, 191.

14. Some description of this can be found, for example, in Sarah M. Griffith, *The Fight for Asian American Civil Rights: Liberal Protestant Activism, 1900–1950* (Urbana: University of Illinois Press, 2018).

15. Gabriel J. Chin, "'A Chinaman's Chance' in Court: Asian Pacific Americans and Racial Rules of Evidence," *University of California, Irvine, Law Review* 3, no. 4 (December 2013): 96; Gotanda, "'Other Non-Whites' in American Legal History," 359–360; Hester, *Deportation*, 18, 23; *People v. Hall*, 4 Cal. 399 (1854). For details on Chinese labor in the South, see Moon-Ho Jung, *Coolies and Cane: Race, Labor, and Sugar in the Age of Emancipation* (Baltimore: Johns Hopkins University Press, 2006); Lew-Williams, *The Chinese Must Go*, 26–27, 32.

16. Gotanda, "'Other Non-Whites' in American Legal History," 361; Kim, *A Legal History of Asian Americans*, 95–96, 126–127; Parker, *Making Foreigners*, 161–162; *Yick Wo v. Hopkins* 118 U.S. 356 (1886).

17. *Brown v. Board of Education of Topeka, Kansas* 347 U.S. 483 (1954); *Loving v. Virginia*, 388 U.S. 1 (1967); *Shelley v. Kraemer* 334 U.S. 1 (1948).

18. *Final Report of the Administrator of the Refugee Relief Act of 1953, as Amended*

(Washington, DC: U.S. Government Printing Office, 1958), 76–77; Xiaojian Zhao, *Remaking Chinese America: Immigration, Family, and Community, 1940–1965* (New Brunswick, NJ: Rutgers University Press, 2002), 1–3.

19. *Yellow Claw*, nos. 1–4 (October 1956, December 1956, February 1957, April 1957), Atlas Comics, New York. The character of the FBI agent, Jimmy Woo, is still in continuity in the Marvel Cinematic Universe, played by Randall Park in *The Ant-Man and the Wasp* (2018): I am indebted to Jeremy Dauber for the reference and Louie Rivers III for help with placing Woo's character. Richard LaPiere to Pardee Lowe, letter, January 3, 1941, and others, folder MSS *The Golden Mountains*, box 335, PL.

20. Works mentioned are Buwei Yang Chao, *Autobiography of a Chinese Woman*, trans. Yuen Ren Chao (New York: John Day, 1947); Buwei Yang Chao, *How to Cook and Eat in Chinese* (New York: John Day, 1945); Helena Kuo, *I've Come a Long Way* (New York: D. Appleton, 1942); Mai-mai Sze, *Echo of a Cry, A Story Which Began in China* (New York: Harcourt, Brace, 1945).

21. This division roughly follows Hsu's division among "front-gate," "side-door," and "back-door" immigrants. This classification and biographical information on C. Y. Lee is in Hsu, *The Good Immigrants*, 5, 104. Lin Yutang's use of Lowe is mentioned in Richard Jean So, "Collaboration and Translation: Lin Yutang and the Archive of Asian American Literature," *Modern Fiction Studies* 56, no. 1 (2010): 56–57.

22. Rocío G. Davis, *Relative Histories: Mediating History in Asian American Family Memoirs* (Honolulu: University of Hawai'i Press, 2011), 2.

23. Wu, *The Color of Success*, 4–5. See also Ali Behdad, *A Forgetful Nation: On Immigration and Cultural Identity in the United States* (Durham, NC: Duke University Press, 2005); Christina Klein, *Cold War Orientalism: Asia in the Middlebrow Imagination, 1945–1961* (Berkeley: University of California Press, 2003).

24. Lisa Lowe, *Immigrant Acts: On Asian American Cultural Politics* (Durham, NC: Duke University Press, 1996).

25. Richard Harvey Brown and Beth Davis-Brown, "The Making of Memory: The Politics of Archives, Libraries and Museums in the Construction of National Consciousness," *History of the Human Sciences* 11, no. 4 (1998): 18–19; Jacques Derrida, "Archive Fever: A Freudian Impression," *Diacritics* 25, no. 2 (1995): 9–63.

26. Brown and Davis-Brown, "The Making of Memory," 30; Gayatri Chakravorty Spivak, "The Rani of Sirmur: An Essay in Reading the Archives," *History and Theory* 24, no. 3 (1985): 271.

27. See Daniel Marshall, Kevin P. Murphy, and Zeb Tortorici, "Queering Archives: Historical Unravelings," *Radical History Review* 120 (Fall 2014): 1–2.

28. Derrida, "Archive Fever," 51. Frank Abe, referring to Chin's archived transcripts, notes that this is a fictionalized story that supports Chin's own politics. The transcript instead suggests that Dorothy Okada had written to UCLA, gotten no response, and then thrown away the papers. I cite the story here because of its imaginative importance to the narrative of Asian American literature. See Frank Abe, "Review: 'The Great Japanese American Novel,'" *Amerasia* 30, no. 2 (2004): 111; Colleen Lye, "Reading for Asian American Literature," in *A Companion to American Literary Studies*, edited by Caroline F. Levander and Robert S. Levine (Malden, MA: John Wiley and Sons, 2011), 485–487; Min Song, *The Children of 1965: On Writing, and Not Writing, as an Asian American* (Durham, NC: Duke University Press, 2013), 60.

29. Edward W. Said, *Culture and Imperialism* (New York: Vintage, 1994), 51.

30. So, "Collaboration and Translation," 59.

31. Davis, *Relative Histories*, 3.

CHAPTER 1

1. Maxine Hong Kingston, *The Woman Warrior: Memoirs of a Girlhood among Ghosts*, repr. ed. (New York: Vintage International, 1989), 184–185. Hereafter, page numbers from this work are cited parenthetically in the text.

2. Peter Kwong and Dušanka Miščević, *Chinese America: The Untold Story of America's Oldest New Community* (New York: New Press, 2005), 206–207; Xiaojian Zhao, *The New Chinese America: Class, Economy, and Social Hierarchy* (New Brunswick, NJ: Rutgers University Press, 2010), 74, 81.

3. In a report in the same year, the INS wrote, "The purpose of the program was two-fold. The humanitarian aspect was to free these otherwise law-abiding persons from the constant pressure of living with a lie. At the time, the Service wanted to terminate permanently the machinery which facilitated a steady influx of illegal aliens." In other words, the program ostensibly fulfilled two purposes, one humanitarian and one practical, particularly in its language about those of "tender years": U.S. Department of Labor, *Annual Report of the Immigration and Naturalization Service* (Washington, DC: U.S. Government Printing Office, 1956–1957), 13, accessed via HathiTrust, June 12, 2017, emphasis added. These reports cover the fiscal year. See also Mae M. Ngai, *Impossible Subjects: Illegal Aliens and the Making of Modern America* (Princeton, NJ: Princeton University Press, 2004), 12, 17, 210, 222; Office of the Attorney General, ed., *Annual Report of the Attorney General of the United States* (Washington, DC: U.S. Government Printing Office, 1957), 442; Xiaojian Zhao, *Remaking Chinese America: Immigration, Family, and Community, 1940–1965* (New Brunswick, NJ: Rutgers University Press, 2002), 160–162.

4. The conversation runs:

> MHK [Kingston]: Well, I was just a child, but I had a sense that people did not trust that any Exclusion Acts were lifted. There was not a sudden relief, as if now we could bring more relatives from China. There continued to be a figuring out of how to get around immigration laws. People still thought about how to do that. Also, throughout my parents' lives, there was worry about how they would protect themselves from being deported. Every once in a while there would be some announcement from the government that it was all right to come forward and apply for certain papers or apply for certain benefits. My parents *never* came forward. Everybody in town would say 'You do that and they're going to get you and you're going to get deported.'
>
> JSW [Jade Snow Wong]: Somebody's in trouble.
>
> PRHC [moderator]: So nobody ever came forward?
>
> MHK: Nobody came forward! I think there was never a sense that we could trust any Exclusion Acts being changed.

("You Just Have to Burn to Get Your Message Out: A Conversation with JSW and Maxine Hong Kingston" [Transcript of 2005 Pacific Regional Humanities Center event] 23, box 4, folder 35, Other Writings and Notes series, JSW. See also Fae Myenne Ng, "My Confusion Program, an Inheritance of Indecision," *Ploughshares* 35, nos. 2–3 [2009]: 117, 119.)

5. Fanny Butcher, "The Literary Spotlight," *Chicago Daily Tribune*, July 29, 1951, H2.

6. U.S. Department of Labor, *Annual Report of the Immigration and Naturalization Service* (Washington, DC: U.S. Government Printing Office, 1950–1951), 46–47, accessed June 12, 2017, https://catalog.hathitrust.org/Record/000546059.

7. Jade Snow Wong, *Fifth Chinese Daughter*, repr. ed. (Seattle: University of Washington Press, 1993). Hereafter, page numbers from this work are cited parenthetically in the text.

8. Amy Ling, *Between Worlds: Women Writers of Chinese Ancestry* (New York: Pergamon, 1990), 120. See also Leslie Bow, *Betrayal and Other Acts of Subversion: Feminism, Sexual Politics, Asian American Women's Literature* (Princeton, NJ: Princeton University Press, 2001), chap. 3.

9. Typescript of *Chinese American*, 258, folder CBP_014 2003 Manuscript, *Chinese American: Burden and Prize* (CBP) Series, JSW.

10. Ibid., 259. See also transcript of interview by Shan Te-hsing, San Francisco, August 11, 1995, folder SPT 004, Scripts and Transcripts Series, JSW.

11. Bow, *Betrayal and Other Acts of Subversion*, 84; Bow, "Introduction: Jade Snow Wong's Giftshop and Travel Service," *Fifth Chinese Daughter* (Seattle: University of Washington Press, 2019), xxiii; Judy Yung to Wong, letter, August 28, 1997, and Wong to Yung, letter, September 25, 1997, folder COR_073, Correspondence Series, JSW; typescript of *Chinese America* marked original ms., undated, 103, folder CBP_004, CBP series, JSW.

12. Jade Snow Wong, "Exclusion [Letter to the Editor]," *San Francisco Chronicle*, June 21, 1943, clipping in box 6, Scrapbook Series, JSW.

13. George Sessions Perry, "The Wongs," *Saturday Evening Post*, October 16, 1948. Hereafter, page numbers from this article are cited parenthetically in the text. Wu more heavily stresses the Americanizing narrative in her interpretation of this piece in Ellen D. Wu, *The Color of Success: Asian Americans and the Origins of the Model Minority* (Princeton, NJ: Princeton University Press, 2014), 126. The list of families is from the compilation volume by George Sessions Perry, *Families of America; Where They Come From and How They Live* (New York: Whittlesey House/McGraw-Hill, 1949), 137.

14. Jade Snow Wong, "Daddy," *Common Ground* (Winter 1945): 25–29; Jade Snow Wong, "Jon," *Common Ground* (Autumn 1945): 39–44. For more on these early articles, see also Jaime Cleland, "Breaking the 'Chinese Habit': Jade Snow Wong in First Person," *MELUS* 37, no. 1 (2012): 61–82. These essays commence her attention to humor and a highly united family. However, by focusing on eponymous individuals in two family-focused essays, "Daddy" and "Jon," she avoided the problem of explaining her family dynamics or immigration, though the entire family is a clear presence in each.

15. "Interview with Esther Wong, Native-born Chinese, San Francisco, California, 1924 July 1," Survey of Race Relations Records, box 28, Hoover Institution Archives, Stanford University, Stanford, CA. The original is available online through the digitized collection as of December 2016 (see https://purl.stanford.edu/cb681cm3403).

The survey was carried out from 1905 to 1934, directed by sociologists at Stanford University and the University of Chicago and with funding from the Institute of Social and Religious Research: finding aid, Register of the Survey of Race Relations Records, Hoover Institution Archives, Online Archives of California, http://www.oac.cdlib.org/findaid/ark:/13030/tf2q2n98s9/entire_text.

Esther and Virginia returned to the United States in 1937 when they were "bombed out of their home in Canton," Wong mentions (112). Sometime in this period, she married (presumably a man of her own choice), and as of 1948, according to Perry, "The Wongs," 107, she had a grocery store with her husband in Oakland. See also Judy Yung, *Unbound Voices: A Documentary History of Chinese Women in San Francisco* (Berkeley: University of California Press, 1999), 299–305; Judy Yung, *Unbound Feet: A Social History of Chinese Women in San Francisco* (Berkeley: University of California Press, 1995), 121.

16. Typescript bound draft of *No Chinese Stranger*, 36, folder NCS_006, *No Chinese Stranger* (NCS) Series, JSW; Wong to George and Claire [Perry], letter (typescript copy), August 13, 1948, folder COR_036 Personal Correspondence 1947–50, COR Series, JSW.

Jade Snow Wong, *No Chinese Stranger* (New York: Harper and Row, 1975), 4. Hereafter, page numbers from this work are cited parenthetically in the text.

17. Claire Perry to Connie [Wong], letter, August 9, 1948, 2, folder COR_036 Personal Correspondence 1947–50, COR Series, JSW.

18. Wong to Stuart and Esther Strong, letter, March 18, 1948, April 9, 1948, folder COR_036, COR Series, JSW.

19. Federal census records for this period are not yet available. In California records, a John Wong's birth appears in 1942, around the correct time, with a mother whose maiden name is Shee, quite possibly a mistaken listing for Jang Shee. No information is given about the father in this and other similar records of the period. Ancestry.com, *California Birth Index*, 1905–1995 (Provo, UT: Ancestry.com Operations, 2005).

20. Wong to Harriet [Bradley Tegart], letter (typescript copy), September 26, 1944, folder 39, *Fifth Chinese Daughter* (FCD) Correspondence, COR Series, JSW

21. "Mlle Merit Awards," *Mademoiselle*, December 30, 1948, 97; "California '49ers," *House & Garden*, July 1949: 46.

22. Elizabeth Lawrence to Connie [Wong], letter, February 25, 1947, 1, folder 29, FCD Correspondence, COR Series, JSW.

23. Richard J. Walsh to Y. T. [Lin Yutang], letter, June 29, 1948, 1, box 258, folder 10, JDP. The information about Lawrence is in Al Silverman, *The Time of Their Lives: The Golden Age of Great American Book Publishers, Their Editors, and Authors* (New York: Truman Talley, 2008). Lawrence tried to mold another Asian writer into a "marketable mold," writing to Santha Rama Rau to emphasize the "woman angle" when Rau wrote to her for guidance on how to shape a book: Antoinette M. Burton, *The Postcolonial Careers of Santha Rama Rau* (Durham, NC: Duke University Press, 2007), 8. I refer to Cold War orientalism, as outlined in Christina Klein, *Cold War Orientalism: Asia in the Middlebrow Imagination, 1945–1961* (Berkeley: University of California Press, 2003).

24. Elaine H. Kim, *Asian American Literature: An Introduction to the Writings and Their Social Context* (Philadelphia: Temple University Press, 1982). This ought not to be construed as a disparaging comment from Wong. Wong's relationship with Lawrence was extremely strong and personally friendly, and she relied strongly on Lawrence's suggestions. One key aspect of the writing for which Wong has been critiqued was entirely her own; correspondence reveals that the use of third person was at her own insistence. Elizabeth Lawrence to Jade Snow or Connie [Wong], letters, January 9, 1946, November 21, 1949; Wong to Lawrence, letter, November 27, 1949, folder 29, FCD Correspondence, COR Series, JSW; undated typescript draft of *Fifth Chinese Daughter*, folder 007, FCD Series, JSW. Cuts are marked on various pages—notably, in chapters 14 and 15.

25. For examples of her post-publication publicity, see Butcher, "The Literary Spotlight"; Charles Poore, "Books of *The Times*," *New York Times*, December 13, 1950; Joyce Geary, "A Chinese Girl's World," *New York Times*, October 29, 1950; Clara Ingram Judson, "The Colorful Home Life of Chinese Girl," *Daily Chicago Tribune*, October 1, 1950; Joseph Henry Jackson, "Bookman's Notebook," *Los Angeles Times*, September 21, 1950. The quote is from *This is San Francisco*, KCBS radio, transcript, 2, September 25, 1950, folder COR_083, COR Series, JSW. Cleland suggests that this transition from the very traditional Chinese father of *Fifth Chinese Daughter* can better be viewed as Wong returning to the more liberal earlier depiction of her father in "Daddy": Cleland, "Breaking the 'Chinese Habit.'" However, "Daddy" portrays a decidedly comic figure.

26. "U.S. Inquiry Hurts Chinatown Trade; $100,000 Weekly Loss Laid to Fear in Passport Check," *New York Times*, March 17, 1956; Everett F. Drumright, "Report on the Problem of Passport Fraud at Hong Kong," *Foreign Service Dispatch* 931 (December 9,

1955): 1–89; Everett F. Drumright, "Proposals to Better Cope with Problem of Fraud at Hong Kong," *Foreign Service Dispatch* 942 (December 13, 1955): 1–6; Wolfgang Saxon, "Everett F. Drumright, 86, Is Dead; Envoy to Taiwan in Tense Period," *New York Times*, April 27, 1993, accessed August 17, 2017, http://www.nytimes.com/1993/04/27/obituaries/everett-f-drumright-86-is-dead-envoy-to-taiwan-in-tense-period.html.

27. "H[ong] K[ong] Consul General Charges Passport Fraud Racket," *Chinese World*, March 5, 1956, 1; "Bureau of Far Eastern Affairs Testimony," January 13, 1956, in *Departments of State and Justice, Judiciary, and Related Agencies, Appropriations for 1957: Hearings before the Subcommittee of the Committee on Appropriations, House of Representatives, 84th Congress, Second Session* (Washington, DC: U.S. Government Printing Office, 1956), 219, 226. See also "Bureau of Security and Consular Affairs," February 12, 1957, *Departments of State and Justice, the Judiciary, and Related Agencies Appropriations for 1958: Hearings before the Subcommittee of the Committee on Appropriations, House of Representative, 85th Congress, First Session* (Washington, DC: U.S. Government Printing Office, 1957). The previous year's testimony, when funding was given for eight more employees to deal with fraud in Hong Kong, is quoted on pages 276, 287, and 304. Most testimony for 1957 is given by Scott McLeod and then by Frances G. Knight.

28. Quoted in Charlotte Brooks, *Between Mao and McCarthy: Chinese American Politics in the Cold War Years* (Chicago: University of Chicago Press, 2015), 76. See also ibid., 113–114, 149, 151; "Dai-ming Lee is Dead," *New York Times*, March 20, 1961.

29. Dai-Ming Lee, "The Mountain Labored and Brought Forth a Mouse," *Chinese World*, May 9, 1956, 1; "Commentary on Drumright Report Published by *Chinese World*," *Chinese World*, May 28, 1956, 1.

30. Dai-Ming Lee, "The Sins of Fathers and Grandfathers," *Chinese World*, April 19, 1956, 1; Dai-Ming Lee, "Drumright's Exclusion Laws," *Chinese World*, April 28, 1956, 1.

31. The biographical information is from a number of sources. *Ly Shew v. Acheson*, 110 F. Supp. 50. (1953); *Ly Shew v. Dulles*, 219 F.2d. 413 (1954). *Customs Passenger Lists of Vessels Arriving at San Francisco*, NAI no. 4478116, Records of the Immigration and Naturalization Service, 1787–2004, Record Group (RG) 85, U.S. National Archives, Washington, DC, accessed via Ancestry.com. "Chow Faces Quiz by U.S. Grand Jury," *Oakland Tribune*, September 27, 1956. Entries show the children in 1952: *Passenger Lists of Vessels Arriving at San Francisco, California*, NAI no. 4498993, Records of the Immigration and Naturalization Service, 1787–2004, RG 85, U.S. National Archives, Washington, DC, accessed via Ancestry.com; *California, Passenger and Crew Lists, 1882–1959* (Provo, UT: Ancestry.com Operations, 2008).

32. "Albert Chow to Appear before Grand Jury," *Chinese World*, September 28, 1956, 1; "Chow Faces Quiz by U.S. Grand Jury." In both articles, Ly Shew's son Ly Gway Sang appears as an addendum to the interrogation of Chow, a former president of the Six Companies, who had also been subpoenaed by the grand jury: "Immigration Case Cook Talks; Freed," *Chinese World*, September 29, 1956, 1.

"Immigration Law Violations Admitted," *Oakland Tribune*, January 20, 1957, 6A. Ly Shue Ngor is clearly named in one of the court cases as entering in 1947: *Ly Shew v. Dulles*; "Illegal Arrest Charged in Passport Case," *Chinese World*, November 23, 1956, 1.

33. "Mercy for Mother in Alien Case," *Oakland Tribune*, February 8, 1957, 1; "U.S. Passport Fraud Figure Hangs Himself," *Oakland Tribune*, January 29, 1957, 1; Dai-Ming Lee, "Deportations to Red China," *Chinese World*, January 30, 1957, 1.

34. Lee, "Deportations to Red China." See also "How Thousands of Chinese Get into U.S. Told: Hong Kong Racketeers Paid $3,000 a Head," *Chicago Daily Tribune*, March 24, 1956, 3. The Supreme Court ruled against the petitioners Leng May Ma, in *Leng*

May Ma v. Barber (1958), and the Quan family, in the companion case *Rogers v. Quan*, 357 U.S. 193 (1958), in 5–4 decisions from which Chief Justice Earl Warren and Justices William Douglas, Hugo Black, and William Brennan dissented. Clark's opinions for the court rested on statutory grounds, specifying that Ma had not technically gained entry and therefore was not eligible for the benefactions of law due to those who had entered the United States. Douglas's dissent on behalf of all four preferred to read the "spirit of the law" less "narrowly" and focused heavily on the question of "Communist China—a country which the Immigration and Naturalization Service itself has told us is inhospitable to refugees." In the footnotes, the opinion cites an INS report on "Red China" and the unknown nature of its "persecution" of individuals in China. Douglas concludes that "this case is one of those where the Attorney General is authorized to save a human being from persecution in a Communist land": *Leng May Ma v. Barber*; *Rogers v. Quan*; Ngai, *Impossible Subjects*, 23, 221.

35. *Application of the Presidents, Secretaries, Treasurers, and Custodians of Records of Certain Chinese Family Benevolent and District Associations to Quash Grand Jury Subpoenas duces tecum*, 19 FRD 97 (1956), 101–102.

36. "Six Companies Protests Calumny Heaped on Entire Chinese Community: Inference of Wholesale Wrongdong [*sic*] Resented by Chinese Organizations," *Chinese World*, March 16, 1956, 1.

37. "60 New York Chinese Groups Protest 'Blanket' Probe of S[an] F[rancisco] Organizations," *Chinese World*, March 13, 1956, 1; "Complete Text of Statement Issued by Chinese Confab in Washington," *Chinese World*, March 12, 1957, 1; "Text of Resolutions Adopted by Chinese Conference in Washington," *Chinese World*, March 13, 1957, 1; "More on D.C. Conference Resolutions," *Chinese World*, March 15, 1957, 1; "More on D.C. Conference," *Chinese World*, March 14, 1957, 1.

38. Dai-Ming Lee, "Press Acclaims Judicial Decision on Subpoenas," *Chinese World*, March 27, 1956, 1. I am indebted to Jared Brown-Rabinowitz for his advice on the historical case law.

39. "Six Companies Protests Calumny Heaped on Entire Chinese Community."

40. Ibid.; Jade Snow Wong, "How to Get the Best Chinese Food," *Holiday*, vol. 18, October 1955, 67, 133.

41. *Application of the Presidents*, 102.

42. Drumright, "Report on the Problem of Passport Fraud at Hong Kong," 2, 4–5, 7. Foster Rhea Dulles was a well-published historian who wrote multiple books on U.S. relations with China and Japan, as well as on labor and the Civil Rights Commission.

43. Ibid., 7, 88.

44. Lee, "The Sins of Fathers and Grandfathers"; "Drumright's Amazing Charges," *Chinese World*, April 20, 1956, 1; "History of Chinese Six Companies in San Francisco Reviewed," *Chinese World*, March 17, 1956, 1.

45. Lee, "Drumright's Exclusion Laws"; Dai-Ming Lee, "Drumright Indicts an Entire Race," *Chinese World*, April 29, 1956, 1; Dai-Ming Lee, "Drumright Report Lacks Accuracy, Objectivity," *Chinese World*, May 4, 1956, 1.

46. Lee, "Drumright Report Lacks Accuracy, Objectivity."

47. *United States ex rel. Lee Kum Hoy et al. v. Murff*, 355 U.S. 169 (1957); *United States ex rel. Lee Kum Hoy v. Murff*, oral argument transcript, accessed August 16, 2017, https://www.oyez.org/cases/1957/32. For further discussion, see chapter 3 in this volume. See also Lloyd H. Burke et al., *Appellee's Brief in Ly Shew v. Dulles 9th Cir. (1953)* (San Francisco: Pernau-Walsh [1953?]); *Ly Shew v. Acheson* (1953).

48. Kingston, *The Woman Warrior*, 115. Hereafter, page numbers from this work are cited parenthetically in the text.

49. Michael Bérubé, "Disability and Narrative," *PMLA* 120, no. 2 (2005): 571. From the Immigration and Nationality Act, Public Law 82-414, 66 Stat. 163 (1952), 182. Thereafter followed the insane, psychopathic, epileptic, mentally defective, addicts, alcoholics, the diseased, those unable to support themselves, and many more, including stowaways, those denied visas, and political troublemakers.

CHAPTER 2

1. Rose Hum Lee, *The Chinese in the United States of America* (Hong Kong: Hong Kong University Press, 1960), 185.

2. Elaine Tyler May, *Homeward Bound: American Families in the Cold War Era* (New York: Basic, 1988), 3, 21, 208; Stephanie Coontz, *The Way We Never Were: American Families and the Nostalgia Trap* (New York: Basic, 1992), 28.

3. Daniel Patrick Moynihan, *The Negro Family: The Case for National Action*, U.S. Department of Labor (Washington, DC: U.S. Government Printing Office, 1965), digitized without original page numbers or charts on the Department of Labor's website, accessed August 16, 2017, https://www.dol.gov/oasam/programs/history/webid-meynihan.htm [*sic*], emphasis added. See also Hortense J. Spillers, "Mama's Baby, Papa's Maybe: An American Grammar Book," *Diacritics* 17, no. 2 (1987): 64–81.

4. "Success Story of One Minority Group in U.S.," *U.S. News and World Report*, December 26, 1966, 73–74, 76; William Petersen, "Success Story, Japanese-American Style," *New York Times Magazine*, January 9, 1966, 41; Myron Cohen, *House United, House Divided: The Chinese Family in Taiwan* (New York: Columbia University Press, 1976), 228–229.

5. Chiou-ling Yeh, "'A Saga of Democracy': Toy Len Goon, American Mother of the Year, and the Cultural Cold War," *Pacific Historical Review* 81, no. 3 (August 2012): 446–447; Jacqueline Field, "Mud Silk and the Chinese Laundress: From the South China Silk Industry to Mud Silk Suits in Maine," *Textile History* 45, no. 2 (November 2014): 234–260.

6. Ellen D. Wu, *The Color of Success: Asian Americans and the Origins of the Model Minority* (Princeton, NJ: Princeton University Press, 2014), 186–187, 200–201. See also Peter Kwong, *Chinatown, New York: Labor and Politics, 1930–1950* (New York: New Press, 2001), 147; S. W. Kung, *Chinese in American Life: Some Aspects of Their History, Status, Problems, and Contributions* (Seattle: University of Washington Press, 1962), 207–210; Betty Lee Sung, *Mountain of Gold: The Story of the Chinese in America* (New York: Macmillan, 1967), 186; Jade Snow Wong, "My Chinatown," *Forum* (San Francisco Junior College), Spring 1940, 37–39, copy found in folder OWN_082, Other Writings and Notes Series, JSW.

7. Erin Ninh, "Model Minority Narratives and the Asian American Family," in *The Cambridge Companion to Asian American Literature*, edited by Daniel Y. Kim and Crystal Parikh (New York, NY: Cambridge University Press, 2015), 114. Ninh also discusses the family as a site of capitalist enterprise in *Ingratitude: The Debt-Bound Daughter in Asian American Literature* (New York: New York University Press, 2011).

8. Robert G. Lee, *Orientals: Asian Americans in Popular Culture* (Philadelphia: Temple University Press, 1999); Colleen Lye, *America's Asia: Racial Form and American Literature, 1893–1945* (Princeton, NJ: Princeton University Press, 2005); Elaine Tyler May, *Great Expectations: Marriage and Divorce in Post-Victorian America* (Chicago: University of Chicago Press, 1980), 22.

9. See Moon-Ho Jung, *Coolies and Cane: Race, Labor, and Sugar in the Age of Emancipation* (Baltimore: Johns Hopkins University Press, 2006). Jung's discussion also addresses the question of voluntary migration, so that Asians have been more recently contextualized as part of the American dream as hardworking, willing immigrants, while at the time coolies were first a racial category, then a legal category used to differentiate them from slaves and "real" immigrants—that is, the more desirably raced immigrants from Europe.

10. Erika Lee, *At America's Gates: The Exclusion Era, 1882–1943* (Chapel Hill: University of North Carolina Press, 2003), 97.

11. Supreme Court Justice Frank Murphy later cited such prejudices in his dissenting opinion in *Korematsu v. United States*, 323 U.S. 214 (1944).

12. Frank Chin, Shawn Wong, Jeffery Paul Chan, and Lawson Fusao Inada, "An Introduction to Chinese and Japanese Literature," in *Aiiieeeee! An Anthology of Asian American Writers*, edited by Frank Chin, Shawn Wong, Jeffery Paul Chan, and Lawson Fusao Inada (New York: Mentor, 1991), 17. The term "mutilated family" was coined by Charles F. Marden in *Minorities in American Society* (New York: American Book, 1952). See also Sung, *Mountain of Gold*, 156, 186.

13. Everett F. Drumright, "Report on the Problem of Passport Fraud at Hong Kong," *Foreign Service Dispatch* 931 (December 9, 1955), 48.

14. I compiled and calculated the demographic information from the 1950 Census of Population, vol. 4, Special Reports, sec. 6, "Nonwhite Population by Race," tables 5 and 12; 1960 Census of the Population, vol. 2, Subject Reports, pt. 1C, "Nonwhite Population by Race," table 12.

15. Cindy I-fen Cheng, *Citizens of Asian America: Democracy and Race during the Cold War* (New York: New York University Press, 2013), 72–73; Nayan Shah, *Contagious Divides: Epidemics and Race in San Francisco's Chinatown* (Berkeley: University of California Press, 2001), 42, 234.

16. Cheng, *Citizens of Asian America*, 78; original ms. in red folder, 293, folder CBP_004, CBP Series, JSW.

17. *Moore v. City of East Cleveland, Ohio*, 431 U.S. 494 (1977).

18. "You Just Have to Burn to Get Your Message Out: A Conversation with JSW and Maxine Hong Kingston" (Transcript of 2005 Pacific Regional Humanities Center event), 3, box 4, folder 35, Other Writings and Notes Series, JSW. I have silently corrected the spelling of Anna May Wong's name in the transcript.

19. Con[stance] [Wong] to Harriet [Bradley Tegart], letter, February 3, 1942, folder COR_039, COR series, JSW.

20. Ibid.

21. Ibid.

22. Lin Yutang, *Chinatown Family* (New Brunswick, NJ: Rutgers University Press, 2007), 55. Hereafter, page numbers from this work are cited parenthetically in the text. See also Katherine A. Karle, "Flamingos and Bison: Balance in Chinatown Family," *MELUS* 15, no. 2 (1988): 95.

23. May, *Homeward Bound*, 88.

24. [Richard J. Walsh] to Y. T. [Lin Yutang], letter, May 9, 1948, box 258, folder 10, JDP. Much of the correspondence is preserved in typescript carbons that lack Walsh's signature.

25. [Richard J. Walsh] to Y. T. [Lin Yutang], letter, May 26, 1948, box 258, folder 10, JDP.

26. Ibid. Walsh's leadership on the exclusion repeal can be seen in numerous contemporary articles, such as "Committee to Fight Exclusion of Chinese," *New York Times*, July 7, 1943.

27. Lin Yutang to Dick [Richard J. Walsh], letter, May 27, 1948, folder 10, box 258, JDP.

28. Lin Yutang to Dick [Richard J. Walsh], attachment to letter, June 16, 1948, folder 10, box 258, JDP. I am obligated here to correct some of Richard Jean So's critique, which is based on the drafts and misses that this passage was largely composed by Walsh and not by Lin, which complicates So's thoughts on this entangled and aggressive editing. So makes the suggestion, based on an examination of the drafts, that the last line of this passage, "But the thing was done," is Lin's reflection of Walsh's edict that he must insert an explanation of the Fong family's immigration, "But it has to be done" (Richard Jean So, "Collaboration and Translation: Lin Yutang and the Archive of Asian American Literature," *Modern Fiction Studies* 56, no. 1 [Spring 2010]: 47). Instead, however, we might see this as Walsh echoing himself, sending Lin a passage that is just as emphatic as his correspondence.

29. R. J. Walsh to M. Minton (Mel), memorandum, July 5, 1948, folder 10, box 258, JDP. Walsh called the book "third-rate." Negative commentary appears elsewhere: see Betty Harold to Mr. Walsh Sr., memorandum, July 12, 1948, Cecil Goldbeck to [Walsh?], letter, [July 1948], both in folder 10, box 258, JDP. Goldbeck wrote, "It's inferior Lin Yutang." Lin Yutang to Dick [Richard J. Walsh], letter, June 16, 1948, folder 10, box 258, JDP.

30. Walsh to Lin, May 26, 1948. The scandal he spoke of is covered in "Passport Sale Charted: Philadelphia Jury indicts Two Former U.S. Commissioners," *New York Times*, April 15, 1948, 16.

31. Lin to [Walsh], attachment to letter, June 16, 1948.

32. Henry Koster, dir., *Flower Drum Song*, film, 133 min., Universal Pictures, 1961. The Broadway production was *Flower Drum Song*, by Richard Rodgers and Oscar Hammerstein II, directed by Gene Kelly, which ran at the St. James Theatre in New York from 1958 to 1960.

33. For example, Kenneth Tynan, "Tiny Chinese Minds," *New Yorker*, December 13, 1958, clipping in book 35, 22, RR. Tynan's review is a particularly famous one for its excoriation of the musical, which he called "a world of woozy song," drawing a punning parallel with *The World of Suzie Wong*. See also Michael Grieg, "How the Public Boomed a Hit out of 'Flower Drum Song' despite the Critics," *Highlight Magazine* (*San Francisco Examiner*), August 14, 1960[?], clipping in book 35, 43, RR.

34. Oscar Hammerstein to Dorothy Derry Shaw, letter, December 4, 1958, 2, box 3 of 9 (banker's box), 1958 January–December O. H. Written Notes December folder, OH. The plot element of communism was added back by David Henry Hwang in his 2006 revision of the book of *Flower Drum Song*, and he removed the stress on illegal immigration. See John Farrar to Kenneth Wilson, typescript letter, *Reader's Digest*, February 28, 1956, Lee, Chin Y., General Correspondence 1956–1971 folder, FSG.

35. Typescript draft, undated, 2–6-7, Flower Drum Song Scripts box, Flower Drum Song folder, OH.

36. Fastened script of "The Flower Drum Song," undated, 2–7-28, 2–7-29, (Flower Drum Song) box, OH.

37. Loose typescript page 2–7-4, undated, Flower Drum Song scripts box, (Flower Drum Song) folder, OH.

38. Elinor Hughes, "Final Polishing Job Gives 'Flower Drum' New Luster," *Boston Herald*, November 26, 1958, clipping in book 35, 8, RR. Correspondence with the publishers of the libretto also shows complaints that the script changed from week to week, and the publishers could not set a date for a final print: see various letters and memos from 1959 in box 197, Lee, Chin Y., The Flower Drum Song (play) General, Foreign, Publicity 1949–59 folder, FSG. James Hammerstein's comments are in Stephen Citron, *The Wordsmiths: Oscar Hammerstein 2nd and Alan Jay Lerner* (New York: Oxford University Press, 1995), 297. We can identify who James Hammerstein meant, as his terminology presumably contrasts the "Chinese boy" with the white men who initially played Sammy Fong in yellowface onstage. (The Japanese American actor Jack Soo initially played Frankie, the nightclub host, and only later took over the role of Sammy, which he played in the film.) Putting aside the dismissive tone and objectification of Kenney that this implies, it is ironic that he should remember Ed Kenney as "the Chinese boy" when several critics eagerly pointed out Kenney's mixed race or his non-Chineseness.

39. Mae M. Ngai, *Impossible Subjects: Illegal Aliens and the Making of Modern America* (Princeton, NJ: Princeton University Press, 2004), 56, 58–61, 139, 149.

40. Oscar Hammerstein II and Joseph A. Fields, *Flower Drum Song: A Musical Play* (New York: Farrar, Straus and Cudahy, 1959), 140.

41. Anne Anlin Cheng, *The Melancholy of Race* (Oxford: Oxford University Press, 2000), 43–44. Madam Liang's big number, the famous "Chop Suey," was originally a full-on paean to Americanness entitled "Independence," with garbled words taken from the Declaration of Independence, the Constitution, and the Bill of Rights, as if she were reciting material learned in her citizenship school: see undated pages in Flower Drum Song scripts box, (Old Script Pages and Notes) folder, OH.

42. What is more, Fong's grown-up son Richard, who was entangled in the divorce through the transfer of various assets, had previously been convicted of conspiracy and illegal surgery to perform abortions, as well as being prosecuted for a narcotics charge, during which his father was extorted by an underworld figure: "Fong Wan, Chinese Herbalist," *San Francisco Chronicle*, June 19, 1949, http://www.sfmuseum.org/hist8/fongwan1.html; "Herbalist's Wife Testifies in Divorce Trial," *Chinese World*, March 16, 1956, 2; "'Jane Russell' of Hong Kong Sues Dr. Fong Wan for $175,000 Damages," *Oakland Tribune*, May 21, 1950, 60A; "John Rossi to Face Trial in Fong Wan Bribe Case," *Oakland Tribune*, August 29, 1953, 18D; "Jury Convicts Fong in Illegal Surgery Case," *Oakland Tribune*, August 19, 1953, D3; "Litigious Fong Family Makes Headlines Again," *Chinese World*, March 30, 1956, 2; "Mrs. Fong Is Given Divorce and Million," *Oakland Tribune*, November 24, 1956, 4E.

43. "Ronald Reagan at Charlie Low's Forbidden City," Virtual Museum of the Museum of the City of San Francisco, accessed March 25, 2019, http://www.sfmuseum.org/hist10/forbidcity.html. See also Don Steele's "Going Places" column in the *Oakland Tribune* on September 24, 1949, June 11, 1949 (also the advertisement below for Club Oakland), August 6, 1949, September 24, 1949, and January 24, 1953. Sammy Tong was later known as Sammee Tong and became famous for playing Peter Tong, the valet on television show "Bachelor Father."

44. On Helen and William Fong, see "'Color' Testimony Charged at Concubine Trial," *Chinese World*, July 12, 1956, 2; "U.S. Witnesses Testify at Concubine Trial," *Chinese World*, July 13, 1956, 2; "'Concubine' Trial Defendant Had Change Of Heart," *Chinese World*, July 14, 1956, 2; "'Concubine' Trial Defendant Pleads Guilty," *Chinese World*, July 16, 1956, 2; "Concubine Case Defendant Guilty," *Chinese World*, July 19, 1956, 2; "Concubine Case Woman to Be Deported," *Chinese World*, September 20, 1956,

2. On the Walter Fongs, see "Concubine Case Defendants Arraigned," *Chinese World*, May 25, 1957, 2; "Concubine Case Figure Fined $2,000," *Chinese World*, June 1, 1957, 2.

Lee was not much involved in the adaptation, although he took Fields and Hammerstein on a tour of San Francisco Chinatown. Unfortunately, exactly what they did was not specified anywhere I could find, but we can speculate that Lee took Fields and Hammerstein to various nightclubs that inspired the show. In a column mentioning their visit, Lee mentions that he took Groucho Marx, who had written him a fan letter, to dinner in Chinatown and then to the nightclub Bimbo's, which was not exclusively Chinese but likely featured "Oriental" acts: C. Y. Lee, "Came the Year of the Rooster—Luck Made a 90-Degree Turn," *San Francisco Chronicle*, February 2, 1958, clipping in my personal collection. As is well known, Lee later helped director Gene Kelly scout talent for the shows, which eventually turned Jack Soo, a performer whom Kelly "discovered" at Forbidden City, into a beloved film and television star.

45. Loose typescript pages dated December 23, 1957, 1-1-2, Flower Drum Song Scripts box, Flower Drum Song Miscellaneous Typescripts (Outline and Scenario) folder, OH.

46. Cheng, *The Melancholy of Race*, 46. See also Lynn Spigel, *Make Room for TV: Television and the Family Ideal in Postwar America* (Chicago: University of Chicago Press, 1992).

47. Typescript of *Chinese America*, 258, folder CBP_014 2003 ms., CBP Series, JSW.

48. Original ms. in red folder, 236; typescript of *Chinese America*, 182.

49. Typescript of *Chinese America*, 22.

CHAPTER 3

1. Maxine Hong Kingston, *The Woman Warrior: Memoirs of a Girlhood among Ghosts*, repr. ed. (New York: Vintage International, 1989), 1. Hereafter, page numbers from this work are cited parenthetically in the text.

2. Everett F. Drumright, "Report on the Problem of Passport Fraud at Hong Kong," *Foreign Service Dispatch* 931 (December 9, 1955): 2.

3. *Loving v. Virginia*, 388 U.S. 1 (1967); *Naim v. Naim*, 197 Va. 734 (1955).

4. Drumright, "Report on the Problem of Passport Fraud at Hong Kong," 28, 34, 44–45, 49; Gabriel J. Chin, Cindy Hwang Chiang, and Shirley S. Park, "The Lost *Brown v. Board of Education* of Immigration Law," *North Carolina Law Review* 91, no. 5 (2013): 1675–1676.

5. Drumright, "Report on the Problem of Passport Fraud at Hong Kong," 2; Everett F. Drumright, "Proposals to Better Cope with Problem of Fraud at Hong Kong," *Foreign Service Dispatch* 942 (December 13, 1955): 4–5.

6. Accounts of the Chaplin paternity suit appear in many different places. A few different perspectives are available in Jacqueline R. Braitman and Gerald F. Uelmen, *Justice Stanley Mosk: A Life at the Center of California Politics and Justice* (Jefferson, NC: McFarland, 2012); Joyce Milton, *Tramp: The Life of Charlie Chaplin* (New York: Open Road Media, 2014). A literal textbook example is in Benjamin A. Pierce, *Genetics: A Conceptual Approach* (New York: Macmillan, 2008), which explains the science of the ABO blood testing. Some historians suggest that Chaplin may have bribed or otherwise altered the results of the blood tests, but that is not relevant to the tests' being legally inadmissible to evidence.

7. A. Frederick Harris, "Some Observations on the Un-Uniform Act on Blood Tests to Determine Paternity," *Villanova Law Review* 9, no. 1 (1963): 76, fn. 1, text of the act, sec. 5. However, the presumption of legitimacy could be overturned prior to the act in

cases of impotence, nonaccess (the putative father being absent at the time of conception), or a child who was visibly of a "different race": Robert Johnston, "Public Policy Considerations in Rulings on the Uniform Act on Blood Tests to Determine Paternity," *William and Mary Law Review* 4, no. 2 (1963): 149, 156, 159. Presumption of legitimacy therefore guarded not only marital sanctity but also the racial sanctity of the family unit. Modern versions of this, known as the Uniform Parentage Act, now take into consideration other technologies of genetic testing, as well the many possible options of adoptive or assisted parenthood, such as egg donation, surrogacy, and so on.

8. *Lue v. Brownell*, 220 F.2d. 187 (1955).

9. "Benjamin Gim: A Great Life Remembered," American Immigration Lawyers Association, January 26, 2010, accessed August 18, 2017, http://www.aila.org/about/announcements/in-memoriam/benjamin-gim; *United States ex rel. Lee Kum Hoy v. Murff*, oral argument transcript, accessed August 16, 2017, https://www.oyez.org/cases/1957/32, emphasis added. I have silently corrected the Oyez Project's transcript where obvious errors appear that do not align with the audio recording, which is also available at the site as of the accessed date. See also Chin, Chiang, and Park, "The Lost *Brown v. Board of Education* of Immigration Law," 1693–1694.

10. *United States ex rel. Lee Kum Hoy v. Murff*, oral argument transcript. Lawyers were allowed to speak at much greater length in the 1950s court than they are today. Felix Frankfurter, Earl Warren, and Hugo Black particularly questioned Gim and Davis about Drumright's report, being evidently concerned that it might have been declassified (or not) solely for this case and about whether it was a public enough document for them to take judicial notice of or for the petitioners to have had access to its information: The information about private deliberations is in Chin, Chiang, and Park, "The Lost *Brown v. Board of Education* of Immigration Law," 1684, 1686.

11. Louis Chu, *Eat a Bowl of Tea* (Seattle: University of Washington Press, 1961), 227. Hereafter, page numbers from this work are cited parenthetically in the text.

12. Madeline Yuan-yin Hsu, "Unwrapping Orientalist Constraints: Restoring Homosocial Normativity to Chinese American History," *Amerasia Journal* 29, no. 2 (2003): 229–253.

13. *United States ex rel. Lee Kum Hoy v. Shaughnessy*, 115 F. Supp. 302 (1953).

14. Charlotte Brooks, *Between Mao and McCarthy: Chinese American Politics in the Cold War Years* (Chicago: University of Chicago Press, 2015), 167; Peter Kwong, *Chinatown, New York: Labor and Politics, 1930–1950* (New York: New Press, 2001), 147, 158.

15. See Alan Nadel, *Containment Culture: American Narratives, Postmodernism, and the Containment Age* (Durham, NC: Duke University Press, 1995).

16. Elaine Tyler May, *Homeward Bound: American Families in the Cold War Era* (New York: Basic, 1988), 151–152.

17. Wong's correspondence notes that her younger sister eloped to Reno to marry a white man (an older divorced man with four children) sometime before the publication of *Fifth Chinese Daughter*. The stress had evidently thrown Mama into a depression. Wong to Paul [Wong], December 8, [1947–50?], folder COR_036 Personal Correspondence 1947–1950, COR Series, JSW.

18. D. W. Griffith, dir., *Broken Blossoms*, film, 90 min., United Artists, 1919.

19. Emma Jinhua Teng, *Eurasian: Mixed Identities in the United States, China, and Hong Kong, 1842–1943* (Berkeley: University of California Press, 2013), 15. Kingston later wrote that this wife was from Nicaragua: Maxine Hong Kingston, *I Love a Broad Margin to My Life* (New York: Knopf, 2011), 178, 181.

20. Teng, *Eurasian*, 6, 23–26, 29. Louisa May Alcott, *Rose in Bloom* (Boston: Roberts Brothers, 1876). Accounts of Chinese-black intermarriage can be found in James Loewen, *The Mississippi Chinese: Between Black and White* (Cambridge, MA: Harvard University Press, 1971). See also the fascinating account "A White Woman Compares Marriage to Chinese and Japanese Husbands, circa 1924," in Lon Kurashige and Alice Yang Murray, eds., *Major Problems in Asian American History* (Boston: Houghton Mifflin, 2003), 218–223. Kurashige and Murray's volume contains more historical documentation of the problematic racial positioning of Filipino men in interracial relationships, including "A Filipino Immigrant Is Shocked by Sexual Freedom in the United States, circa 1924" (224–225), "Sociologist Emory Bogardus Analyzes an Anti-Filipino Riot, 1930" (225–228), and "*Time* Magazine Reveals Sexual Basis for Filipino Repatriation, 1936" (228–229), as well as Rhacel Salazar Parrenas's essay "Alliances between White Working-Class Women and Filipino Immigrant Men" (241–246).

21. Teng, *Eurasian*, 44, 86–91. For discussion of the rise of antimiscegenation law, see Peggy Pascoe, *What Comes Naturally: Miscegenation Law and the Making of Race in America* (Oxford: Oxford University Press, 2009), chaps. 2–4. Cable Act, Public Law 67-346, 42 Stat. 1021 (1922). For discussion of Filipino marriage, see Pascoe, *What Comes Naturally*, 152–159, 196; Parrenas, "Alliances between White Working-Class Women and Filipino Immigrant Men," 247. *Perez v. Sharp*, 32 Cal.2d 711 (1948).

22. Pardee Lowe, "Mixed Marriage: A Chinese Husband and American Wife Are Put to Test," *Asia* (January 1937): 7–10. The clippings files are in PL. *Perez v. Sharp*.

23. Lin Yutang, *Chinatown Family* (New Brunswick, NJ: Rutgers University Press, 2007), 45. Hereafter, page numbers from this work are cited parenthetically in the text.

24. Gregory Michael Dorr, "Principled Expediency: Eugenics, *Naim v. Naim*, and the Supreme Court," *American Journal of Legal History* 42, no. 2 (1998): 119–159. Dorr's archival work contains the important elements that I recap here, though he stresses very different threads of the legal and personal aspects of *Naim*.

25. Dorr, "Principled Expediency," 129–130.

26. Ibid.

27. Ibid.

28. Drumright, "Report on the Problem of Passport Fraud at Hong Kong," 71.

29. Dorr, "Principled Expediency," 130, 132.

30. See *Loving v. Virginia*, oral argument transcript, accessed August 18, 2017, https://www.oyez.org/cases/1966/395. Leslie Bow discusses *Naim* in *Partly Colored: Asian Americans and Racial Anomaly in the Segregated South* (New York: New York University Press, 2010), 51–53. The antimiscegenation suit of Henry Oyama and his wife is not to be confused with *Oyama v. California* (1948), the case that struck down aspects of the Alien Land laws in California: see Pascoe, *What Comes Naturally*, 237–238.

31. Anne Anlin Cheng, *The Melancholy of Race* (Oxford: Oxford University Press, 2000), 53.

32. C. Y. Lee, *The Flower Drum Song*, repr. ed. (London: Pan, [1957] 1960), 10. Hereafter, page numbers from this work are cited parenthetically in the text.

33. Typescript draft of review of "*The Flower Drum Song* by Chin Y. Lee," folder COR_096 Curtis Brown, Agent, COR Series, JSW. The published review is Jade Snow Wong, "The Four Loves of Wang Ta," *Saturday Review*, May 25, 1957, 16, 29. Unfortunately for posterity, the dialogue between these two very different chroniclers of Chinatown was carried no further. Even though the final printed form without the critique of morality was relatively mild, Lee was bothered enough by Wong's review to write to his editor about it, a letter that was not preserved. Farrar replied, "About the

Saturday Review—it [*sic*] think it would be very unwise to do anything. I do not hesitate to quarrel with them, and I think this choice of reviewers was probably silly, but a discussion would not, I believe, be good publicity for the book, and I hope you will trust me on this": John Farrar to C. Y. Lee, letter, June 3, 1957, box 197, Lee, Chin Y., The Flower Drum Song Publicity 1957–63 folder, FSG.

34. C. Y. Lee, *Lover's Point* (New York: Farrar, Straus and Cudahy, 1958), 186. Hereafter, page numbers from this work are cited parenthetically in the text.

35. Joshua Logan, dir., *Sayonara*, film, 147 min., Warner Brothers, 1957. See Caroline Chung Simpson, *An Absent Presence: Japanese Americans in Postwar American Culture, 1945–1960* (Durham, NC: Duke University Press, 2001); Naoko Shibusawa, *America's Geisha Ally: Reimagining the Japanese Enemy* (Cambridge, MA: Harvard University Press, 2006). The ACLU's search is described in Pascoe, *What Comes Naturally*, 234.

36. War Brides Act, Public Law 271 59, Stat. 659. Some Asian women were permitted to enter by a separate act in 1946: Rose Hum Lee, *The Chinese in the United States of America* (Hong Kong: Hong Kong University Press, 1960), 18, 218; Xiaojian Zhao, *Remaking Chinese America: Immigration, Family, and Community, 1940–1965* (New Brunswick, NJ: Rutgers University Press, 2002), 80–82; "Airlift Brings War Brides: Orientals Rushing to U.S. to Beat Law Expiration Tuesday," *New York Times*, December 24, 1948, 4; "5 Indicted Here on 'War Bride' Fraud Charges," *Chicago Daily Tribune*, April 28, 1950, 5; "War Brides Getting 'Airlift,'" *New York Times*, December 14, 1948, 14.

37. Cited in Zhao, *Remaking Chinese America*, 148–149.

38. Christina Klein, *Cold War Orientalism: Asia in the Middlebrow Imagination, 1945–1961* (Berkeley: University of California Press, 2003), 175.

39. *United States v. Yin Liu and four other cases*, 190 U.S. 400 (1951); *United States v. Jeu Foon, United States v. Fong Nong, United States v. Gee Gong*, 193 U.S. 117 (1951). Referring to Supreme Court decisions from 1925 and 1900, which followed the aforementioned flurry of post-exclusion cases, the appeals courts held that the Exclusion Act and the Immigration and Naturalization Act of 1924 did not revoke the terms of the Treaty of Commerce and Navigation between the United States and China of 1880, by which merchants and scholars and their households could enter: see *Cheung Sum Shee v. Nagle*, 268 U.S. 336 (1925); *United States v. Mrs. Gue Lim*, 176 U.S. 459 (1900).

40. C. Y. Lee, "Lover's Point: He Is Free," *Chinese World*, August 18, 1956, 2.

41. C. Y. Lee, *The Land of the Golden Mountain* (New York: Meredith, 1967), 227. Hereafter, page numbers from this work are cited parenthetically in the text.

42. The case is discussed in Zhao, *Remaking Chinese America*, 133–134; Sui Sin Far, *Mrs. Spring Fragrance* (Peterborough, ON: Broadview, 2011).

43. "It made the people laugh to hear it," she concludes. Correspondence with her editor suggests that the distinction was instead a cultural/racial one; similarity to the Midas myth impelled its change—implying concern over its lack of distinctive Chineseness. "True, if it weren't for good old Midas the first ending would have been preferable," her editor wrote. Speaking to C. Lok Chua, Kingston could scarcely remember the revision, but mused, "Maybe I switched them because of gender," the king and king's son being male and Ts'ai Yen being female and therefore better suited to a book called *The Woman Warrior*: typescript draft of *The Woman Warrior*, 280–81, box 1, folder 7, MHK; C. Lok Chua, "On Maxine Hong Kingston's Manuscript Revisions of *The Woman Warrior* and *China Men*: An Anecdotal Account," in *On the Legacy of Maxine Hong Kingston: The Mulhouse Book*, edited by Sami Ludwig and Nicoleta Alexoae-Zagni (Zurich: LIT Verlag Munster, 2014), 117; Charles Elliott to Kingston,

letter, October 29, 1975, box 15, folder 6, MHK. Elliott and other readers worried about the "elliptical" quality of the ending: Charles Elliott to Kingston, letter, October 31, 1975, box 15, folder 6, MHK.

CHAPTER 4

1. Rocío G. Davis, *Relative Histories: Mediating History in Asian American Family Memoirs* (Honolulu: University of Hawai'i Press, 2011), 17.

2. Estelle T. Lau, *Paper Families: Identity, Immigration Administration, and Chinese Exclusion* (Durham, NC: Duke University Press, 2006), 125.

3. Timothy P. Fong, *The First Suburban Chinatown: The Remaking of Monterey Park, California* (Philadelphia: Temple University Press, 1994), 28; Xiaojian Zhao, *Remaking Chinese America: Immigration, Family, and Community, 1940–1965* (New Brunswick, NJ: Rutgers University Press, 2002), 189. I calculated the demographic information from the 1970 Census of Population, vol. 2, sec. 1G, Subject Reports: Japanese, Chinese, and Filipinos in the United States, tables 17–18, 22, U.S. Government Printing Office, Washington, DC, 1971. See also Peter Kwong, *The New Chinatown* (New York: Hill and Wang, 1996), 40; Victor G. Nee and Brett de Bary Nee, *Longtime Californ': A Documentary Study of an American Chinatown* (New York: Pantheon, 1973), xxi–xxvii, 253–261.

4. Cindy I-fen Cheng, *Citizens of Asian America: Democracy and Race during the Cold War* (New York: New York University Press, 2013), 205. Brooks, *From Mao to McCarthy*, 123.

5. Zhao, *Remaking Chinese America*, 188–189; Peter Kwong, *Chinatown, New York: Labor and Politics, 1930–1950* (New York: New Press, 2001), 8.

6. King-Kok Cheung, *Articulate Silences: Hisaye Yamamoto, Maxine Hong Kingston, Joy Kogawa* (Ithaca, NY: Cornell University Press, 1993), 15.

7. Diane Simmons, "Appendix: A Conversation with Maxine Hong Kingston," in *Maxine Hong Kingston*, edited by Diane Simmons (New York: Twayne, 1999), 164.

8. Maxine Hong Kingston, *The Woman Warrior: Memoirs of a Girlhood among Ghosts*, repr. ed. (New York: Vintage International, 1989), 183.

9. Frank Chin, "This Is Not an Autobiography," *Genre* 18, no. 2 (1985): 130; Frank Chin, "Come All Ye Asian American Writers of the Real and the Fake," in *The Big Aiiieeeee! An Anthology of Chinese American and Japanese American Literature*, edited by Frank Chin, Shawn Wong, Jeffery Paul Chan, and Lawson Fusao Inada, 3. Ironically, Chin's head-on assertion of history and authenticity has conflicted with his own work to rebuild that history. Chin's narratives send their protagonists out to research history and build solidarity to compensate for what has been lost in white institutions, while his public work to establish (for example) the Manzanar Japanese American incarceration camp pilgrimage has been foundational for Asian American identity.

10. Diane Johnson, "Ghosts," *New York Review of Books*, February 3, 1977, accessed May 28, 2020, https://www.nybooks.com/articles/1977/02/03/ghosts. Johnson is better known for her novels, such as *Persian Nights* and *Le Divorce*. She reviewed *The Woman Warrior* in conversation with N. Scott Momaday's *The Names* and the less remembered *Encounter with an Angry God*, a memoir by Carobeth Laird, an ethnographer of the Chemehuevi, but her focus is very much on Laird and Kingston in the review.

11. Jeffery Paul Chan and Diane Johnson, "The Mysterious West," *New York Review of Books*, April 28, 1977, accessed May 28, 2020, https://www.nybooks.com/arti

cles/1977/04/28/the-mysterious-west; Katheryn M. Fong, "An Open Letter/Review of Maxine Hong Kingston, *The Woman Warrior*," *Bulletin of Concerned Asian Scholars* 9, no. 4 (1977): 67.

12. Fong, "An Open Letter," 68–69. Kingston particularly expressed this view in "Cultural Mis-Readings by American Reviewers," in *Asian and Western Writers in Dialogue: New Cultural Identities*, edited by Guy Amirthanayagam (London: Macmillan, 1982), 55–65.

13. Genny Lim and Judy Yung, "Our Parents Never Told Us," *California Living*, January 23, 1977, 6. Hereafter, page numbers from the work are cited parenthetically in the text. For other accounts, see Mark Lai, Genny Lim, and Judy Yung, eds., *Island: Poetry and History of Chinese Immigrants on Angel Island, 1910–1940* (Seattle: University of Washington Press, 2014); Connie Young Yu, "Rediscovered Voices: Chinese Immigrants and Angel Island," *Amerasia* 4, no. 2 (1977): 123–139.

14. Lau, *Paper Families*, 166, fn. 15.

15. Judy Yung, "Chi Am Corner: New Job, New Challenge," *East/West*, March 10, 1976, clipped in scrapbook 3, Scrapbook Series, JSW, emphasis added. After telling another unrelated, cute anecdote about life in Chinatown, Yung continues, "Back to books, I recommend Jade Snow Wong's *No Chinese Stranger*," although she draws no direct connection between Wong's narrative and her own. Instead, Yung's focus on oral history would eventually culminate in her studies *Unbound Voices: A Documentary History of Chinese Women in San Francisco* (Berkeley: University of California Press, 1999), and *Unbound Feet: A Social History of Chinese Women in San Francisco* (Berkeley: University of California Press, 1995), in which she brought women's stories together to tell the history of San Francisco Chinatown.

16. Erika Lee and Judy Yung, *Angel Island: Immigrant Gateway to America* (Oxford: Oxford University Press, 2010), 301–309.

17. First/second draft (continued), 82–83, box 5, folder 2, MHK.

18. Ibid, 83.

19. Jade Snow Wong, *No Chinese Stranger* (New York: Harper and Row, 1975), 42. Hereafter, page numbers from this work are cited parenthetically in the text.

20. Lim's original translation appears in Lim and Yung, "Our Parents Never Told Us." Another version, presumably in collaboration, appears in Lee and Yung, *Angel Island*, 134–135 (poem and figure 69). Both versions mention the "Mexican exclusion" law(s). I am indebted to Jared Brown-Rabinowitz for his assistance with elucidating the original Chinese.

21. A turn to the food writing that made her early work so popular was fortunately removed by either Wong or her editor at some point but still leaves a very disjointed ending: ms. of *No Chinese Stranger*, folder NCS_002, NCS Series, JSW.

22. Timothy Pfaff, "Talk with Mrs. Kingston," *New York Times Book Review*, June 15 1980, 25.

23. 1st/2nd draft, 59; 1st/2nd draft (continued), 72.

24. David Leiwei Li, "Re-presenting *The Woman Warrior*: An Essay of Interpretive History," in *Critical Essays on Maxine Hong Kingston*, edited by Laura E. Skandera-Trombley (New York: G. K. Hall, 1998), 198–199.

25. "Statement of Plans," Guggenheim application, box 4, folder 1, MHK.

26. Linda Ching Sledge, "Maxine Kingston's *China Men*: The Family Historian as Epic Poet," *MELUS* 7, no. 4 (1980): 4, cited on 22.

27. Notes and early draft, box 4, folder 3; unnumbered handwritten pages and first/second draft, 62–63, in box 5, folder 1, MHK.

28. "A History of Chinese-Americans," 1, 29–30, box 10, folder 1, MHK.

29. Notes and early draft, box 4, folder 3; unnumbered handwritten page; 1st/2nd draft (continued), 229–230. FOB stands for "fresh off the boat," a phrase used (often pejoratively) to describe new immigrants from China and other parts of Asia. "Refugitude" or "refugeetude" are terms originated by Khatharya Um and Vinh Nguyen, respectively, around the same time: see Khatharya Um, *From the Land of Shadows: War, Revolution, and the Making of the Cambodian Diaspora* (New York: New York University Press, 2015); Vinh Nguyen, "Refugeetude: When Does a Refugee Stop Being a Refugee?" *Social Text* 37, no. 2 (2019): 109–131.

30. *Wong Kim Ark v. United States*, 169 U.S. 649 (1898); typescript fragments, 273, 275, 271, box 5, folder 7, MHK, emphasis added.

31. Typescript fragments, 276. Another version appears in "A History of Chinese-Americans," 1–3.

32. Typescript fragments, 277–[278]. A similar version appears in another draft: "The way in which I am not different from other Chinamen is that I am and always have been afraid of being deported to a country which is more alien than any other on earth, the one at the opposite end of the planet. And if not me, then my relatives. It tempers my actions, limits freedom. Makes me want to be inconspicuous, not take leadership in political activities, not to get arrested for any reason, even political demonstrations, to be as conventional as possible but none of this would matter, except that it stops me from reporting well. I listen and am warned when the Chinamen say, 'Don't tell.' Otherwise, what stories, what lost stories": 1st/2nd draft, box 5, folder 3, 232.

33. 5th/6th draft, 219, box 6, folder 4, MHK. Other versions are in box 7, folder 3, 199, and box 6, folder 4, 219, MHK.

34. The case that Kingston refers to, *Mao v. Brownell*, 207 F.2d 142 (1953), deals with a Chinese legal resident in the United States who wanted to return to China and had been temporarily barred. Remittances to the People's Republic of China were prosecuted in the early 1950s under the Trading with the Enemy Act of 1917, as described in Meredith Oyen, *The Diplomacy of Migration: Transnational Lives and the Making of U.S.-Chinese Relations in the Cold War* (Ithaca, NY: Cornell University Press, 2015).

35. Maxine Hong Kingston, "San Francisco's Chinatown: A View from the Other Side of Arnold Genthe's Camera," *American Heritage*, 30, no. 1 (December 1978): 36–47. A transcribed version without photos was available at https://www.americanheritage.com/san-franciscos-chinatown as of the production of this book. Hereafter, page numbers from this work are cited parenthetically in the text. See also Alan G. Artner, "Photography: Genthe's Slighted Contribution Gets a New Exposure," *Chicago Tribune*, December 7, 1975, D10; Will Irwin, *Old Chinatown: A Book of Pictures*, edited by Arnold Genthe (New York: Mitchell Kennerley, 1913); Carleton Jones, "Rare Photos Sold for $27 Now Valued in Five Figures: Baltimore Find Was Made at an Auction for Kitchen Equipment," *Baltimore Sun*, December 12, 1976, SM28-30; Renee Renouf, "'The Chinese in America' Is an Eloquent Tale Told in Photos," *Christian Science Monitor*, December 12, 1980, 19; John Kuo Wei Tchen, ed., *Genthe's Photographs of San Francisco's Old Chinatown* (New York: Dover, 1984).

36. Tchen, *Genthe's Photographs of San Francisco's Old Chinatown*, 33, 39, 41, 45.

37. Folder labeled "History of Chinese Americans" [hand-numbered "page 18"], box 44, MHK.

38. See also Thy Phu, "Spectacles of Citizenship and Civility: Arnold Genthe and the Photography of Chinatown," *Genre* 39, no. 3 (2006): 57–82.

39. Mae M. Ngai, *Impossible Subjects: Illegal Aliens and the Making of Modern America* (Princeton, NJ: Princeton University Press, 2004), 205.

40. Pardee Lowe, *Father and Glorious Descendant* (Boston: Little, Brown, 1943), 3.

41. When Lowe advocates for and attempts to adopt three Chinese Nicaraguan orphans who speak not Chinese or English but a kind of "Spanish-Indian patois," he fails, as "there could be only one fate for aliens in transit: deportation." Unlike Lowe, his father, when reminiscing about this emotional time, "doesn't condemn, as I do, the inhumanity of this country's immigration laws," Lowe writes. "He merely chants an old Chinese proverb: 'Men do not toil either willingly or effectively for hard masters.'" In a wartime climate, one leading to the end of exclusion, Lowe could afford to make such an open critique, though he waters down the younger generation's anger with the older generation's exotic philosophy: ibid., 197, 206.

42. Yoon Sun Lee, "Type, Totality, and the Realism of Asian American Literature," *Modern Language Quarterly* 73, no. 3 (2012): 415–432.

43. Jade Snow Wong, "Daddy," bound first draft, 42, folder NCS_006, NCS Series, JSW.

44. Original ms. in red folder, 77, folder CBP_004, CBP Series, JSW.

45. Ibid., 78.

46. Ibid., 101.

47. Affidavit of Wong Hang, October 25, 1904; partnership list of Sang Wo Sang and Company, April 3, 1906; In re Wong Hang, October 3, 1906, all in CBP_011, CBP Series, JSW. See also original ms. in red folder, 103.

48. Original ms. in red folder, 103.

EPILOGUE

1. Jeff Yang, "Is Obama Still the 'First Asian American President'?" *Wall Street Journal*, February 11, 2013, accessed November 1, 2019, https://blogs.wsj.com/speakeasy/2013/02/11/is-obama-still-the-first-asian-american-president. This was a question he first asked Christopher P. Lu in 2008. See Eric Chang, "On the First Asian-American President," *Vogue*, December 21, 2016, accessed November 1, 2019, https://www.vogue.com/article/barack-obama-first-asian-american-president; Konrad Ng and Maya Soetoro-Ng, in "Asian-American Leaders Reflect on Obama's Legacy for the Community," *NBC News*, January 8, 2017, accessed November 1, 2019, https://www.nbcnews.com/storyline/president-obama-the-legacy/asian-american-leaders-reflect-obama-s-legacy-community-n673526. Jennifer Ho also spoke publicly on this idea.

2. Gardner Harris and Abby Goodnough, "Obama Was Unaware of Aunt's Status, Aides Say," *New York Times*, November 1, 2008, accessed March 25, 2019, https://www.nytimes.com/2008/11/02/us/politics/02campaign.html; Ryan J. Reilly and Elise Foley, "ICE Official Who Leaked Obama's Aunt's Immigration Status Thought Americans Had 'A Right to Know,'" *Huffington Post*, September 5, 2013, accessed March 25, 2019, https://www.huffpost.com/entry/obama-aunt-immigration_n_3874048; Aamer Madhani, "Obama's Aunt, Who Fought Immigration Battle, Dies at 61," *USA Today*, April 8, 2014, accessed March 25, 2019, https://www.usatoday.com/story/news/politics/2014/04/08/obama-aunt-asylum-kenya/7478801; Sam Tanenhaus, "North Star: Populism, Politics, and the Power of Sarah Palin," *New Yorker*, November 29, 2009, accessed November 1, 2019, https://www.newyorker.com/magazine/2009/12/07/north-star-2.

3. For more information on the attacks on Obama's identity, see, e.g., Claire Jean Kim, "President Obama and the Polymorphous 'Other' in U.S. Political Discourse," *Asian American Law Journal* 18 (2011): 165–175; Tom Olds, "Marginalizing the President: The Concerted Effort to 'Other' Obama," *Race, Gender and Class* 18, nos. 3–4 (2011): 100–

109; Emily Stewart, "Watch John McCain Defend Barack Obama against a Racist Voter in 2008," Vox.com, September 1, 2018, accessed November 1, 2019, https://www.vox.com/policy-and-politics/2018/8/25/17782572/john-mccain-barack-obama-statement-2008-video.

4. Allan Smith, "Trump Says Congresswomen of Color Should 'Go Back' and Fix the Places They 'Originally Came From,'" *NBC News*, July 15, 2019, accessed November 1, 2019, https://www.nbcnews.com/politics/donald-trump/trump-says-progressive-congresswomen-should-go-back-where-they-came-n1029676. A few months later, he attacked Representative Ilhan Omar directly amid other attacks on refugees, repeating a right-wing blog's assertion that she had married her brother to obtain a green card for him: Grace Panetta, "Here's Everything We Know about the Persistent but Unproven Rumors that Rep. Ilhan Omar Married Her Brother, Which Trump Repeated at a Recent Rally," BusinessInsider.com, October 11, 2019, accessed November 1, 2019, https://www.businessinsider.com/unproven-allegations-ilhan-omar-married-her-brother-explained-2019-7.

5. Melissa Blasius, "Congressman Biggs defends stance against DACA and DREAM act," ABC15.com, January 24, 2018, accessed March 25, 2019, https://www.abc15.com/news/region-southeast-valley/gilbert/congressman-biggs-defends-stance-against-daca-and-dream-act; Janet Napolitano, "Exercising Prosecutorial Discretion with Respect to Individuals Who Came to the United States as Children," Department of Homeland Security, June 15, 2012, accessed October 11, 2019, https://www.dhs.gov/xlibrary/assets/s1-exercising-prosecutorial-discretion-individuals-who-came-to-us-as-children.pdf; Janell Ross, "What's Happening to Two Undocumented Texas Valedictorians Says It All about the Immigration Debate," *Washington Post*, June 12, 2016, accessed March 25, 2019, https://www.washingtonpost.com/news/the-fix/wp/2016/06/12/whats-happening-to-two-undocumented-texas-valedictorians-says-it-all-about-the-immigration-debate.

6. "CAPAC Members Demand End to Deportation of Southeast Asian Refugees," *Rafu Shimpo* (Los Angeles), December 27, 2018, accessed March 25, 2019, http://www.rafu.com/2018/12/capac-members-demand-end-to-detention-deportation-of-southeast-asian-refugees; "The Devastating Impact of Deportation on Southeast Asian Americans," Southeast Asia Resource Action Center, April 2018, accessed March 25, 2019, http://www.searac.org/wp-content/uploads/2018/04/The-Devastating-Impact-of-Deportation-on-Southeast-Asian-Americans-1.pdf; Sang-hun Choe, "Deportation a 'Death Sentence' to Adoptees after a Lifetime in the U.S.," *New York Times*, July 2, 2017, https://www.nytimes.com/2017/07/02/world/asia/south-korea-adoptions-phillip-clay-adam-crapser.html. See also Elizabeth Shim, "Bill Aims to Protect Korean-American Adoptees from Deportation," UPI.com, May 29, 2019, accessed May 27, 2020, https://www.upi.com/Top_News/World-News/2019/05/29/Bill-aims-to-protect-Korean-American-adoptees-from-deportation/2051559102228. Legislation to regularize the status of those who were adopted to the United States under the age of eighteen has consistently stalled in Congress to date. Such stories certainly illustrate the enduring peril of mixed-race Asian children (see Chapter 3).

7. Jeffrey S. Passel and D'vera Cohn, "As Mexican Share Declined, U.S. Unauthorized Immigrant Population Fell in 2015 below Recession Level," Pew Research Center, April 25, 2017, accessed March 25, 2019, http://www.pewresearch.org/fact-tank/2017/04/25/as-mexican-share-declined-u-s-unauthorized-immigrant-population-fell-in-2015-below-recession-level; "Unauthorized Immigrant Population Trends for States, Birth Countries, and Regions," Pew Research Center: Hispanic Trends, November 27, 2018, accessed March 25, 2019, http://www.pewhispanic.org/interactives/unauthorized-trends.

8. Nina Bernstein, "U.S. Relieves Judge of Duties in Courtroom," *New York Times*, March 13, 2007; Casey Miner, "Judges on the Verge of a Nervous Breakdown," *Mother Jones*, November–December 2010, accessed May 29, 2020, https://www.motherjones.com/politics/2010/11/immigration-judge-case-overload. See also Mark S. Hurwitz, "Removing Judges: The Cases of Immigration Judges Jeffrey Chase and Noel Ferris," *Justice System Journal* 31, no. 1 (2010): 114–116. Thanks to Jared Brown-Rabinowitz for bringing the Chase episode to my notice. See Maya Kosoff, "Steve Bannon's Racist Comments about Silicon Valley Are Also Wildly Inaccurate," Vanityfair.com, November 17, 2016, accessed March 25, 2019, https://www.vanityfair.com/news/2016/11/steve-bannon-racist-comments-silicon-valley-inaccurate; Andy J. Semotiuk, "Recent Changes to the H1B Visa Program and What Is Coming in 2019," Forbes.com, January 2, 2019, accessed March 25, 2019, https://www.forbes.com/sites/andyjsemotiuk/2019/01/02/recent-changes-to-the-h1b-visa-program-and-what-is-coming-in-2019.

9. Ha Jin, *A Good Fall* (New York: Pantheon, 2009).

Bibliography

LITERARY TEXTS (ESSAYS, FICTION, FILM/STAGE, MEMOIR)

Alcott, Louisa May. *Rose in Bloom*. Boston: Roberts Brothers, 1876.

Chao, Buwei Yang. *Autobiography of a Chinese Woman*. Trans. Yuen Ren Chao. New York: John Day, 1947.

———. *How to Cook and Eat in Chinese*. New York: John Day, 1945.

Chu, Louis. *Eat a Bowl of Tea,* repr. ed. New York: Citadel, [1961] 1990.

Far, Sui Sin. *Mrs. Spring Fragrance*. Peterborough, ON: Broadview, 2011.

Flower Drum Song. By Richard Rodgers and Oscar Hammerstein II. Directed by Gene Kelly. St. James Theatre, New York, 1958–1960.

Griffith, D. W., dir. *Broken Blossoms*. Film, 90 min., United Artists, 1919.

Hammerstein, Oscar, II, and Joseph A. Fields. *Flower Drum Song: A Musical Play*. New York: Farrar, Straus and Cudahy, 1959.

Jin, Ha. *A Good Fall*. New York: Pantheon, 2009.

Kingston, Maxine Hong. *China Men*, repr. ed. New York: Vintage International, 1989.

———. "Cultural Mis-readings by American Reviewers." In *Asian and Western Writers in Dialogue: New Cultural Identities*, edited by Guy Amirthanayagam, 55–65. London: Macmillan, 1982.

———. *The Fifth Book of Peace*. New York: Vintage, 2003.

———. *I Love a Broad Margin to My Life*. New York: Knopf, 2011.

———. "San Francisco's Chinatown: A View from the Other Side of Arnold Genthe's Camera." *American Heritage* 30, no. 1 (December 1978): 36–47.

———. *The Woman Warrior: Memoirs of a Girlhood among Ghosts*, repr. ed. New York: Vintage International, 1989.

Koster, Henry, dir. *Flower Drum Song*. Film, 133 min., Universal Pictures, 1961.

Kuo, Helena. *I've Come a Long Way*. New York: D. Appleton, 1942.

Lee, C. Y. *The Flower Drum Song*, repr. ed. London: Pan, [1957] 1960.

———. *The Land of the Golden Mountain*. New York: Meredith, 1967.
———. *Lover's Point*. New York: Farrar, Straus and Cudahy, 1958.
Lin, Yutang. *Chinatown Family*. New Brunswick, NJ: Rutgers University Press, 2007.
Logan, Joshua, dir. *Sayonara*. Film, 147 min, Warner Brothers, 1957.
Lowe, Pardee. *Father and Glorious Descendant*. Boston: Little, Brown, 1943.
Ng, Fae Myenne. "My Confusion Program, an Inheritance of Indecision." *Ploughshares* 35, nos. 2–3 (2009): 116–120.
Perry, George Sessions. "The Wongs." *Saturday Evening Post*, October 16, 1948, 24–25, 102, 105–107, 109–110, 112.
Sze, Mai-mai. *Echo of a Cry, A Story Which Began in China*. New York: Harcourt, Brace, 1945.
Wong, Jade Snow. "Daddy." *Common Ground* (Winter 1945): 25–29.
———. *Fifth Chinese Daughter*. New York: Harper and Brothers, 1950.
———. "The Four Loves of Wang Ta." *Saturday Review*, May 25, 1957, 16, 29.
———. "How to Get the Best Chinese Food." *Holiday*, vol. 18, October 1955, 65, 67, 133–35.
———. "Jon." *Common Ground* (Autumn 1945): 39–44.
———. "My Chinatown," *Forum* (San Francisco Junior College) (Spring 1940): 37–39.
———. *No Chinese Stranger*. New York: Harper and Row, 1975.
Yellow Claw, nos. 1–4 (October 1956, December 1956, February 1957, April 1957). Atlas Comics, New York.

BOOKS AND ACADEMIC ARTICLES

Abe, Frank. "Review: 'The Great Japanese American Novel.'" *Amerasia Journal* 30, no. 2 (2004): 107–112.
Behdad, Ali. *A Forgetful Nation: On Immigration and Cultural Identity in the United States*. Durham, NC: Duke University Press, 2005.
Bérubé, Michael. "Disability and Narrative." *PMLA* 120, no. 2 (March 2005): 568–576.
Bow, Leslie. *Betrayal and Other Acts of Subversion: Feminism, Sexual Politics, Asian American Women's Literature*. Princeton, NJ: Princeton University Press, 2001.
———. "Introduction: Jade Snow Wong's Giftshop and Travel Service." In *Fifth Chinese Daughter*, by Jade Snow Wong, ix-xxx. Seattle: University of Washington Press, 2019.
———. *Partly Colored: Asian Americans and Racial Anomaly in the Segregated South*. New York: New York University Press, 2010.
Braitman, Jacqueline R., and Gerald F. Uelmen. *Justice Stanley Mosk: A Life at the Center of California Politics and Justice*. Jefferson, NC: McFarland, 2012.
Brooks, Charlotte. *Between Mao and McCarthy: Chinese American Politics in the Cold War Years*. Chicago: University of Chicago Press, 2015.
Brown, Richard Harvey, and Beth Davis-Brown. "The Making of Memory: The Politics of Archives, Libraries and Museums in the Construction of National Consciousness." *History of the Human Sciences* 11, no. 4 (1998): 17–32.
Burton, Antoinette M. *The Postcolonial Careers of Santha Rama Rau*. Durham, NC: Duke University Press, 2007.
Chang, Robert S. *Disoriented: Asian Americans, Law, and the Nation-State*. New York: New York University Press, 1999.
Cheng, Anne Anlin. *The Melancholy of Race*. Oxford: Oxford University Press, 2000.
Cheng, Cindy I-fen. *Citizens of Asian America: Democracy and Race during the Cold War*. New York: New York University Press, 2013.

Cheung, King-Kok. *Articulate Silences: Hisaye Yamamoto, Maxine Hong Kingston, Joy Kogawa*. Ithaca, NY: Cornell University Press, 1993.

Chin, Frank. "Come All Ye Asian American Writers of the Real and the Fake." In *The Big Aiiieeeee! An Anthology of Chinese American and Japanese American Literature*, edited by Frank Chin, Shawn Wong, Jeffery Paul Chan, and Lawson Fusao Inada, 1–92. New York: Meridian, 1991.

———. "This Is Not an Autobiography." *Genre* 18, no. 2 (Summer 1985): 109–130.

Chin, Frank, Jeffery Paul Chan, Lawson Fusao Inada, and Shawn H. Wong. "An Introduction to Chinese and Japanese Literature." In *Aiiieeeee! An Anthology of Asian-American Writers*, edited by Frank Chin, Shawn Wong, Jeffery Paul Chan, and Lawson Fusao Inada, 3–38. New York: Mentor, 1991.

Chin, Gabriel J. "'A Chinaman's Chance' in Court: Asian Pacific Americans and Racial Rules of Evidence." *University of California, Irvine, Law Review* 3, no. 4 (December 2013): 965–90.

Chin, Gabriel J., Cindy Hwang Chiang, and Shirley S. Park. "The Lost *Brown v. Board of Education* of Immigration Law." *North Carolina Law Review* 91, no. 5 (2013): 1657–98.

Chua, C. Lok. "On Maxine Hong Kingston's Manuscript Revisions of *the Woman Warrior* and *China Men*: An Anecdotal Account." In *On the Legacy of Maxine Hong Kingston: The Mulhouse Book*, edited by Sami Ludwig and Nicoleta Alexoae-Zagni, 113–124. Zurich: LIT Verlag Munster, 2014.

Citron, Stephen. *The Wordsmiths: Oscar Hammerstein 2nd and Alan Jay Lerner*. New York: Oxford University Press, 1995.

Cleland, Jaime. "Breaking the 'Chinese Habit': Jade Snow Wong in First Person." *MELUS* 37, no. 1 (Spring 2012): 61–82.

Cohen, Myron. *House United, House Divided: The Chinese Family in Taiwan*. New York: Columbia University Press, 1976.

Coontz, Stephanie. *The Way We Never Were: American Families and the Nostalgia Trap*. New York: Basic, 1992.

Davis, Rocío G. *Relative Histories: Mediating History in Asian American Family Memoirs*. Honolulu: University of Hawai'i Press, 2011.

Derrida, Jacques. "Archive Fever: A Freudian Impression." *Diacritics* 25, no. 2 (1995): 9–63.

Dorr, Gregory Michael. "Principled Expediency: Eugenics, *Naim v. Naim*, and the Supreme Court." *American Journal of Legal History* 42, no. 2 (April 1998): 119–159.

Field, Jacqueline. "Mud Silk and the Chinese Laundress: From the South China Silk Industry to Mud Silk Suits in Maine." *Textile History* 45, no. 2 (November 2014): 234–260.

Fong, Katheryn M. "An Open Letter/Review of Maxine Hong Kingston, *The Woman Warrior*." *Bulletin of Concerned Asian Scholars* 9, no. 4 (1977): 67–69.

Fong, Timothy P. *The First Suburban Chinatown: The Remaking of Monterey Park, California*. Philadelphia: Temple University Press, 1994.

Gotanda, Neil. "'Other Non-Whites' in American Legal History: A Review Essay on *Justice at War*." *Journal of Gender, Race, and Justice* 13, no. 2 (Winter 2010): 333–369.

Griffith, Sarah M. *The Fight for Asian American Civil Rights: Liberal Protestant Activism, 1900–1950*. Urbana: University of Illinois Press, 2018.

Haney López, Ian. *White by Law: The Legal Construction of Race*. New York: New York University Press, 2006.

Harris, A. Frederick. "Some Observations on the Un-Uniform Act on Blood Tests to Determine Paternity." *Villanova Law Review* 9, no. 1 (Fall 1963): 59–76.

Hester, Torrie. *Deportation: The Origins of U.S. Policy.* Philadelphia: University of Pennsylvania Press, 2017.

Hing, Bill Ong. *Making and Remaking Asian America through Immigration Policy, 1850–1990.* Stanford, CA: Stanford University Press, 1993.

Hirobe, Izumi. *Japanese Pride, American Prejudice: Modifying the Exclusion Clause of the 1924 Immigration Act.* Stanford, CA: Stanford University Press, 2001.

Honig, Bonnie. *Democracy and the Foreigner.* Princeton, NJ: Princeton University Press, 2001.

Hsu, Madeline Yuan-yin. *The Good Immigrants: How the Yellow Peril Became the Model Minority.* Princeton, NJ: Princeton University Press, 2015.

———. "Unwrapping Orientalist Constraints: Restoring Homosocial Normativity to Chinese American History." *Amerasia Journal* 29, no. 2 (2003): 229–253.

Hurwitz, Mark S. "Removing Judges: The Cases of Immigration Judges Jeffrey Chase and Noel Ferris." *Justice System Journal* 31, no. 1 (2010): 114–116.

Irwin, Will, and Arnold Genthe. *Old Chinatown: A Book of Pictures by Arnold Genthe.* New York: Mitchell Kennerley, 1913.

Johnston, Robert. "Public Policy Considerations in Rulings on the Uniform Act on Blood Tests to Determine Paternity." *William and Mary Law Review* 4, no. 2 (1963): 149–159.

Jung, Moon-Ho. *Coolies and Cane: Race, Labor, and Sugar in the Age of Emancipation.* Baltimore: Johns Hopkins University Press, 2006.

Karle, Katherine A. "Flamingos and Bison: Balance in Chinatown Family," *MELUS* 15, no. 2 (1988): 93–99.

Kim, Claire Jean. "President Obama and the Polymorphous 'Other' in U.S. Political Discourse," *Asian American Law Journal* 18 (2011): 165–175.

Kim, Elaine H. *Asian American Literature: An Introduction to the Writings and Their Social Context.* Philadelphia: Temple University Press, 1982.

Kim, Hyung-chan. *A Legal History of Asian Americans, 1790–1990.* Westport, CT: Greenwood, 1994.

Klein, Christina. *Cold War Orientalism: Asia in the Middlebrow Imagination, 1945–1961.* Berkeley: University of California Press, 2003.

Kung, S. W. *Chinese in American Life: Some Aspects of Their History, Status, Problems, and Contributions.* Seattle: University of Washington Press, 1962.

Kurashige, Lon, and Alice Yang Murray, eds. *Major Problems in Asian American History.* Boston: Houghton Mifflin, 2003.

Kwong, Peter. *Chinatown, New York: Labor and Politics, 1930–1950.* New York: New Press, 2001.

———. *The New Chinatown.* New York: Hill and Wang, 1996.

Kwong, Peter, and Dušanka Miščević. *Chinese America: The Untold Story of America's Oldest New Community.* New York: New Press, 2005.

Lai, H. Mark, Genny Lim, and Judy Yung, eds. *Island: Poetry and History of Chinese Immigrants on Angel Island, 1910–1940.* Seattle: University of Washington Press, 2014.

Lau, Estelle T. *Paper Families: Identity, Immigration Administration, and Chinese Exclusion.* Durham, NC: Duke University Press, 2006.

Lee, Erika. *At America's Gates: The Exclusion Era, 1882–1943.* Chapel Hill: University of North Carolina Press, 2003.

Lee, Erika, and Judy Yung. *Angel Island: Immigrant Gateway to America.* Oxford: Oxford University Press, 2010.

Lee, Robert G. *Orientals: Asian Americans in Popular Culture*. Philadelphia: Temple University Press, 1999.

Lee, Rose Hum. *The Chinese in the United States of America*. Hong Kong: Hong Kong University Press, 1960.

Lee, Yoon Sun. "Type, Totality, and the Realism of Asian American Literature." *Modern Language Quarterly* 73, no. 3 (2012): 415–432.

Lew-Williams, Beth. *The Chinese Must Go: Violence, Exclusion, and the Making of the Alien in America*. Cambridge, MA: Harvard University Press, 2018.

Li, David Leiwei. "Re-presenting *The Woman Warrior*: An Essay of Interpretive History." In *Critical Essays on Maxine Hong Kingston*, edited by Laura E. Skandera-Trombley, 182–203. New York: G. K. Hall, 1998.

Ling, Amy. *Between Worlds: Women Writers of Chinese Ancestry*. New York: Pergamon, 1990.

Loewen, James. *The Mississippi Chinese: Between Black and White*. Cambridge, MA: Harvard University Press, 1971.

Lowe, Lisa. *Immigrant Acts: On Asian American Cultural Politics*. Durham, NC: Duke University Press, 1996.

Lye, Colleen. *America's Asia: Racial Form and American Literature, 1893–1945*. Princeton, NJ: Princeton University Press, 2005.

———. "Reading for Asian American Literature." In *A Companion to American Literary Studies*, edited by Caroline F. Levander and Robert S. Levine, 483–499. Malden, MA: John Wiley and Sons, 2011.

Marden, Charles F. *Minorities in American Society*. New York: American Book, 1952.

Marshall, Daniel, Kevin P. Murphy, and Zeb Tortorici. "Queering Archives: Historical Unravelings." *Radical History Review* 120 (Fall 2014): 1–11.

May, Elaine Tyler. *Great Expectations: Marriage and Divorce in Post-Victorian America*. Chicago: University of Chicago Press, 1980.

———. *Homeward Bound: American Families in the Cold War Era*. New York: Basic, 1988.

Milton, Joyce. *Tramp: The Life of Charlie Chaplin*. New York: Open Road Media, 2014.

Motomura, Hiroshi. *Immigration outside the Law*. Oxford: Oxford University Press, 2014.

Nadel, Alan. *Containment Culture: American Narratives, Postmodernism, and the Containment Age*. Durham, NC: Duke University Press, 1995.

Nee, Victor G. and Brett de Bary Nee. *Longtime Californ': A Documentary Study of an American Chinatown*. New York: Pantheon, 1973.

Ngai, Mae M. *Impossible Subjects: Illegal Aliens and the Making of Modern America*. Princeton, NJ: Princeton University Press, 2004.

Nguyen, Vinh. "Refugeetude: When Does a Refugee Stop Being a Refugee?" *Social Text* 37, no. 2 (2019): 109–131.

Ninh, Erin. "Model Minority Narratives and the Asian American Family." In *The Cambridge Companion to Asian American Literature*, edited by Daniel Y. Kim and Crystal Parikh, 114–28. New York, NY: Cambridge University Press, 2015.

Ninh, erin Khuê. *Ingratitude: The Debt-Bound Daughter in Asian American Literature*. New York: New York University Press, 2011.

Olds, Tom. "Marginalizing the President. 'The Concerted Effort to "Other" Obama.'" *Race, Gender and Class* 18, nos. 3–4 (2011): 100–109.

Oyen, Meredith. *The Diplomacy of Migration: Transnational Lives and the Making of U.S.-Chinese Relations in the Cold War*. Ithaca, NY: Cornell University Press, 2015.

Parker, Kunal. *Making Foreigners: Immigration and Citizenship Law in America, 1600–2000*. New York: Cambridge University Press, 2015.

Pascoe, Peggy. *What Comes Naturally: Miscegenation Law and the Making of Race in America*. Oxford: Oxford University Press, 2009.

Perry, George Sessions. *Families of America; Where They Come from and How They Live*. New York: Whittlesey House/McGraw-Hill, 1949.

Phu, Thy. "Spectacles of Citizenship and Civility: Arnold Genthe and the Photography of Chinatown." *Genre* 39, no. 3 (2006): 57–82.

Pierce, Benjamin A. *Genetics: A Conceptual Approach*. New York: Macmillan, 2008.

Said, Edward W. *Culture and Imperialism*. New York: Vintage, 1994.

Shah, Nayan. *Contagious Divides: Epidemics and Race in San Francisco's Chinatown*. Berkeley: University of California Press, 2001.

Shibusawa, Naoko. *America's Geisha Ally: Reimagining the Japanese Enemy*. Cambridge, MA: Harvard University Press, 2006.

Silverman, Al. *The Time of Their Lives: The Golden Age of Great American Book Publishers, Their Editors, and Authors*. New York: Truman Talley, 2008.

Simmons, Diane. "Appendix: A Conversation with Maxine Hong Kingston." In *Maxine Hong Kingston*, edited by Diane Simmons, 163–167. New York: Twayne, 1999.

Simpson, Caroline Chung. *An Absent Presence: Japanese Americans in Postwar American Culture, 1945–1960*. Durham, NC: Duke University Press, 2001.

Sledge, Linda Ching. "Maxine Kingston's China Men: The Family Historian as Epic Poet." *MELUS* 7, no. 4 (Winter 1980): 3–22.

So, Richard Jean. "Collaboration and Translation: Lin Yutang and the Archive of Asian American Literature." *Modern Fiction Studies* 56, no. 1 (Spring 2010): 40–62.

Song, Min. *The Children of 1965: On Writing, and Not Writing, as an Asian American*. Durham, NC: Duke University Press, 2013.

Spigel, Lynn. *Make Room for TV: Television and the Family Ideal in Postwar America*. Chicago: University of Chicago Press, 1992.

Spillers, Hortense J. "Mama's Baby, Papa's Maybe: An American Grammar Book." *Diacritics* 17, no. 2 (1987): 64–81.

Spivak, Gayatri Chakravorty. "The Rani of Sirmur: An Essay in Reading the Archives." *History and Theory* 24, no. 3 (1985): 247–272.

Sung, Betty Lee. *Mountain of Gold: The Story of the Chinese in America*. New York: Macmillan, 1967.

Tchen, John Kuo Wei, ed. *Genthe's Photographs of San Francisco's Old Chinatown*. New York: Dover, 1984.

Teng, Emma Jinhua. *Eurasian: Mixed Identities in the United States, China, and Hong Kong, 1842–1943*. Berkeley: University of California Press, 2013.

Um, Khatharya. *From the Land of Shadows: War, Revolution, and the Making of the Cambodian Diaspora*. New York: New York University Press, 2015.

Wong, K. Scott. *Americans First: Chinese Americans and the Second World War*. Cambridge, MA: Harvard University Press, 2005.

Wu, Ellen D. *The Color of Success: Asian Americans and the Origins of the Model Minority*. Princeton, NJ: Princeton University Press, 2014.

Yeh, Chiou-ling. "'A Saga of Democracy': Toy Len Goon, American Mother of the Year, and the Cultural Cold War." *Pacific Historical Review* 81, no. 3 (Aug 2012): 432–461.

Young, Elliott. *Alien Nation: Chinese Migration in the Americas from the Coolie Era through World War II*. Chapel Hill: University of North Carolina Press, 2014.

Yu, Connie Young. "Rediscovered Voices: Chinese Immigrants and Angel Island." *Amerasia Journal* 4, no. 2 (1977): 123–39.

Yung, Judy. *Unbound Feet: A Social History of Chinese Women in San Francisco.* Berkeley: University of California Press, 1995.

———. *Unbound Voices: A Documentary History of Chinese Women in San Francisco.* Berkeley: University of California Press, 1999.

Zhao, Xiaojian. *The New Chinese America: Class, Economy, and Social Hierarchy.* New Brunswick, NJ: Rutgers University Press, 2010.

———. *Remaking Chinese America: Immigration, Family, and Community, 1940–1965.* New Brunswick, NJ: Rutgers University Press, 2002.

NEWSPAPER/MAGAZINE ARTICLES

"Airlift Brings War Brides: Orientals Rushing to U.S. to Beat Law Expiration Tuesday." *New York Times*, December 24, 1948, 4.

"Albert Chow to Appear before Grand Jury." *Chinese World*, September 28, 1956, 1.

Artner, Alan G. "Photography: Genthe's Slighted Contribution Gets a New Exposure." *Chicago Tribune*, December 7, 1975, D10.

"Benjamin Gim: A Great Life Remembered." American Immigration Lawyers Association, January 26, 2010. Accessed August 18, 2017. http://www.aila.org/about/announcements/in-memoriam/benjamin-gim.

Bernstein, Nina. "U.S. Relieves Judge of Duties in Courtroom." *New York Times*, March 13, 2007.

Blasius, Melissa. "Congressman Biggs Defends Stance against DACA and DREAM Act." ABC15.com, January 24, 2018. Accessed March 25, 2019. https://www.abc15.com/news/region-southeast-valley/gilbert/congressman-biggs-defends-stance-against-daca-and-dream-act.

Butcher, Fanny. "The Literary Spotlight." *Chicago Daily Tribune*, July 29, 1951, H2.

"California '49ers." *House and Garden*, July 1949, 45–47.

"CAPAC Members Demand End to Deportation of Southeast Asian Refugees," *Rafu Shimpo* (Los Angeles), December 27, 2018. Accessed March 25, 2019. http://www.rafu.com/2018/12/capac-members-demand-end-to-detention-deportation-of-southeast-asian-refugees.

Chan, Jeffery Paul, and Diane Johnson. "The Mysterious West." *New York Review of Books*, April 28, 1977. Accessed May 26, 2020. https://www.nybooks.com/articles/1977/04/28/the-mysterious-west.

Chang, Eric. "On the First Asian-American President." *Vogue*, December 21, 2016. Accessed November 1, 2019. https://www.vogue.com/article/barack-obama-first-asian-american-president.

Choe, Sang-hun, "Deportation a 'Death Sentence' to Adoptees after a Lifetime in the U.S." *New York Times*, July 2, 2017. Accessed March 25, 2019. https://www.nytimes.com/2017/07/02/world/asia/south-korea-adoptions-phillip-clay-adam-crapser.html.

"Chow Faces Quiz by U.S. Grand Jury." *Oakland Tribune*, September 27, 1956, 10.

"'Color' Testimony Charged at Concubine Trial." *Chinese World*, July 12, 1956, 2.

"Commentary on Drumright Report Published by Chinese World." *Chinese World*, May 28, 1956, 1.

"Committee to Fight Exclusion of Chinese." *New York Times*, July 7, 1943, 19.

“Complete Text of Statement Issued by Chinese Confab in Washington.” *Chinese World*, March 12, 1957, 1.
“Concubine Case Defendant Guilty.” *Chinese World*, July 19, 1956, 2.
“Concubine Case Defendants Arraigned.” *Chinese World*, May 25, 1957, 2.
“Concubine Case Figure Fined $2,000.” *Chinese World*, June 1, 1957, 2.
“Concubine Case Woman to Be Deported.” *Chinese World*, September 20, 1956, 2.
“‘Concubine’ Trial Defendant Had Change of Heart.” *Chinese World*, July 14, 1956, 2.
“‘Concubine’ Trial Defendant Pleads Guilty.” *Chinese World*, July 16, 1956, 2.
“Dai-Ming Lee Is Dead.” *New York Times*, March 20, 1961.
“The Devastating Impact of Deportation on Southeast Asian Americans.” Southeast Asia Resource Action Center, April 2018. Accessed March 25, 2019. http://www.searac.org/wp-content/uploads/2018/04/The-Devastating-Impact-of-Deportation-on-Southeast-Asian-Americans-1.pdf.
“5 Indicted Here on ‘War Bride’ Fraud Charges.” *Chicago Daily Tribune*, April 28, 1950, 5.
“Fong Wan, Chinese Herbalist,” *San Francisco Chronicle*, June 19, 1949. Accessed March 25, 2019. http://www.sfmuseum.org/hist8/fongwan1.html.
Geary, Joyce. “A Chinese Girl’s World.” *New York Times*, October 29, 1950, 201.
Harris, Gardner, and Abby Goodnough. “Obama Was Unaware of Aunt’s Status, Aides Say.” *New York Times*, November 1, 2008. Accessed March 25, 2019. https://www.nytimes.com/2008/11/02/us/politics/02campaign.html.
“Herbalist’s Wife Testifies in Divorce Trial.” *Chinese World*, March 16, 1956, 2.
“History of Chinese Six Companies in San Francisco Reviewed.” *Chinese World*, March 17, 1956, 1.
“H[ong] K[ong] Consul General Charges Passport Fraud Racket.” *Chinese World*, March 5, 1956, 1.
“How Thousands of Chinese Get into U.S. Told: Hong Kong Racketeers Paid $3,000 a Head.” *Chicago Daily Tribune*, March 24, 1956, 3.
“Illegal Arrest Charged in Passport Case.” *Chinese World*, November 23, 1956, 1.
“Immigration Case Cook Talks; Freed.” *Chinese World*, September 29, 1956, 1.
“Immigration Law Violations Admitted.” *Oakland Tribune*, January 20, 1957, 6A.
Jackson, Joseph Henry. “Bookman’s Notebook.” *Los Angeles Times*, September 21, 1950, A5.
“‘Jane Russell’ of Hong Kong Sues Dr. Fong Wan for $175,000 Damages.” *Oakland Tribune*, May 21, 1950, 60A.
“John Rossi to Face Trial in Fong Wan Bribe Case.” *Oakland Tribune*, August 28, 1953, 18D.
Johnson, Diane. “Ghosts.” *New York Review of Books*, February 3, 1977.
Jones, Carleton. “Rare Photos Sold for $27 Now Valued in Five Figures: Baltimore Find Was Made at an Auction for Kitchen Equipment.” *Baltimore Sun*, December 12, 1976, SM28–30.
Judson, Clara Ingram. “The Colorful Home Life of Chinese Girl.” *Chicago Daily Tribune*, October 1, 1950, O5.
“Jury Convicts Fong in Illegal Surgery Case.” *Oakland Tribune*, August 19, 1953, D3.
Kosoff, Maya. “Steve Bannon’s Racist Comments about Silicon Valley Are Also Wildly Inaccurate.” VanityFair.com, November 17, 2016. Accessed March 25, 2019. https://www.vanityfair.com/news/2016/11/steve-bannon-racist-comments-silicon-valley-inaccurate.
Lee, C. Y. “Came the Year of the Rooster—Luck Made a 90-Degree Turn.” *San Francisco Chronicle*, February 2, 1958.
———. “Lover’s Point: He Is Free.” *Chinese World*, August 18, 1956, 4.

Lee, Dai-Ming. "Deportations to Red China." *Chinese World*, January 30, 1957, 1.

———. "Drumright Indicts an Entire Race." *Chinese World*, April 29, 1956, 1.

———. "Drumright Report Lacks Accuracy, Objectivity." *Chinese World*, May 4, 1956, 1.

———. "Drumright's Amazing Charges." *Chinese World*, April 20, 1956, 1.

———. "Drumright's Exclusion Laws." *Chinese World*, April 28, 1956, 1.

———. "The Mountain Labored and Brought Forth a Mouse." *Chinese World*, May 9, 1956, 1.

———. "Press Acclaims Judicial Decision on Subpoenas." *Chinese World*, March 27, 1956, 1.

———. "The Sins of Fathers and Grandfathers." *Chinese World*, April 19, 1956, 1.

———. "Time for Unity in Chinatown." *Chinese World*, March 23, 1956, 1.

Lim, Genny, and Judy Yung. "Our Parents Never Told Us." *California Living*, January 23, 1977, 6–9.

"Litigious Fong Family Makes Headlines Again." *Chinese World*, March 30, 1956, 2.

Lowe, Pardee. "Mixed Marriage: A Chinese Husband and American Wife Are Put to Test." *Asia* (January 1937): 7–10.

Madhani, Aamer. "Obama's Aunt, Who Fought Immigration Battle, Dies at 61." *USA Today*, April 8, 2014. Accessed March 25, 2019. https://www.usatoday.com/story/news/politics/2014/04/08/obama-aunt-asylum-kenya/7478801.

"Mercy for Mother in Alien Case." *Oakland Tribune*, February 8, 1957, 15E.

Miner, Casey. "Judges on the Verge of a Nervous Breakdown." *Mother Jones*, November–December 2010. Accessed May 29, 2020. https://www.motherjones.com/politics/2010/11/immigration-judge-case-overload.

"Mlle Merit Awards." *Mademoiselle*, December 30, 1948, 95–97.

"More on DC Conference." *Chinese World*, March 14, 1957, 1.

"More on DC Conference Resolutions." *Chinese World*, March 15, 1957, 1.

"Mrs. Fong Is Given Divorce and Million," *Oakland Tribune*, November 24, 1956, 4E.

Ng, Konrad, and Maya Soetoro-Ng. "Asian-American Leaders Reflect on Obama's Legacy for the Community." *NBC News*, January 8, 2017. Accessed November 1, 2019. https://www.nbcnews.com/storyline/president-obama-the-legacy/asian-american-leaders-reflect-obama-s-legacy-community-n673526.

Panetta, Grace. "Here's Everything We Know about the Persistent but Unproven Rumors That Rep. Ilhan Omar Married Her Brother, Which Trump Repeated at a Recent Rally." BusinessInsider.com, October 11, 2019. Accessed November 1, 2019. https://www.businessinsider.com/unproven-allegations-ilhan-omar-married-her-brother-explained-2019-7.

Passel, Jeffrey S., and D'vera Cohn. "As Mexican Share Declined, U.S. Unauthorized Immigrant Population Fell in 2015 below Recession Level." Pew Research Center, April 25, 2017. Accessed March 25, 2019. http://www.pewresearch.org/fact-tank/2017/04/25/as-mexican-share-declined-u-s-unauthorized-immigrant-population-fell-in-2015-below-recession-level.

"Passport Sale Charted: Philadelphia Jury Indicts Two Former U.S. Commissioners." *New York Times*, April 15, 1948, 16.

Petersen, William. "Success Story, Japanese-American Style." *New York Times Magazine*, January 9, 1966, 20–21, 33, 36, 38, 40–41, 43.

Pfaff, Timothy. "Talk with Mrs. Kingston." *New York Times Book Review*, June 15, 1980, 1, 25–27.

Poore, Charles. "Books of *The Times*." *New York Times*, December 13, 1950, 33.

Reilly, Ryan J., and Elise Foley. "ICE Official Who Leaked Obama's Aunt's Immigration Status Thought Americans Had 'A Right to Know.'" *Huffington Post*, September 5,

2013. Accessed March 25, 2019. https://www.huffpost.com/entry/obama-aunt-immi gration_n_3874048.

Renouf, Renee. "'The Chinese in America' Is an Eloquent Tale Told in Photos." *Christian Science Monitor*, December 12, 1980, 19.

Ross, Janell. "What's Happening to Two Undocumented Texas Valedictorians Says It All about the Immigration Debate." *Washington Post*, June 12, 2016. Accessed March 25, 2019. https://www.washingtonpost.com/news/the-fix/wp/2016/06/12 /whats-happening-to-two-undocumented-texas-valedictorians-says-it-all-about -the-immigration-debate.

Saxon, Wolfgang. "Everett F. Drumright, 86, Is Dead; Envoy to Taiwan in Tense Period." *New York Times*, April 27, 1993. Accessed August 17, 2017. http://www.nytimes .com/1993/04/27/obituaries/everett-f-drumright-86-is-dead-envoy-to-taiwan-in tense-period.html.

Semotiuk, Andy J. "Recent Changes to The H1B Visa Program and What Is Coming in 2019." Forbes.com, January 2, 2019. Accessed March 25, 2019. https://www.forbes .com/sites/andyjsemotiuk/2019/01/02/recent-changes-to-the-h1b-visa-program -and-what-is-coming-in-2019.

Shim, Elizabeth. "Bill Aims to Protect Korean-American Adoptees from Deportation," UPI.com, May 29, 2019. Accessed May 27, 2020. https://www.upi.com/Top_News /World-News/2019/05/29/Bill-aims-to-protect-Korean-American-adoptees-from -deportation/2051559102228.

"Six Companies Protests Calumny Heaped on Entire Chinese Community: Inference of Wholesale Wrongdong [*sic*] Resented by Chinese Organizations." *Chinese World*, March 16, 1956, 1.

"60 New York Chinese Groups Protest 'Blanket' Probe of S[an] F[rancisco] Organizations." *Chinese World*, March 13, 1956, 1.

Smith, Allan. "Trump Says Congresswomen of Color Should 'Go Back' and Fix the Places They 'Originally Came From.'" *NBC News*, July 15, 2019. Accessed November 1, 2019. https://www.nbcnews.com/politics/donald-trump/trump-says-progressive -congresswomen-should-go-back-where-they-came-n1029676.

Stewart, Emily. "Watch John McCain Defend Barack Obama against a Racist Voter in 2008." Vox.com, September 1, 2018. Accessed November 1, 2019. https://www.vox .com/policy-and-politics/2018/8/25/17782572/john-mccain-barack-obama-state ment-2008-video.

"Success Story of One Minority Group in U.S." *U.S. News and World Report*, December 26, 1966, 73–76.

Tanenhaus, Sam. "North Star: Populism, Politics, and the Power of Sarah Palin." *New Yorker*, November 29, 2009. Accessed November 1, 2019. https://www.newyorker .com/magazine/2009/12/07/north-star-2.

"Text of Resolutions Adopted by Chinese Conference in Washington." *Chinese World*, March 13, 1957, 1.

"Unauthorized Immigrant Population Trends for States, Birth Countries, and Regions." Pew Research Center: Hispanic Trends, November 27, 2018. Accessed March 25, 2019. http://www.pewhispanic.org/interactives/unauthorized-trends.

"U.S. Inquiry Hurts Chinatown Trade; $100,000 Weekly Loss Laid to Fear in Passport Check." *New York Times*, March 17, 1956, 1, 4.

"U.S. Passport Fraud Figure Hangs Himself." *Oakland Tribune*, January 29, 1957, 1.

"U.S. Witnesses Testify at Concubine Trial." *Chinese World*, July 13, 1956, 2.

"War Brides Getting 'Airlift.'" *New York Times*, December 14, 1948, 14.
Yang, Jeff. "Is Obama Still the 'First Asian American President'?" *Wall Street Journal*, February 11, 2013. Accessed November 1, 2019. https://blogs.wsj.com/speakeasy/2013/02/11/is-obama-still-the-first-asian-american-president.
Yung, Judy. "Chi Am Corner: New Job, New Challenge." *East/West*, March 10, 1976, 6.

GOVERNMENT DOCUMENTS AND LEGAL CASES (HIGHLIGHTS)

Application of the Presidents, Secretaries, Treasurers, and Custodians of Records of Certain Chinese Family Benevolent and District Associations to Quash Grand Jury Subpoenas Duces Tecum. 19 FRD 97 (1956).
Brown v. Board of Education of Topeka, Kansas. 347 U.S. 483 (1954).
Burke, Lloyd H., et al. *Appellee's Brief in Ly Shew v. Dulles 9th Cir. (1953)*. San Francisco: Pernau-Walsh, 1953[?].
Cable Act. Public Law 67–346, 42 Stat. 1021 (1922).
Cheung Sum Shee v. Nagle. 268 U.S. 336 (1925).
Departments of State and Justice, Judiciary, and Related Agencies, Appropriations for 1957: Hearings before the Subcommittee of the Committee on Appropriations, House of Representatives, 84th Congress, Second Session. Washington, DC: U.S. Government Printing Office, 1956.
Departments of State and Justice, the Judiciary, and Related Agencies Appropriations for 1958: Hearings before the Subcommittee of the Committee on Appropriations, House of Representative, 85th Congress, First Session (Washington, DC: U.S. Government Printing Office, 1957).
Drumright, Everett F. "Proposals to Better Cope with Problem of Fraud at Hong Kong." *Foreign Service Dispatch* 942 (December 13, 1955): 1–6.
———. "Report on the Problem of Passport Fraud at Hong Kong." *Foreign Service Dispatch* 931 (December 9, 1955): 1–89.
Final Report of the Administrator of the Refugee Relief Act of 1953, as Amended. Washington, DC: U.S. Government Printing Office, 1958.
Fong Yue Ting v. United States. 149 U.S. 698 (1893).
Immigration and Nationality Act. Public Law 82-414, 66 Stat. 163 (1952).
Korematsu v. United States. 323 U.S. 214 (1944).
Leng May Ma v. Barber. 357 U.S. 185 (1958).
Loving v. Virginia. 388 U.S. 1 (1967).
Loving v. Virginia. Oral argument transcript. Accessed August 18, 2017. https://www.oyez.org/cases/1966/395.
Lue v. Brownell. 220 F.2d. 187 (1955).
Ly Shew v. Acheson. 110 F. Supp. 50 (1953).
Ly Shew v. Dulles. 219 F.2d. 413 (1954).
Mao v. Brownell. 207 F.2d 142 (1953).
Moore v. City of East Cleveland, Ohio. 431 U.S. 494 (1977).
Moynihan, Daniel Patrick. *The Negro Family: The Case for National Action*. U.S. Department of Labor. Washington, DC: U.S. Government Printing Office, 1965.
Naim v. Naim. 197 Va. 734 (1955).
Napolitano, Janet. "Exercising Prosecutorial Discretion with Respect to Individuals Who Came to the United States as Children." Department of Homeland Security, June 15,

2012. Accessed October 11, 2019. https://www.dhs.gov/xlibrary/assets/s1-exercising-prosecutorial-discretion-individuals-who-came-to-us-as-children.pdf.
Office of the Attorney General, ed. *Annual Report of the Attorney General of the United States*. Washington, DC: U.S. Government Printing Office, 1957.
People v. Hall. 4 Cal. 399 (1854).
Perez v. Sharp. 32 Cal. 2d 711 (1948).
Rogers v. Quan. 357 U.S. 193 (1958).
Shelley v. Kraemer. 334 U.S. 1 (1948).
Takao Ozawa v. United States. 260 U.S. 178 (1922).
United States ex rel. Lee Kum Hoy et al. v. Murff. 355 U.S. 169 (1957).
United States ex rel. Lee Kum Hoy v. Murff. Oral argument transcript. Accessed August 16, 2017. https://www.oyez.org/cases/1957/32.
United States ex rel. Lee Kum Hoy v. Shaughnessy. 115 F. Supp. 302 (1953).
United States v. Jeu Foon, United States v. Fong Nong, United States v. Gee Gong. 193 U.S. 117 (1951).
United States v. Mrs. Gue Lim. 176 U.S. 459 (1900).
United States v. Thind. 261 U.S. 204 (1923).
United States v. Yin Liu and Four Other Cases. 190 U.S. 400 (1951).
U.S. Department of Labor. *Annual Report of the Immigration and Naturalization Service*. Washington, DC: U.S. Government Printing Office, 1950–1951. Accessed June 12, 2017. https://catalog.hathitrust.org/Record/000546059.
———. *Annual Report of the Immigration and Naturalization Service*. Washington, DC: U.S. Government Printing Office, 1956–1957.
War Brides Act. Public Law 271, 59 Stat. 659.
Wong Kim Ark v. United States. 169 U.S. 649 (1898).
Yick Wo v. Hopkins. 118 U.S. 356 (1886).

ARCHIVAL COLLECTIONS

Citations to archival collections in the endnotes use abbreviations. An asterisk denotes that a collection is not fully processed, and citations provide as much identifying detail as possible according to the system in use at the time of access.

FSG	Farrar, Straus and Giroux, Inc., Manuscripts and Archives Division, New York Public Library
JDP	Archives of John Day Company (C0123), Rare Books and Special Collections, Princeton University Library, Princeton, NJ
JSW	Jade Snow Wong Papers, Asian-American Pacific Islander Collection, Asian Reading Room, Library of Congress, Washington, DC*
MHK	Maxine Hong Kingston Papers, Bancroft Library, University of California, Berkeley
OH	Oscar Hammerstein II Papers, Music Division, Library of Congress, Washington, DC*
PL	Pardee Lowe Papers, Hoover Institution Archives, Stanford University, Stanford, CA
RR	Richard Rodgers Scrapbooks, Music Division, New York Public Library

Index

Page numbers followed by the letter f *refer to figures.*

Heidi Kim is Associate Professor of English and Comparative Literature at the University of North Carolina at Chapel Hill. She is the author of *Invisible Subjects: Asian Americans in Postwar Literature* and editor of *Taken from the Paradise Isle: The Hoshida Family Story.*

Additional titles in this series:

Kieu-Linh Caroline Valverde, *Transnationalizing Viet Nam: Community, Culture, and Politics in the Diaspora*
Lan P. Duong, *Treacherous Subjects: Gender, Culture, and Trans-Vietnamese Feminism*
Kristi Brian, *Reframing Transracial Adoption: Adopted Koreans, White Parents, and the Politics of Kinship*
Belinda Kong, *Tiananmen Fictions outside the Square: The Chinese Literary Diaspora and the Politics of Global Culture*
Bindi V. Shah, *Laotian Daughters: Working toward Community, Belonging, and Environmental Justice*
Cherstin M. Lyon, *Prisons and Patriots: Japanese American Wartime Citizenship, Civil Disobedience, and Historical Memory*
Shelley Sang-Hee Lee, *Claiming the Oriental Gateway: Prewar Seattle and Japanese America*
Isabelle Thuy Pelaud, *This Is All I Choose to Tell: History and Hybridity in Vietnamese American Literature*
Christian Collet and Pei-te Lien, eds., *The Transnational Politics of Asian Americans*
Min Zhou, *Contemporary Chinese America: Immigration, Ethnicity, and Community Transformation*
Kathleen S. Yep, *Outside the Paint: When Basketball Ruled at the Chinese Playground*
Benito M. Vergara Jr., *Pinoy Capital: The Filipino Nation in Daly City*
Jonathan Y. Okamura, *Ethnicity and Inequality in Hawai'i*
Sucheng Chan and Madeline Y. Hsu, eds., *Chinese Americans and the Politics of Race and Culture*
K. Scott Wong, *Americans First: Chinese Americans and the Second World War*
Lisa Yun, *The Coolie Speaks: Chinese Indentured Laborers and African Slaves in Cuba*
Estella Habal, *San Francisco's International Hotel: Mobilizing the Filipino American Community in the Anti-eviction Movement*
Thomas P. Kim, *The Racial Logic of Politics: Asian Americans and Party Competition*
Sucheng Chan, ed., *The Vietnamese American 1.5 Generation: Stories of War, Revolution, Flight, and New Beginnings*
Antonio T. Tiongson Jr., Edgardo V. Gutierrez, and Ricardo V. Gutierrez, eds., *Positively No Filipinos Allowed: Building Communities and Discourse*
Sucheng Chan, ed., *Chinese American Transnationalism: The Flow of People, Resources, and Ideas between China and America during the Exclusion Era*
Rajini Srikanth, *The World Next Door: South Asian American Literature and the Idea of America*
Keith Lawrence and Floyd Cheung, eds., *Recovered Legacies: Authority and Identity in Early Asian American Literature*
Linda Trinh Võ, *Mobilizing an Asian American Community*
Franklin S. Odo, *No Sword to Bury: Japanese Americans in Hawai'i during World War II*
Josephine Lee, Imogene L. Lim, and Yuko Matsukawa, eds., *Re/collecting Early Asian America: Essays in Cultural History*
Linda Trinh Võ and Rick Bonus, eds., *Contemporary Asian American Communities: Intersections and Divergences*

Sunaina Marr Maira, *Desis in the House: Indian American Youth Culture in New York City*

Teresa Williams-León and Cynthia Nakashima, eds., *The Sum of Our Parts: Mixed-Heritage Asian Americans*

Tung Pok Chin with Winifred C. Chin, *Paper Son: One Man's Story*

Amy Ling, ed., *Yellow Light: The Flowering of Asian American Arts*

Rick Bonus, *Locating Filipino Americans: Ethnicity and the Cultural Politics of Space*

Darrell Y. Hamamoto and Sandra Liu, eds., *Countervisions: Asian American Film Criticism*

Martin F. Manalansan IV, ed., *Cultural Compass: Ethnographic Explorations of Asian America*

Ko-lin Chin, *Smuggled Chinese: Clandestine Immigration to the United States*

Evelyn Hu-DeHart, ed., *Across the Pacific: Asian Americans and Globalization*

Soo-Young Chin, *Doing What Had to Be Done: The Life Narrative of Dora Yum Kim*

Robert G. Lee, *Orientals: Asian Americans in Popular Culture*

David L. Eng and Alice Y. Hom, eds., *Q & A: Queer in Asian America*

K. Scott Wong and Sucheng Chan, eds., *Claiming America: Constructing Chinese American Identities during the Exclusion Era*

Lavina Dhingra Shankar and Rajini Srikanth, eds., *A Part, Yet Apart: South Asians in Asian America*

Jere Takahashi, *Nisei/Sansei: Shifting Japanese American Identities and Politics*

Velina Hasu Houston, ed., *But Still, Like Air, I'll Rise: New Asian American Plays*

Josephine Lee, *Performing Asian America: Race and Ethnicity on the Contemporary Stage*

Deepika Bahri and Mary Vasudeva, eds., *Between the Lines: South Asians and Postcoloniality*

E. San Juan Jr., *The Philippine Temptation: Dialectics of Philippines–U.S. Literary Relations*

Carlos Bulosan and E. San Juan Jr., eds., *The Cry and the Dedication*

Carlos Bulosan and E. San Juan Jr., eds., *On Becoming Filipino: Selected Writings of Carlos Bulosan*

Vicente L. Rafael, ed., *Discrepant Histories: Translocal Essays on Filipino Cultures*

Yen Le Espiritu, *Filipino American Lives*

Paul Ong, Edna Bonacich, and Lucie Cheng, eds., *The New Asian Immigration in Los Angeles and Global Restructuring*

Chris Friday, *Organizing Asian American Labor: The Pacific Coast Canned-Salmon Industry, 1870–1942*

Sucheng Chan, ed., *Hmong Means Free: Life in Laos and America*

Timothy P. Fong, *The First Suburban Chinatown: The Remaking of Monterey Park, California*

William Wei, *The Asian American Movement*

Yen Le Espiritu, *Asian American Panethnicity*

Velina Hasu Houston, ed., *The Politics of Life*

Renqiu Yu, *To Save China, To Save Ourselves: The Chinese Hand Laundry Alliance of New York*

Shirley Geok-lin Lim and Amy Ling, eds., *Reading the Literatures of Asian America*

Karen Isaksen Leonard, *Making Ethnic Choices: California's Punjabi Mexican Americans*

Gary Y. Okihiro, *Cane Fires: The Anti-Japanese Movement in Hawaii, 1865–1945*

Sucheng Chan, *Entry Denied: Exclusion and the Chinese Community in America, 1882–1943*